SEMIOTEXT(E) FOREIGN AGENTS SERIES

The publication of this book was supported by the French Ministry of Foreign Affairs through the Cultural Services of the French Embassy, New York. "Ouvrage publié avec le concours du Ministère français chargé de la Culture– Centre nationale du livre".

Original published as "Le Ludique et le policier," Paris, Sens & Tonka, 2001 Jean Baudrillard/Jean-Louis Violeau, "A Propos d'Utopie," Paris, Sens & Tonka, 2005

Published by Semiotext(e)
501 Philosophy Hall, Columbia University, New York, NY 10027
2007 Wilshire Blvd., Suite 427, Los Angeles, CA 90057
www.semiotexte.com

Special thanks to Jean-Louis Voileau, Craig Buckley, Andrew Berardini, Nicholas Zurko and Ardevan Yaghoubi.

Cover Photography by Hervé Véronèse
© Centre G. Pompidou/Bibliothèque Kandinsky
Back Cover Photography by Sylvère Lotringer
Design by Hedi El Kholti

ISBN: 1-58435-033-4
Distributed by The MIT Press, Cambridge, Mass. and London, England
Printed in the United States of America

Utopia Deferred

Jean Baudrillard

Writings from *Utopie* (1967-1978)

Translated by Stuart Kendall

Table of Contents

1

On *Utopie*, an interview

with Jean Baudrillard

Jean-Louis Voileau: *How could Utopie express an "ideal-specific" relationship between architects and "intellectuals"?*

Jean Baudrillard: The equivalent of a symbiosis between a few architects and young intellectuals effectively occurred at the end of the 1960s, but at that time, it seems to me that architecture didn't have the façade, the surface that it has today. And since these architects were still unknown, they could take more risks in a certain way, leave their "technical" space so as to see elsewhere. I don't know if this is still the case today. It is not the same situation. Basically, the intention was to surpass architecture as such, just as urbanism as such had been surpassed and as the Situationists had liquidated the space of the university as such... Everyone was trying to liquidate his own discipline. There was a mode of disappearance through excess in which each of us could rediscover himself. Today, I have the impression that between architects and intellectuals, or artists and intellectuals or philosophers—because artists also participate in this movement—it's more a question of a friendly contract. We pass in the halls. The conditions are no longer the same. Fusion can no longer be envisioned. Within *Utopie*—and besides this is what *Utopie* was—we were in search of a point of intellectual gravity from which it would have been possible to radiate out to all disciplines. Thus, each of us eventually set out from his own point of view, but in the end sought to transverse all the themes of the period. Today, I truly believe that it is much more of a graft, or even a search for justification. In fact, a search for "intellectual salvation" founded on the will to save the discipline of architecture—architecture as such—or to rehabilitate it, or rediscover its meaning, etc. Because it too is experiencing a mental crisis, in its foundations, even if it isn't the sole cause, since everything, everywhere around, it is, evidently... Today we are seeing an attempt at consolidation, at re-foundation, such that, at that time, the intention was the opposite: to go as far as possible toward disappearance, just to see what would happen out there. Today, I have the impression that the intellectual is perceived as a resource. This is only an impression... I myself have not really sounded this one out... Compromise imposes itself everywhere. Politics and culture support one another. If there is a political crisis, it is surpassed in the holy alliance with culture. We see it with Le Pen[1]... There is a crisis in contemporary art, but we've switched it to the extreme right, and made it a political accusation, exchanging at once processes and combinations. But I don't want to discredit it entirely for that. It is good that these exchanges have taken place, that these dialogues have taken place, but all of this remains on the order of exchange and dialogue. *Utopie* was not on this order. *Utopie* was a bit of a fusion, of a superfusion. We were looking for something other than simple dialogue...

Was there a conscious intention to renew architectural thought or urbanism?

We were effectively part of such a postulate, nourished by sociology —more precisely by the thought of Henri Lefebvre. It was about questioning architecture and every formal and symbolic practice in terms of historicity and radicality. All of this reviewed across every intellectual sphere, at once of everyday life and of history, which deformalized and deprofessionalized architectural practice.

The urban as "separated" space...

Yes, the end of the urban, the process of the disappearance of the urban and more precisely of the urban utopia. This wasn't so much my project as it was that of Lefebvre as a philosopher, and of Hubert Tonka, as an architect, even if it was already clearly exposed in architectural practice. This inquiry anticipated 1968, of course, a "moment" during which any even slightly formalized, slightly professionalized activity was called into question... This movement came before 1968, undoubtedly. And besides, in fact, *Utopie* could hardly continue for very long after 1968, even if it nevertheless endured for several years, though with some wandering... The ascendant period, when there had not yet been any kind of event— or "non-event"...—like 1968, was more interesting. The 1968 event came, in some way, "to realize" the project, though also, in the same blow, to extinguish a little of its potential.

How did you meet Hubert Tonka?

This whole thing began started with Lefebvre. I had known Lefebvre at the beginning of the 1960s. He was at the center of a group interested in urbanism. He taught at the *Institut d'urbanisme* and Tonka was his assistant. We got to know one another in 1962 and

1963. *Utopie* truly began at Lefebvre's place at Navarrenx, in the Pyrenees, in 1966. Lefebvre and Lourau were already there... There, in 1966, I got to know the group. In fact, just before 1968. All of this really began right before 1968...

What was your relationship to the "enrages" at Nanterre?

Nanterre... the sociology department... Cohn-Bendit... the 22nd of March[2]... We were at the center of the "events." We participated in AG, we went to the barricades... The "spirit of May" circulated for several years at Nanterre. We still had a certain power. The students were behind us. We defended the department of sociology above all. This situation lasted until 1973-74. I stayed on a few more years, through inertia. During the work of mourning, for me, there was no longer any activity. I had passed to the side of theory. Leftism, or what it had become, closed militarism, was no longer an option.

You were never tempted by Vincennes...

Why not? Lourau went there, Lyotard too... Tonka... Undoubtedly I should have gone, but I made a bet, I said: no, I'll stay here, I'll stay till the end, I want to see what happens, in the end, at Nanterre. I haven't regretted having made this choice, even when it was clear that I couldn't stay at Nanterre any longer. It was simply too late to go to Vincennes. The story, for me, ended at Nanterre...

Yes, but from that moment, you were among the references for the students...

Yes. I was very friendly with Lyotard, with Guattari, all of them... I was already at the center of that group even if I remained on the margins of the "elite." I worked with groups like *Utopie*, which was nevertheless a "cell," a little on the margin, or I worked largely alone. In the end, I always preferred working alone.

Where do you situate Utopie *in this intellectual and political context?*

There were a number of movements like it during those years, analogous anticipations that wanted to be marginal. We should remember that there was still a phobia about official political action and about parties, a refusal of all political and intellectual nomenclature. The Situationists were closest to us, but the Situationists didn't want to see anyone else. And we didn't really seek them out. We had known them, with Tonka, at the beginning of the 1960s, just before their break with Lefebvre. The position of the Situationists, in 1968, became very problematic. Previously, at Nanterre, between the anarchists, Cohn-Bendit, and the Situationists, there was an extraordinary focal point, but the workers councils the Situationists extolled in 1968 seemed irrelevant to us. We had the feeling of having surpassed this kind of initiative. Debord disappointed us in 1968, with his "old moons," and again twenty years later, rereading what he had written, cloning himself by saying: nothing has changed, what I said was absolutely true, there is nothing more to say about it. While completely recognizing the value of what happened before, he was nevertheless already fossilized for us. The 1960s were really extraordinary, more than the 1970s, which were more "spectacular." The 1960s were more rich, more complex, even if it was also during these years that I began mourning "politics." For us, 1968 was already more than politics. It was symbolic, almost "metahistorical." Thereafter, it was all over. In the 1970s, we passed beyond the end. Thereafter, we passed entirely to the side of theory. This moment is also the moment that *Utopie* effectively ceased all engaged activity, even all activity relative to architecture. We passed inexorably toward disappearance, a disappearance tending toward the most radical…

What role did Aspen play in this process?

We were simply delegates in Aspen. It's true that we created a "moment," a little event in Aspen, in passing.[3] But in the end, the scene was too large for it to be of any importance. No, if I had to think of an influence, I would more likely reference *The System of Objects*, which provoked a small event, an event that went beyond me and beyond *Utopie* as well. Aspen, it's true, was the place where a counter culture expressed itself and is therefore worthy of interest. This "counter culture" was foreign to us. We were very "French," therefore very "metaphysical," a French metaphysics of revolt, of insubordination, while the counter culture that expressed itself in Aspen was largely American. Aspen was a "moment" and not an event, even if, at that time, despite a certain vigor in the American movement which persisted, the decline was nevertheless in the air. Even if Vietnam and Cambodia were still going on, even if violence still followed, even if we had discovered the occasion, I think that the "counter cultural flash" was already a little "metastasized," even if the trip, it's true, nevertheless remains a revelation. America truly started things, an illuminating trip, even if we didn't bring much back to France when we returned. How could we do something here in France? There was no way to metabolize this contribution in a French context dominated by the "politico-careerist" New Left, even if, from that moment on, things simultaneously began to decline here too. We were already on the road to the great recycling, to the restoration, to rehabilitation... I lived through this recycling at Nanterre, at the university level. We really saw the recycling, the restoration of things, the return of the authorities to their jobs, etc. We struggled for several years against it, but it was inexorable. We moved toward an integrated society. Integration, even if I should admit that this grand recycling wasn't entirely negative. Architecture, for example, was reborn, but this time, in a professional form, at another level... Evidently, in the eyes of our initial transversal utopia, this rebirth was undoubtedly a revision, revisionism, but architecture started over, just the same, from that situation, with other means, other technologies, other minds. What remains of it today? Someone like Stinco, for example, "makes architecture"... He does his job, in a certain way. Nouvel is a foundational spirit, but he is also a true professional. He would truly ask himself, Nouvel... In the end, he could be both completely unique and retain the first class, high tech image, which he really has, of course... But he still has concerns... This vast movement gave us the people that we know today: Portzamparc, Nouvel, Gaudin... Free spirits, troubled... But in the end, architects. Today it's no longer about questioning all of that. Today I no longer see what might question the postulates of this evolution.

How did you see the role of the architects—among others...—refusing to build immediately after 1968?

I have never been very libertarian, nor spontaneous... The idea that creativity was everywhere and that there was no longer any need for architects always left me indifferent. I never really believed it. It's appealing, certainly, but in a "virtuality," in a dream space, a dream of equality… And this—even if I brought the entire group to a theoretical level—to the only level that it was possible to think and create. With theory, one can work alone, do what one wants, and, on this point, I have never compromised. The University was nothing. I never found myself caught up in having to return to a "conventional" activity. This problem is much more complicated for people like architects, pragmatists, those who do things, real operators. I have never been anything, but a virtual, theoretical operator, and in theory I have complete freedom. Having eliminated the few constraints that I felt on a political level at a given moment, I have been perfectly free. I choose this freedom, but people like Tonka, who wanted to be both theoretically radical and to nevertheless maintain the working method of a group and a communitarian practice, never got out. Besides, Hubert is still at the center of this insoluble dilemma, a dilemma that, with his build, he gives a rather unique character. But this is a situation for which there can be absolutely no model. One cannot even offer an example. This is a very, very particular case. For those who have wanted to maintain the essence of a collective, utopian imaginary and to continue to work in the sharpest way, it is very difficult. I believe that one really has to choose. I chose to distance myself. I chose to do what I wanted to do, practically alone. For a time, a journal like *Traverses* was the locus of a collective activity, a structure of reception, but never my unique center of gravity. It was a thematic journal that invested in the world, but even this kind of journal was already no longer possible on the fringes of the 1980s…

What really happened at the beginning of the 1980s… I am thinking, notably, of those three great expositions of architecture in Paris, and more particularly, of one of them, La Modernité ou l'esprit du temps, *curated by Jean Nouvel, in which you participated, with François Barré... In 1981,* Présence de L'Histoire, l'après modernisme, *the Venice Biennale that came to Paris in 1980. The following year, in response to Nouvel and to Chemetov,* Modernité, un projet inachevé, *which made its appeal to Habermas' caution, all of this in the midst of the modern/postmodern controversy... A controversy wrapped up in the promises of modernity, unfinished because unfinishable according to Chemetov, finished in Venice around Portoghesi, and finished in a completely different way by Nouvel... What is your view of what has been called postmodernism in architecture?*

I've never had anything but an amateur's eye for this. I never followed the history of architectural ideas. On a theoretical level, on the contrary, I had enormous reservations since the beginning, and even an absolute distrust about concepts like these. In part, besides, because I have been classed in a certain abrupt fashion among the supporters of postmodernism. I found myself bound by a certain etiquette, having enjoyed undeserved success based on a total misunderstanding. In fact, I didn't see what this label corresponded too. People took "simulation" for postmodernism, and I became a guru of postmodernism... In regard to this controversy, I've always stayed at arms' length. I don't like the so-called "postmodern" architectural displays. It is clear that I resisted this kind of architecture. I remained modern in the sense that I refer to Manhattan, in its truly modern version. What happened afterward didn't please me at all, at all. In my eyes, the referencing of past forms incarnated a movement that was not only a regression, but also a reversal. I did not see it as a sign of renewal in any way, but more as *bricolage* at the highest level, reusing all past forms. We've seen similar phenomena elsewhere in art, in theory, and in philosophy. This movement is still going on. Luc Ferry and his group do postmodernism, in their way. We don't call it that, but they are in the process of cobbling together a subject, a weak humanism…

The old moral ground…

Exactly. An old moral ground that reappears, the replacement of a system of values… After 1968, a liquidation was sought. It was necessary at least to go to the end of that, and not return to these things to work with the past. We destroyed—or deconstructed—the old moral ground. We analyzed it joyfully, if you will, and today we see all these people applying themselves to reconstructing the past in distress, in any case out of sadness. All of this is not very comforting. I never adhered to an intellectual program, but in foreign countries, in all the other countries, I'm always asked about it, always questioned about it… Certain habits are tough. One would have thought that all this would pass away bit by bit. This is more or less the case in France, since, after all, we have never spoken much about it in France. But elsewhere, no, the label persists, incarnating an entire period, an entire era… And then, it is useless to want to clear up a misunderstanding. No one can correct anything. You are pegged once and for all, that's it.

It is true that the vision of architecture offered by the catalogue of Jean Nouvel's exposition is practically the opposite of that offered by the catalogue of Paolo Portoghesi's. In the end, it is not "postmodern" in the sense that the term was primarily defined at the time. Elsewhere, the exposition was called Modernity or the spirit of the times…

Yes, yes, absolutely… But here I might fool you. I was never close to the ambiance of architecture, the evolution of the 1980s… I would not even be capable of offering a "religion," an opinion about it. I followed events like that, through chance relations and friendships, but the stakes of these things, I cannot say that I followed that. I'm not really a good resource about them.

Rather your interest in this was through your friendship with Jean Nouvel…

Yes, Nouvel. Even if it was not really a choice. It happened that I knew him best, and that what he did pleased me, though I still didn't really know why… I went to New York to see Tschumi a little in the same spirit. To the extent that these people thought they found things that inspired them in what I was doing—why not?—but truthfully, I never really understood what excited them about my work. The problem posed itself in the same way with the artists. I saw more or less clearly what they found in my work—at least what they gathered from it…—but reciprocation was hardly required. I cannot say that I never found myself inspired by their work. The only text that I had to write on architecture was on La Villette for Tonka, for the book *Parc Ville Villette*.[4] A text that has certain architectural elements but which is more "metaphysical"… Similarly, in regard to painting, I was certainly interested in Warhol and Duchamp, but I situate myself on the fringes of painting. Something else is at stake, a metaphysics of the object, of the image… It is the same for architecture: Beaubourg interested me, but as an object, and not strictly as architecture. Besides, I have no real understanding of architecture. As an object, on the other hand, Beaubourg, this "monster," was interesting to me. In the end, the architectural "monsters" were interesting to me... I'm really only a wild amateur and I don't really know how to slip out of this amateur's taste. Once, Nouvel, Tonka and I did a long dialogue. Yes, we felt that there were several points of intersection, but there was no real point of anchorage, like there was, even if the complicities were a little forced, between Tschumi and Derrida or Eisenmann, even if, between them, there was a very determined will, a common project. It was something else. In my opinion, the transplantation of deconstruction into architecture was not very convincing. Fundamentally, I don't really believe in this kind of contamination, even if, for those who attempt it, it should certainly reveal itself to be very exciting. For myself, I never entered into any game that was so advanced. The "contamination" eventually occurred only through simple affinities. I certainly acquired the equivalent of credit on the basis of *The System of Objects*, of design, since the people that worked in these areas, including architecture, used me as a reference. There was an entire movement, but in the end, I always flirted with all that, without... And I don't know, from their side, if the flirting went very far anyway... I can't say that the ideas circulating in architecture or in architectural debates were really influenced by my work. My trajectory passed, like that, through architecture, just as it has passed through philosophy. Without any privilege. For me, even the history of ideas is a field with which I flirt, at its limits, but I only pass through. I work more at a distance. I never really return to the heart of a discipline. For the rest of them it's a question of recurrence: whether it be psychoanalysis, semiology, architecture or linguistics... I never came back to the details of things, the structures of things, to make an internal critique because I saw too clearly that if one entered too deeply into a discipline, one would never get out. Of course, my point of view can seem a bit cavalier, but I've preserved this reaction because it prevents me from truly investing myself in the details of things. If alchemy worked better with architects, as in the *Utopie* group, it is because they were also avoiding the details of their activity. They wanted to make something else. They had an ambition that was different than building, if I may say so.

So this relationship with Nouvel is of an entirely different nature than the one that you entertained with the architects of the Utopie *group…*

Yes, even if there wasn't an organic relationship with the architects in *Utopie*. We never really worked together, even if, between us, we talked a lot… I don't think that any truly common project could have come of it. With Nouvel, I also don't think that I was involved in any development whatsoever. The way that Tonka was engaged in this kind of collaboration is very different. He always remained linked very closely with architecture, and it was rather through him that I was associated with the architectural milieu with, meanwhile, enormous intermittences.

Tonka's chosen affinities became your own, marginally…

Yes, in echoes, resonances… His ambition is to mediate these exchanges, to be a bit of a "resonator," the spokesman. I was one pole for him, but there were others… And he really wanted to be a bit of the convector for this entire elective cartography. I gladly accepted this ambition. We have been friends for a long time… Our relations have always been woven with resonance, ricochet…

A family…

Yes, the architects are a bit like my cousins, but in the end, they aren't my cousins... It is not a close family, even if I should admit that I don't really have a close family, if only in my head, or really, anywhere else...

Have you been tempted by the experience of Unités pédagogiques *(UP) after 1968?* [5]

No. To enter the universe of the UP, one must possess a certain skill at infiltration, militant infiltration. I was not adept at this relationship of pedagogy and militancy. I was always so conscious of the limits of these enterprises that my strategy has been, each time, to withdraw rather than to enter... And then, it would have been necessary to be the clearest person of one's times, the most activist, and I am not an activist. These groups were already set up, they already had a framework, each was already more or less affiliated with such and such a movement. It must have begun and set itself up within that framework, to recognize positions... Very quickly, that set off intrigue, influence, things that I was afraid of and that depressed me. In fact, I remained quite outside the institutions, a shy partisan of minimal institutional arts...

Did architecture students attend your seminars at Nanterre?

No, I don't think so, even if we can't really know, at a given moment, who precisely attended those seminars... It is true that at the height of the New Left, there must have been an osmosis, in the end, they came because it was Nanterre, and undoubtedly not so much because they were architecture students... There were people who passed through. I remember people who came from elsewhere, from

Belgium, from Germany, linked more or less to architecture, who came to follow the class, even if, in any case, the drainage was not the same as at Vincennes. Besides, Nanterre ended up becoming a desert, more or less abandoned. In fact, I really liked that disaffection. It left me the time and freedom that I needed to work. In the end, through the first years, after 1968, for four or five years, there was such an infatuation and so variable an audience that it was very difficult to delineate the contours of a "devoted" audience...

You weren't interested in the shake-ups at the École *des beaux-arts before 1968, for example?*

I heard echoes, because I knew people there. But I didn't participate or follow the events very closely. I wasn't looking elsewhere for a replacement institution. We broke out during a moment at Nanterre. Then, life at the university little by little resembled that of an asylum. I was part of it, even if I lived much more while traveling in foreign countries. I traveled all over a little, and I was no longer invested here, in Paris, in any case much less than elsewhere. I don't think that it should be a choice.

Is there something American that happened in Utopie...

Nothing much could have. *Utopie* really preceded my departure for America, even if I already had access to American culture, cinema, and literature... There was, it's true, a fascination. Did these things happen in *Utopie*? It's true that since the 1960s, hyperreality, the hyperreal, Warhol, American painting, already interested me... And then, I already knew American literature, certainly that of the previous generation, and film, yes... We swam in that culture since the 1960s, and then, I already had an anti-French prejudice, or in any case a shifted position... There was certainly, at the same moment, a political radicality that was still rather more oriented toward Marxism, at least for a certain time, but it was despite all that an imaginary, an anticipation, which was much more American. Since the 1960s, this imaginary was there. I already had it—I don't know if the others participants had it as much as me...—but I don't think that it could have passed through my writings of the period, at least, not so much that one could presume that it did.

The imaginary of the immoderate?

The imaginary of simulation. There was already *The Consumer Society*, *The System of Objects*, the objects, consumption, through reading Marcuse, the Frankfurt School... I read the Frankfurt School before it was translated. It was an analysis of alienation, effectively repeated in Sartre and many others—Marx...—but reactivated, updated in the American context, as though in a completely different society, where the story of hyperreality became an extreme phenomenon. The context changed all the givens of the analysis. America had been an analyst, in this sense, the equivalent of a shifter. When I arrived in Paris, at the beginning of the 1960s, and when I began to work with Lefebvre, all this was still really in limbo, even if it was also in that moment that there were glimmers, clear indications. Toward the middle of the 1960s, this thought began to be outlined. Certain elements had been perceived since the beginning. One didn't have to wait for the year 2000 to perceive all that was going to take place. It was not even necessary to have a particular gift for anticipation. One could analyze very well, x-ray it. We also had instruments that were new. Sartre had phenomenology as well, but then we also had semiology, psychoanalysis... powerful tools. A series of fundamental discoveries occurred at the same time.

Even if you must have had a particular relationship to structuralism, having been a disciple of Lefebvre...

Yes, but I was never a structuralist. Lefebvre, it's true, was an anti-structuralist. For me, Foucault or Barthes were very interesting. The question didn't come up. Lefebvre had very "phobic" limits in relation to a bunch of things like that... In the end, Lefebvre was never really a reference for me, nor a model. I liked him well enough, we worked together, but I very quickly found certain of his positions a little naïve... Barthes, for example, influenced me much more. It was very pleasant to work with Lefebvre, but he had a rhetoric that was occasionally too set, that didn't suit me. I'm thinking of his disdain, of his contempt for psychoanalysis and for semiology in the name of a rhetorical libertinage, a touch "Old France," if one may say so... We had a lot of affection for him, but that was beside the point. There were much more acute tasks, much more pointed in all these other disciplines, without these "disciplines" being for all that truly autonomous. It was an experimental period, which was nevertheless very powerful, wherein things already no longer came from previously constituted disciplines, nor even from the university, but transversally between methods of analysis. We tried a bit of everything at that moment. My first books, objects, consumption... were the hybrid and intertwined results of all these contributions. These first books were still at once a bit serious and traditional, with an experimental tone at the same time. Thereafter, for me, all this was a little decanted through radicalization. The problem was that of political radicality. I initially passed from a poetic and metaphysical radicality—Hölderlin and Rimbaud…—when I was in my twenties, to a political subversion—the Algerian War, Leftism, etc. Then, there was a passage wherein it was necessary to transform the political radicality that no longer had any stakes—for which we no longer felt any stakes…—into a theoretical radicality. It's an unoriginal path, all things considered, but one which, for me, seemed very clear. Thereafter, things are a little fixed, because beyond this radicality, I no longer see very well what it would be possible to write… The same goes for my path in the institution: I began by being a professor in a provincial school, then I moved to the university, where, at the moment, the dream… 1966, 1968, it was great. But at the end of the moment, it's inexorable, the stage was emptied. And so I passed to the cosmopolitan level, to travel and the world, to the transoceanic level… I stayed there, and there too, I began to get tired. But beyond, there is nothing. I no longer see very clearly what I could undertake beyond, but I certainly cannot go back and include myself in existing or pre-existing institutions. And now I'm too old to look for a place in the intellectual world!

2

Dialectical Utopia

WE WANT TO SITUATE ourselves in the uncrossed interval between theory and praxis. Praxis (conservative) situates itself in the existing order. Grasping the urban totality and all of its contradictions; apprehending every possibility. The social possibilities are presented and remain to be created—in the sense of made to appear—; the urban contains and confines them; it is essentially a question of freeing them and putting their revolutionary potentiality into play.

The existing order is a *topos*. Criticism and analysis of this topos permits the elaboration of *utopia*; the definition and situation of utopia, the criticism of utopia and the updating of its means of realization (philosophical, political, economic…).

Utopia has two fields of possible realization. 1. Existing power, whatever it is, assimilates the means, the criticisms, and the project of utopia, therefore, in a certain measure, its goals, by rejecting them. But, if there had not been a fundamental modification of the existing order, a share of *utopia* nevertheless passed into reactionary praxis. 2. The revolution that destroyed the *topos* theoretically permitted a total realization of *utopia*, which becomes a (revolutionary) *topos*. In advance, one cannot determine what will constitute the revolutionary praxis of this *topos* and what will remain theoretical and reintegrated in theory.

The realized *utopia* is a new *topos,* which will provoke a new critique, then a new utopia. The installation of utopia passes through a (total) urbanism.

And that is the complete process.

Topos (conservative)—critique/utopia/revolution—urbanism/topos (revolutionary and conservative)/new utopia... etc.

We call that *Dialectical Utopia.*

Utopia is the phase of theoretical construction, but it is absolutely indissociable from the other phases and can only exist as part of dialectical utopia. It is only through dialectical utopia that we can elaborate, outside and within the present system, an urban thought.

(To be continued)

3

The Ephemeral...[1]

THE EPHEMERAL IS undoubtedly the truth of our future habitat. Mobile, variable, retractable structures inscribe themselves in the formal demands of architects and in the social and economic demands of modernity. But this is only true in an ideal dimension. One must not lose sight of the fact that:

1. Neither the ephemeral nor the durable are absolute and exclusive values. Only their constant relation, and the multiple play of oppositions between them, founds a logic of cultural significations. One can inflect their rapport, loosen it as a function of social rhythms: in this sense everything pushes us strongly toward the accelerated mortality of objects and structures. Meanwhile these two terms have meaning only relative to one another.

More precisely, if clothes, objects, appliances, and automobiles increasingly obey (but there is a limit threshold) the norms of the ephemeral, nothing says that they do not, taken together, oppose "inhabiting"—which itself constitutes a specific function which could be brutally or ideally assimilated to other aspects of consumption or fashion. Their symbolic schema is that of ventilation and expenditure, the symbolic schema of inhabiting is that of provision and investment. To reduce the two to the same ephemeral synchrony is undoubtedly to liquidate an entire field of very rich contrasts. Lived culture (and thus the logic of sense) only exists through the tension between two poles like these.

2. It is true that the social deficit that modular or pre-fabricated construction, in disposable or durable materials, represents today is colossal. It contradicts economic rationality and social exchange with the irreversible tendency toward greater social mobility, the loosening of infrastructures, etc. Meanwhile one must account for the latent psychological, familial, and collective functions, of the "disposable" and the solid, very powerful functions of integration that also return in the social "budget."

3. The ephemeral will perhaps one day be the collective solution, but for the moment it is the monopoly of a privileged fraction whom its economic and cultural position permits to question the myth of durability.

It is because generations of bourgeois were able to enjoy the permanent and traditional décor of property that certain among them can today grant themselves the luxury to deny to cut stone and delight in the ephemeral: the fad belongs to them. On the other hand, every generation of the lower classes, who had no chance in the past of acceding to the cultural models at the same time as to durable property,—to what does one wish that they aspire if not to live the bourgeois model, and to found in their turn for themselves and their children, a derisory dynasty in the stone buildings and bungalows of the suburbs—how can one demand of these classes, now "promotable," that they regard their buildings as sacred and accept outright the ideality of mobile structures? They have vowed to desire that which lasts and only this aspiration can translate the cultural destiny of their class.

Reciprocally, the cult of the ephemeral ideologically connotes the privilege of the avant-garde: according to the eternal logic of cultural distinction, a privileged fraction savors the instantaneousness and the mobility of architectural structures at the moment when the others accede only just to the quadrature of their walls. Only the privileged classes have the right to the actuality of the models. The others have the right once these models have already changed.

If therefore in the logic of forms the "ephemeral" represents the truth of modernity, if even it represents the future formula for a rational and harmonious society, it still takes an entirely different sense in the present cultural system. In its logical foundation, culture continually plays on the two *distinct* terms: the ephemeral and the durable, of which neither can be made autonomous. In the socio-cultural class system, on the contrary, this relation breaks into two *distinctive* poles, of which one—the ephemeral—becomes autonomous in a culturally superior model, returning the other to its "obsolescence."

This is not at all to disqualify the formal research of the architect: but there is a bitter derision in the fact that that search for social rationality succeeds precisely in reinforcing the irrational logic and the strategy of the cultural class system.

4

Play and the Police

TO SPEAK OF REPRESSION is to speak of the CRS.[1] But this is a dangerous impressionism. The dramatic evidence of repression when it flowers on the surface of cities under the uniform of the Special Brigades mystifies us largely on its latent systematics, which haunts the depths of our consciences. It was one of the victories of the movement of May to have been able to ward off repression, to have brought it to light as the truth of the institution and of the social order, but it was its weakness to only have been able to ward this off under a spectacular form, in its murderous and archaic aspects, upon which of course a tactical solidarity is tied ("Everyone against repression"), but upon which too the movement exhausted itself in a spectacular guerrilla conflict—ending in the fascination of the symbolic street fight, where incarnated repression became, accordingly in the iconography and the obsessional folklore inspired by the CRS, the *number one object of consumption* for the rebellious imagination.

If the movement of May is caught in this trap, this game, this symbolic counter-dependence which is part of our cultural mechanism (that it meanwhile attempted to surpass toward the end in the slogans of commercial self-management), one can admit that it has been reduced by the tactical political conditions and that it's target was, beyond the violence of the police, the fundamental social violence, the repressive essence of politics, the violence of all kinds, sexual, cultural, economic, done to human beings by the social order *because it is an order.*

But it does not suffice to see radical insurrection against society as a carnivorous flower, a political and transpolitical reincarnation of the Bad Mother. If this kind of genetically distant phantasm, intending to subvert even the principle of social reality, has certainly nourished the "contestation of global society," one must still, to explain their resurgence, grasp the specific mechanisms of repression in contemporary society. What new type of repression provokes this new type of insurrection?

1.

IN ORDER TO READ repression, one must unravel not only the schema of the police, but also the empirical schema, vulgarized by psychoanalysis, of vital forces being pushed back, of the frustration of "essential" needs, etc. Repression in civilized countries is no longer a negation, an aggression, it is an *ambiance.* It is pacified everydayness, wherein the distinction between play and the police is effaced. Again, in other words, generalized repression, which translates itself through the internalization of contraries (intellectual and sexual) and wherein the repressive instance becomes *maternal*, is the place of an intense *participation.* Behind the maternalist slang of the environment, of the ambiance, of interest, of participatory values, which substitutes itself for that, normative and judiciary, of Order, of Justice, of Hierarchy, which was the social lexicon of the Word of the Father, the open era of co-repression installed itself. This repression is imponderable because it operates through signs. It won't be warded off in the street, nor

through street fighting, because it is inscribed even in the arrangement of the street, not panning the windows, not in the spectacle of
the street fighting. In co-management, it nourishes the signs themselves (but only the signs) of responsibility and power. This historic
transition of violent forms of repression toward complicit euphoria
can be read in the face of the city: the grand Parisian boulevards, once
the site of insurrection and of its suppression, have become grand
commercial and spectacular arteries. Here social conflicts are no
longer resolved by force, rather they come here to abolish themselves.

2.

THIS REPRESSION, DEFINED at the lived level as *ambiance* and complicity, is defined inversely, in theory, as a systematic totality of
division, of *separation*. Today social violence expresses itself less in
the direct repression of drives, in the physical constraint of individuals or in the open oppression of the class or category than in
the grid of social relations, in the ever more complex, systematic,
geographical, professional, and cultural segregation, in the irreversible technical and social division of labor, in the unlimited
lessening of needs.

The principle of separation, which breaks the unity of desire
and institutes human activity in multiple sectors—to which a certain autonomy and a certain liberty is in isolation attached—is the
most effective principle of neutralization of energies. The public
sphere and the private sphere: Marx traced the historical genesis of
this dissociation: between the two, a negative reciprocal determination. Under the illusory liberty of the private domain, all the
contradictions of the economy and of politics come to strain the
routine and to alter the course of life. Our dream of the domain
"reserved" for leisure. Here one can clearly see the essence of repression:

to index the free aspiration on the schema even of servitude. Doubled in work and leisure, the everyday routine organizes each share in the same way. Those who live parked in public housing or in the promiscuity of the assembly line can only dream, under the same sign of liberty, of overcrowded beaches and a sea of cars. The disconnection between paradise and hell is that people can only dream of a paradise in the image of their hell.

The system of repression takes root in the division of labor. But the violence that exerts itself on the level of production, the human deficit that results from fragmented labor is rarely experienced as freedom: repression is not consummate (in all the senses of the word: it is not perfect and it does not savor its own image). More significantly today for us is that it exerts itself in the division of needs. Because some risk the illusion even of the pleasure principle. All the prophets of the society of consumption extol our freedom from needs, to promote the multiplication of pleasures. In modern man, there would be a virtuality of needs that awaits only the products necessary for their satisfaction. To awaken these needs is to liberate man, it is to tear mankind from millennia of repression. "Liberate yourself from your superego, enjoy life fully, etc." Of course, these neo-sorcerers are mindful to liberate man according to an explosive finality of happiness. The goal is to permit the drives, long blocked by mental authorities (taboos, superego, guilt) from crystallizing on objects or concrete instances in which the explosive force of desire comes to abolish itself and to materialize the ritual repressive function of the social order. The ever more "free" irrationality, the multiplication of needs will at base be equal to more and more strict control at the summit.

What interests us here is these two united aspects: the repression of desire accomplished through the emancipation of needs

(Marcuse's "repressive desublimation")—this emancipation accompanies a differentiation and a forced ventilation of needs, their arrangement and calculated dispersion across the span of products. It is in effect the needs that are induced by the products —or moreover: since the products have the greatest coherence (the needs are absolutely contingent), it is the needs which return to them and come, broken apart, discontinuously, to insert themselves in the span of objects (just as active practices forcefully come to insert themselves within the division of labor—escaping only through the inoffensive regression into *bricolage*). The system of individual needs is in some way indexed, classified, cut up by the objects and the products (cultural products as well). It can therefore be directed (this is the real finality of the system on the socio-economic level).

This is to clarify Marcuse's notion of "repressive needs" and introduce a critique. Having seen that the most subtle modern alienation links itself at this level with the internalization of the extra-economic violence that describes the repressive needs, Marcuse calls for the "determinate negation" of these needs and for raising new needs, which are conscious and concerted in their harmonious finality, which is to say not complicit with the repressive principle of reality, not complicit with the irrational pleasure principle, but on the contrary, which inaugurate a kind of rational and collective pleasure principle. This is illusory: on the one hand, if the needs are historically determined (which Marcuse himself admits, of course), one cannot really see where these non-alienated needs would come from. In particular, this "revolution of needs" is nothing at bottom, but the modern version of the old idealist project of the moral education of humanity, of a revolution in consciousness, etc. We must be clear: neither needs nor any theory of needs will never offer a non-alienated perspective, a revolutionary alternative, because the needs are immediately as such a product of repression, being immediately as such broken apart, divided, ordered. On the other hand, regarding current repressive needs ("determinate negation") in their specificity, one risks inscribing them in advance (negatively) in a problematic that is already that of repression, one risks sealing them off in a negativity without escape, which quickly becomes part of cultural mechanisms. Thus: the anti-theater is impossible, despite the prowess of Grotowski or the Living Theater. It is the institution of the theater itself which should be questioned, with its fundamental inscription of the stage as the place where separated activity is exercised, homologous with the separated institution of Power in every hierarchized society.

Similarly, it is not this or that need, but the institution of needs as separated ends that should be denied. Neither needs nor labor exist as separate. As a historical social fact only the *division of labor* exists and the correlate *division of needs*. And it is this double division that should be analyzed as the foundation of repression. Every theory of needs, even those with revolutionary intentions, can only reorganize the contradiction between the social ends of order and the anomie of desire, can only loosen the code of directed sublimation and supply a theoretical (ideological) basis to super-repression.

By locating repression in the disjunction itself, in the segregation of social and individual practices, one condemns oneself to struggling for the progressive liberalization of separated domains. For sexual "freedom," for example. This is linked to the exercise of sexuality as a need, as a separated activity, as performance, as perversion, as object of consumption, as individual regression (and not as desire). The same with the liberation of labor. And with the sun during vacation: the rehabilitation of the body, concern for beauty, demand for well-being? Yes, but therein separated ends, circumscribed to vacation, puritan satisfactions, parenthesis in work, substituted for desire: *alibis*. Vacation sun is repressive, its real function is to disavow the value of pleasure, because it intervenes as a sign of an *absent* totality. Thus nudism: is it the truth of the body? Not at all: the truth of the body is desire and nudism, usurping nudity as a sign, disavows more completely, omits and censures nudity as flesh. Hypocrisy? No. The logic of repression.

Of course, repression exerts itself directly on certain contents *as well* (mainly sexual). But what one must see is that it is first of all a strategy, which passes through the systematic disjunction of the social body, like a physical body, in zones, in sectors, in disso-ciated activities, by which it is deservedly assigned to a partial end of *need*, which is today devoted to satisfaction (or to frustration) and not to pleasure and transgression. Another example: I am not alienated insofar as I am a consumer of "free" time, of leisure, but to the extent that I live as free a time formally opposed to the time of work, the extent or the effect even of freedom results from the process of the dissociation of the time of work from leisure time. Therein lies repression, and not in the eventual restriction of leisure time.

If we admit (with Marcuse) that, everywhere in affluent society, repression systematizes itself through needs, which is to say in the principle of partial satisfaction linked to regression, and not at all in the pleasure principle linked to transgression, we also admit that all speculation on needs is pious, and that only desire, in its irrational vehemence, in its heretical and insurrectional drive toward totality can offer a revolutionary alternative.

3.

HAVING SEEN HOW the principle of repression is structurally organized, we quickly return to its phantasmatic organization. The
repressive effectiveness of this society comes not only from paternal
authority, that which founds the reality principle, institutes the
rational processes of work, the bureaucratic processes of organization
and of the political processes of power, nor does it come from the
pure and simple substitution of a maternal power for that paternal
power, gratifying, incarnate in society in well-being, which would
serve the energies in the name of a revolution in gentleness. The
effectiveness of the system comes from what it now stakes on a
double authority: the "traditional" repressive Power is still strongly
present, with its technique and social principle of reality, its class
domination, the absolute finality of production, but it has learned
how to avoid the risks of brutal irruption of that which has been
inhibited and of the subversion of its order by setting in play at the
heart even of repression the *signs* of the pleasure principle. It is all
the litany of the gift, of the offering, of gratification, of blossoming,
which haunts advertisement: "See how society as a whole can only
adapt to you and your desires." You haven't produced the object
(wage-earners), you haven't purchased it (wage-earners), you emitted
the desire, and global society (good mother), through its engineers,
its technicians, its services, gratified that desire. But one can
clearly see that this litany is a *political* discourse, the tactic of which
rests on a splitting in two: that of the social reality in a real
authority and in an image, one effacing itself behind the other,
becoming illegible and ceding place only to a schema of absorption
in the maternal ambiance.[2]

When advertisement suggests in essence : "Society adapts itself
completely to you, adapt yourself completely to it," it is clear that

the reciprocity is rigged: an imaginary authority adapts itself to you, while you adapt yourself in exchange to a very real order. In an armchair which "marries the forms of your body," YOU marry the entire technical and political order of society. Society makes itself maternal to better preserve an order of constraints. Besides, behind this system of gratification, we see all the structures of authority reinforce themselves: planning, centralization, bureaucracy —political parties, apparatus, States reinforcing their hold behind this vast maternal image which renders their (real) contestation less and less possible.

We can formulate things differently: the authoritarian repressive apparatus, which wore itself out by forcefully diminishing the contradiction between the reality principle and the pleasure principle, between individual drives and social purposes, today reaches this same end by warding off the drives in a systematics of happiness, which "harmoniously" integrates itself in a dynamic of production. The schema of happiness, the phantasms and the drives anterior to the reality principle are no longer sacrificed: we arouse them, provoke them, satisfy them. *Repression operates through the detour of regression.* Doing so, it helps to reinvest in the reality principle everything that, anterior to it and repressed, risked surging back on it and sinking it.

A good example of this regression/repression is the eroticism of advertisement (which haunts all mass culture, and which says to all good apostles of modernity that our society is on its way to eliminating sexual prohibitions). The eroticism of advertisement is not genital, or adult. It is precisely, beneath a genital poster, the repression of all adult desire through (or across) regressive schema that are pre-genital, maternal, nourishing, narcissistic, of an infantile homosexuality, etc. The entirety of repressed pre-genital sexuality comes to haunt the signs of "liberated" genital sexuality. This is the true content of sexual liberation, and one sees how repression accomplishes its goals much more profoundly here than in puritan repression. No more prohibition, censorship, or moral ideology— but a substitution of inoffensive infantile processes for a dangerous sexual irruption.[3]

This repression through infantilization, powerfully reactivates structures of risk (the irony or the antiphrase of advertising which has no critical value at all, but a *paracritical* value integrated in advance in the effect of advertising, under the same heading as an obligatory smile). In the society of consumption, everything becomes a sign to be wagered and consumed, including the most radical critique of that society. Repression does not escape. Struggling on the barricades, the students exalted at the same time in their aural image on the radio. Society watches itself everywhere, but the human that it puts into self-reflection is not at all critical: it's the humor of *Lui* magazine, of Godard's films, etc.; complacent lucidity is the number one value of spontaneous intellectual discourse.

Better (and it is here that the system subtly closes itself and becomes almost unbeatable) this play of distancing is the proper mode of the consumption of *culpability* which attaches itself to the infantile regression that implicates consumption itself. Open, traditional repression functions in the name of a puritan morality. Modern repression functions in the name of play. In play (the combinative "freedom"), as it blossoms in the mass media, in erotic play, etc., as it culminates in the "critical" play of the intelligentsia, desire resigns itself definitively in play. This play is far from being, as in the child or the work of art, the reconciliation of desire and the reality principle. On the contrary, it masks, behind signs of nonchalance, the intense culpability which attaches itself to this type of regressive gratification. Warded off in this way, in signs of play, culpability consumes itself like any other object.

It is perhaps even the end of the end of consumption for a certain social group: the intellectuals. Culpability is the order of the day, through psychological exegesis. It should be in sociology as well. This is to say, among other things, to analyze how culpability can become the nourishment even of the existence of the group, and be exploited by it toward cultural ends.[4] For the intelligentsia in particular culpability is a distinctive value. Of course, it has individual psychological foundations, but it is *socially orchestrated* overall, like any other way of dressing or behaving, at its limit like an effect of fashion—like an element of the social code.

There is a "culpability value" among Western intellectuals, just as there is a "goat value" in Kikuyu society. A properly social *exchange value*, which has nothing to do with the neurotic disposition of anyone. This culpability does not require psychoanalysis; it is an economic element of the group. It is requires a social crisis, or cultural contact with other groups. That we dream of the delightful malaise that we seek in the Living Theater, in the political masochism of the intellectuals of the Left, etc. More generally, shame is a primary journalistic value. It is a collective drug (which never engages responsibility): thus the great campaigns on the "Wall of Shame," "Biafra: Shame of Civilized Man," etc. Everyday consumption and advertisement are themselves impregnated with culpability. It is one of the aspects of the "malaise of the civilization." The collision of the two moral imperatives: the ascetic ethos and the modern imperative toward delight, finds an escape in a compromise: delight indexed in blame—shameful delight— reintegration of the failure to delight in orgasm, etc. This is *also* "consumption." There is an entire lexicon of exasperated delight in advertisement.

It is therefore not only the position of an isolated group that we are describing: it is the contradiction of an entire civilization which here expresses, as usual, the marginal class of the intellectuals —but at the same time *it seizes this contradiction as a distinctive value*: it monopolizes it, manipulates it and assures it a portion of its power.

All of this defined, faced with the radical negativity of desire, a second negativity of play, become autonomous everywhere today, but more particularly among the "intellectuals" in the *paracritical subculture*. Thus the transgression of hierarchic social values returns in the play of a cultural elite, the subversive call to happiness returns in the game of social differentiation; where repression is properly crowned, where the repressive authority and the forces of transgression coexistent in a veritable conjugal neurosis.

Where do we go from here? Is there a point outside the system, from which the system can flatter itself, in its functionality even, gambling with and evading disruptive forces? What type of political action is possible? Revolution? The principle of Revolution, as it is founded on a historical dialectic of the resolution of social contradictions, is a *rational* principle. It situates itself entirely in the field of the reality principle. It is the motor of the repressive society of the traditional type because it situates itself in the same theoretical and political field, but it is still gearing up in a society of the new type, wherein the fundamental contradictions still exist, but masked, outsmarted by playful and regressive processes, where repressive adjustment leaves room for an agreed upon adjustment, for a systematic complicity and for that euphoria of ambiance discussed above.

An entirely new situation has been created. A situation of *perfect repression*, which through the fact that it exerts itself beyond politics, calls for a kind of transpolitical intervention. It is this type of intervention that we have seen rise up during the events of May, during which in the end, we spoke very little of objective contradictions and of dialectical surpassing, but wherein we saw the irruption of a principle anterior (or ulterior) to the reality principle, intervening in a block like the living contestation of the system, and through this even denouncing it, breaking it down, directing it even more to subvert it, to block it so as to make it shatter contradictions so as to resolve them dialectically. Facing the principles, conjugated in their antagonism, of repressive Power and of Revolution, a third principle is addressed: that of Subversion.

In still other words: the revolutionary dynamic has been able to prevail up to this point, against the established order, and to conserve itself, from the principle of change, of movement, of social progress (at once economically: as the liberator of productive forces, and symbolically). But faced with a society that takes account of every ideology of change and of development, and of which the repressive mode (the "modernist" reality principle) is that of functionality, of productivity, of innovation, in which the mode of appearance is that of a perpetual flux of signs (fashion in all its aspects, consumption in the largest sense), faced with such a society, the Revolution can no longer inscribe itself as the principle of change, it will translate itself on the contrary through interruption, rupture, dysfunction, blockage. When the system comes to balance itself through progressive flight, when it manages to digest its contradictions and profit from its crises, when the hierarchy of functions and relations assumes the form of objective reason and when sexual liberty itself is a by-product of productivity, what remains other than interruption and to address the almost blind demand of the real pleasure principle, the radical demand for transgression, against the massive collusion that passes under the sign of satisfaction? This is what appeared as the "style of intervention" of the active elements of the month of May.

"Historic possibilities should be thought according to the forms that place the accent on rupture more so than on continuity with past history, on negation more than on positivity, on difference more than on progress."[5]

In a society that is no longer exactly a society of repression, but a society of persuasion, of dissuasion of individual goals, only the subversion of the instinctual order can constitute a point exterior to the system. That subversion is nevertheless also political, by the fact that it appears in the political field. But its register is not that of conscious finality nor of contradiction, its mode is not dialectical. Its negativity is radical. Its goal is not a surpassing of contradictions, but an abolition of separations. It intends to restore the totality, not through a dialectical labor on the separated elements, but by a pure act of critical regression.

Because one must say that the contestation of this repressive/regressive society creates itself (we saw it in May) with the help of schema largely borrowed from values and models anterior to the reality principle: the refusal of work, of organization, the drive to happiness, "play without obstacles," etc.[6] In this way, the transfer of this radical subversive action to a class which was not exactly political —the youth—might be clarified; this is to say to a class latent economic and social responsibility, to a class yet to confront economics in its real contradiction, but as a system of values and, on the other hand, ends. Besides, the concept of transgression goes back expressly to archaic societies, societies anterior to the contradictions of our economic order. The highly integrated primitive hierarchal order, which knew nothing of revolution, presumed ritual and periodic transgression. Transgression is a cyclical space of social menstruation, like the order that it inverts periodically. In our rationalized society too transgression is largely integrated in rituals of rebellion (those of the "critical" intelligentsia, see above) or of revolution (socialism de rigueur). But this society remains inferior to primitive societies in its real power of integration. It largely masters conscious oppositional processes, but not yet unconscious oppositional processes, and transgression flowers like a wild resurgence, like a diehard radical who no longer represents the political and moral conscience confronting power, but a vital drive confronting a vital repression, not of this or that political system, but of the social order insofar as it is an order, and not of the order in its contradictions, but in its coherent finality itself. More and more often we will have to deal with these unforeseen transgressions, these convulsions of the value system.

The political problem is to analyze how this radical negativity can articulate itself in the "objective" contradictions, and this not from some metaphysical or metapsychological point of view, but in the reality of the social classes which support it, and in the social struggles that carry them along.

The theoretical analysis itself should, from this moment, set out from the hypothesis not of a polar antagonism, Social classes/ Revolution, but from three terms, Class Institution/Revolution/ Subversion, and from the complex relationships among these three.

5

Technics as Social Practice

EVERY TECHNICAL PRACTICE is a social practice, every technical practice is soaked in social determination. But it doesn't present itself as such: it claims autonomy, innocence, a technical rationality founded on science. This rationality subtends the ideology of faith, which imposes itself on our society as morality, wherein technical practices, separated from social reason, become a technique of the *social*, and more precisely of social manipulation, and therefore a technics of power.

The practical efficiency of technics changes in social efficacy. But this is too general a statement.

It would be interesting to see how, in different epochs, technical assets were seized by the logic of privilege. In the fifteenth and sixteenth centuries, the wealthy reserved avant-garde techniques: they served their festivals. Through the ages, but in a far more evident way during the twentieth century, the leading technical practices have been military, an exclusive domain of power. The directing classes only let those filter down that were strictly for the reproduction of productive forces—sometimes organizing even stagnation or a deliberate technical deficit. In any era, technical knowledge and its use has divided the social body into distinct airs, categories, zones of privilege. Technical discrimination is a given throughout history.

Nevertheless, it is only when technical knowledge definitively emerges from religious, ritual, playful, or corporate constraints, as in the Industrial Revolution, that it becomes a "free" productive force, while at the same time it establishes itself in the totalitarian myth of modern societies. But this, here again, is too simple; it is not the effect of a global authority called technics on a global society that must be analyzed, it is how society stratifies itself as a function of technical knowledge, what relationship diverse groups and classes maintain, each with the others, across technics as practice and as myth—and what type of relationship exists between social discrimination in the order of a system of values called technical knowledge and the social discrimination according to other systems of values—cultural, for example.

Contrary to the myth that demands—in the inverse of culture —the place of an hereditary inequality—that technics should be a "democratic" dimension:

— the myth according to which individuals of every social origin would be more naturally, more spontaneously equal before technics than they are in regard to culture and art (with even an inverse privilege for non-privileged classes, closer, as one would like to say, to the empire and to the mechanical arts),

— the myth according to which technics would be a more rational domain, therefore more democratic, since virtually accessible to everyone through academics training and practice—in contrast to the subtle paths that bring one into culture and political science,

— the myth according to which technics would be an innocent domain, distinct from politics, innocent because linked to the mastery of nature while culture, economics, and politics would be more directly implicated in social organization and mastery.

In fact, technics is only in a first moment, or in a first place, an instrument of the mastery of nature and of the liberation of productive forces. It is therefore simultaneously an instrument for restructuring social relations and for elaborating a social rationale. Once crossed, a certain level of mastery of natural forces (and we crossed this threshold a long time ago), technics becomes despite itself an instrument of mastery and of social control.

This in two ways—directly as an auxiliary of politics—indirectly as a mechanism of acculturation.

1. Politically. Every social imperative was subordinated to that of faith and therefore to the directed exercise of technics, to mastery of technical research conditions and the exclusive control of advanced technological operations (singularly military research) creating, to the profit of power, a radical privilege, on the basis of which the political game unfolded. Every investment and economic rhythm depends on this monopoly. The confinement of sacred devices and secret rituals was never, in any era, in any society, as exclusive as the secret, technological manipulation of the state in our modern societies.

The structures of this monopoly must of course be explored, defining the techno-political decision-making groups in opposition to the pure technicians and traditional politicians—defining the technical ideology proper to these groups in opposition to the technocratic myths available to everyone, etc.

2. Culturally. Technics, far from homogenizing society through knowledge, affects, from level to level, a discrimination as precise, is not as traditional and hereditary, as cultural initiation. This system of differentiation functions, just like the other, through:

— consecrated authorities (Research Institutes, the Academy of Sciences, the Centre nationale de recherche scientifique, Atomic and Space administrations) which sanction technics as a model and universal value at a higher level. At this level, technics sublimates itself in research and science,

— a scholarly system of technical teaching as a subordinate vocation (in our Western societies certainly, but we can ask if the celebration of technical values in the East is not fundamentally linked to economic objectives), which is always ambiguous in its double, shameful relationship with cultural education and education in scientific theory.

THE REMARKABLE INEQUALITIES that this apparatus institutes in the real participation in technics and that tend to mask the diffuse mythology of technology, this hierarchy, official or officious, is the object of a very strong social code. From theoretical practice to vulgar practice, from a noble technical knowledge to applied knowledge or, lower still, to the application of simply technical recipes in manipulation and construction—from access to the treatises on nuclear physics to reading "Science and Life" or the "Manuel of Domestic Techniques," it is all a sliding scale of *status* that we go through. Each of these indices signals a social condition and a relation to others for assigning each group its respective rank.

This is clearly a question of status and not of knowledge. It is not about concrete differences in knowledge, which, logically, have nothing to do with the social hierarchy of people. It is a question of social *distinction*, of class distinction founded on the *quality* of knowledge taken as an index of *value*—therefore of a *properly cultural system*, of a code of social designation not through literary or artistic habitus, for example, but across a more or less elevated level of *initiation* into the technical order.

In the social logic of culture, this system of technical order comes into play in relation to the system founded on "humanist" values, as a parallel *system of acculturation*, relaying the other and supplementing it through mechanisms analogous to the failings of traditional cultural integration.

Technics effectively constitutes one of the most powerful themes of "mass culture." Large strata of the population, at bottom hardly touched by the properly cultural models, integrated only through dreams, impulses, fragmentary understandings that are dispersed to them in the domain of technics.

The vast phenomenon of autodidacticism, the process of cultural education characteristic of the social emergence of the middle classes, nourishes itself in large part through technics. All the givens accounted for in scientific or cultural training are welcomed in one way or the other in technics. Not that that is their natural propensity: it's the logic of the global cultural system that assigns them to this subculture that lives, in unconscious resignation, off of the prestige of science.

To the direct power that it confers through political efficacy, technics connects the parallel power and ideology that it draws from functioning like a pseudo-culture, a second culture more particularly destined to the "uncultivated" classes—but a systematized culture nonetheless, in its equipment, its legitimating authorities, its mechanisms of diffusion, its models and norms—in brief functioning like a total cultural system coming to reinforce the other to clinch the social hierarchy of powers.[1] Thus one can only grasp the ambiguity of technics by analyzing the position that is assigned to it in the order of a global system of values: made sacred as an absolute spring for power over the international economic chessboard, technics remains a shameful academic and cultural value. One must also analyze how our societies fail to make technical values autonomous as full and transcendent values, this failure (or its rationalization) in a universalist myth of technics.

But fundamentally, if our societies fail to rationalize their social practice of technics (and not only their technical practice), this lapse is not at all innocent: to rationalize technical practice equals failing to establish a social strategy on the *mystery* of technics.

In a hierarchical society, technics must, like other things, no longer have a function, but a mystery of functionality. And this mystery, that weighs on each technical product, on each technical articulation of the social body, is a social mystery.

The Mythic Organization of Technics

TECHNICS OPENS DIRECTLY onto the social level, which is to say when one leaves the abstract and rational level of pure technology, as a divided system, as the systematic opposition of two terms where each is the functional alibi of the other: a metatechnics and an everyday practice. A transcendent technics, hypostasized in fiction, and a banal technics, reified in consumption.

This distortion of technics is often formulated in terms of effects: everyday life, maintained (for strategic reasons) in a state of technical infantilism, would meanwhile benefit from high tech "effects." This presumes the thesis of the unequal development of different sectors of social reality, and, behind that, the hypothesis of a theoretical homogeneity, of a technical transparency, the diffusion of which would be opposed only by social structures.

In fact, there is no other technics than that elaborated by men in such a social context, nor another sense of technics than that which it assumes in social logic. This social logic immediately imposes technics as an ideological system with two poles. Not that social organization comes simply to divide unitary technics in principle; it and it alone institutes technics and institutes it as divided, disassociated, and fundamentally, in its status as social signifier, in the logical distance between these two poles. Sublime technics, banal technics. Fiction, everyday. Between the two, neither a split nor "effects," but a logical distance and a contradictory implication.

In this, technics is homologous with culture—both obeying the same social logic. There is no longer an educated culture from which mass culture would be "fallout" (according to the model/series schema)—there is a direct cultural system founded on the logical distance between educated culture and mass culture—one defining itself as a function of the other, one implicating the other, one exclusive of the other—to the evident benefit of educated culture, which maintains absolute models.

In the same way, one can admit that advanced technics is founded, *in its advancement*, only on the principle of the technical segregation of everyday life and of the forced assignment of everyday life to consumer stereotypes. It is therefore not a social accident if everyday life is in a chronic state of technical under-development. It is not a dysfunction: it is a *logical* function of the system, entirely like a flight from scarcity and poverty is a functional element of the "welfare state."

The imagination plays on this tactical division. Advanced technics, cut from everyday technical practice and confusedly identified with science, comes to be able to serve the imaginary of the banal technics of "consumption"—exactly like educated culture fundamentally serves as an imaginary model for mass culture. The spatial, nuclear, futuristic heroization of technics, that entire demiurge, that *science* fiction comes into play and is revealed in domestic gadgets, that would thus not at all be experienced as effects, but transfigured as signs and as the promise of a total technological revolution, whose model is already here, suggested everywhere in the exalted and euphoric discourse on technics (which always doubles as a moral, pessimistic discourse, complicit with the first, and which only reinforces the "dizzying" effect). Across the washing machine's control panel, the average person thinks of himself as a distinct citizen of the techno-logical revolution, though this control panel precisely in its caricature of power is linked to an archaic world of functions, only sends him back to the absence of a total, innovative, structuring technics—and makes him consume it as an absence. The smallest of everyday objects underscores a myth of the absolute functionality of a completely technological world, beyond social contradictions and history. This is the other aspect of the social mystery which we mentioned above.

This technics completes itself in grand mythic oppositions, like that of spatial fusion and the automobile. In fact, the opposition between a prestigious technology and an obsolete technology is only apparent: the concrete dictatorship of the automobile, which has swallowed an entire civilization, and the abstract fascination of spatial adventures are the two poles of a systematic implication in which technics and everyday life are both enclosed and alienated.

A consequence of this division of the system, where one term can imagine the other: the technical objects do not intervene directly in everyday life, as mediators of structures and new social functions, but on the contrary as *already mediated by the idea of technology* and by a metaphysics of rationality.

Concretely, this signifies that the objects or new technologies are not experienced as practical and social innovations but as erratic novelties, drawing their fascination from their complicity with myth, with the future, with the imaginary, and not at all from their possibility of changing the present. This is how they are received as *objects*, which is to say fixed and idealized as *avant-garde* signs, peopling an unreal everyday world. This is how they fall into *consumption*. And, according to this paradox, the more they are technologically new, the more they are perceived as aesthetic and desired for privileged consumption.

Thus technology, submerged in everyday life, realizes itself as science fiction, nourishing all of its powers in the prestige of consumption. What happened to cinema happens a little to every object or technological group. Edgar Morin has clearly demonstrated how, from the immense possibilities for information, communication and social change that cinema initially opened as a scientific technology of the image, it has almost entirely and, it seems irremediably—teetering in the imaginary—become cinema-spectacle, a cinema of consumption.[2]

Conclusion: "All Technics in the Service of Everyday Life?"

IF ONE ADMITS that technics presents itself directly, in the social logic of class, as the system of opposition that we have come to describe, and thereby as a system for the mythic transfiguration of real contradictions (those of everyday life and of social structures).[3] What happened to the revolutionary slogan: "All technics in the service of everyday life" (Henri Lefebvre).

Effectively, so that there could be a technical revolution of everyday life, there would already have to be a revolution of the entire system to make technics something other than what it is.

This hope is founded on the postulate of the fundamental rationality of the technical order, that it would be sufficient to liberate and articulate it within in social reality for the world to be overturned. But this isn't so easy. This rational level of technics really exists: it's technology. But as private individuals or social subjects, we have no other business with technology other than with technics as a system of value and ideology. Can we hope that if technics is the product, in its most effective substance, of a social order that sanctions failure and contradiction, masking them in its prodigious flight and thereby clearing away the chances of resolving them— how can we hope to place it in the service of a social revolution?

Maintaining every proportion, this would be the same illusion as demanding that "the police enter into service for the collectivity"—though it is by definition social, in the service of private interests and of power. One could say the same thing about culture.

In short, one must be careful to consider the dereliction of the technics of everyday life as an accident along the way, such that it would suffice to shift technics to the right path, to liberate its virtualities to change life. One must see that it is our society itself, in its most fundamental organization, that reinvents technics at every moment as a dimension of salvation, and not of knowledge, as a mythic system and strategy of power, and not as a rational instrument and revolutionary social practice.

In every state of the case, it would know to create the revolutionary "irruption" of technology in concrete society. So that technical innovation inaugurates real structural changes, it would first be necessary to initiate a *technical culture*, which is to say the slow and difficult substitution of another system of values for traditional culture, and this through *a radically different educational system*, not so much in its contents as in its educational *techniques*. Finally, one must separate technics from the technical spectacle and from the myth that encloses it, so as to recognize it in its principle, which is that of "capability and rational exercise,"[4] and bring this principle to the root of social training, if one wants to put an end to magical manipulation.

6

Utopia deferred...

UTOPIA HAS BEEN DEFERRED in idealism through a century and a half of triumphant dialectical historical practice. Today it's starting, in its rigorous indefiniteness, to surpass all revolutionary definitions and to refer every model of revolution back to bureaucratic idealism.

Utopia is no-place, the radical deconstruction of every political space. It offers no privileges to revolutionary politics.

There could be no model for utopia nor utopian function, because utopia denies the inscription of all finality, whether unconscious or in the class struggle.

Utopia is not only the denunciation of the simulacra of Revolution, it is also the analysis of the Revolution as a political *model of simulation* of a rational deadline for man which opposes itself to utopia's radicality.

Utopia is never spoken, never on the agenda, always repressed in the identity of political, historical, logical, dialectical orders. It also haunts and crosses them irrevocably, forcing them into an overstatement of rationality. Utopia does not write itself into the future. It is always, from right now, what the order of the day is missing.

In the topic of the sign, Utopia is the gap, the fault, the void that passes between the signifier and the signified and subverts every sign. It passes between every thing and its model, annulling their respective places. It ceaselessly displaces politics and annuls it as such.

Utopia is not the dialectic of the possible and the impossible. It is not what overcomes contradictions dialectically. It transgresses them in their own terms.

Utopia is the ambivalence which crosses every order, every institution, every rationality, even "revolutionary" rationality, every positivity, no matter what, and returns them to their non-place. Utopia is the deconstruction of every unilateral finality of man or history.

Utopia is the smile of the Cheshire cat, the smile that floats in the air before the cat appears and for a time after he disappears. A little before the cat takes his place, a little after he vacates it. This smile annuls the Cheshire cat and is itself mortal.

Utopia, through the abolition of the blade and the disappearance of the handle, gives the knife its power to strike.

That our discourse analyses everyday life, celebrations, strikes, the media, and sexual liberation and denounces everything therein that is subject to phantasms, slogans, and current revolutionary models—that it appeals, beyond the code, to the radicality of the symbolic and of ambivalence: therein lies a fundamental contradiction—worse than a contradiction—the insoluble position of every theoretical discourse which is irremediably rational, didactic, and political and whose speech fails to subvert the code of the analysis. Too bad. Before canceling itself out through some more radical practice, something must be said.

7

Strike Story

October 1971

DOES A REVOLUTIONARY event unmask the logic of an entire situation, the knots and mechanisms of an entire regime? In this sense, the ten day strike of the metro conductors is a revolutionary event. It questioned all of the givens of today's society, revealed all the conditions of a social struggle in modernist society, provoked and woke up so as to unmask all the future phantasms of this new society.

1.

IT WAS AN "egoistic" struggle of a "privileged caste," a purely and deliberately catagorial action. Regression, perversion, betrayal in regard to solidarity and transcendental proletarian internationalism? Not at all! This translates the objective reality (and not dialectical twaddle) of the hierarchal and technocratic socialization of labor in this society. Labor increasingly but gradually atomized, such that it integrates the whole society in a single and same movement. It happens today, at least in the exploitation of labor power, in discrimination, in social categorization, in an infinite fragmentation of statutes, interests, privileges. The "jungle," as journalists from *Le Monde* put it. In this business of social dislocation, one finds a capitalism still more savage than in the first phase of industrialization. Hence, to be clear, and, without dreaming of words on the order of reformism, pious with solidarity, linked to the *ideal type* of proletariat, and not at all with the present reality of the new contradictions and savages of the system—say that the metro conductors have gone much further than all strikes in unity, scrupulously "designated" by the unions, in taking into account and in exacerbating this categorical *alienation*, in making a weapon of their objective condition. And one needs a certain nerve for this, when one dreams of the mystique of the masses, of mass action, of contact with the masses,—the masses as *medium*, mass *medium* of political action, as absolutely referential, for which there is no point of salvation, the masses as caution for political reality, the masses as the objective reason of politics, the phantasm culminating in the myth of the general strike, or the masses reflecting triumphantly, in the most beautiful vein of the Hegelian spirit. The metro conductors put an end to the myth of solidarity and of the general strike ("if the comrades of the Régie strike, we'll return to work") which for a longtime now has turned against the strikers themselves. We saw it in May '68, we saw it in Mans in the OS strike, we just saw it in the metro: everywhere the unions use the tactic of diffusing the strike to dilute it, to "hear a solution" and control it. It's the police that they exercise with the label of the regime. A wild strike is minoritary. That this minority confounds itself with a professional category doesn't matter; this is what gives it its power. Therein, the conductors were irreducible: no matter their "motives" (an entirely hypocritical, demobilizing moral vision is unrelenting against them, from the left and the right)—for wanting to be minoritary, in refusing mediatisation at all costs, the mass mediatisation of their strike, they made clear the resort to a political *radicality* that we have largely forgotten in the language of mass socialism. Only this "immoral" determination permitted them to bring the edifice of the system to a critical threshold, an explosive situation, in ten days.

2.

ANOTHER ASPECT OF this radicalization: for the first time, it was a wild strike against not only the bosses and the unions (in a certain way this is not new, insofar as, for the unions, this strike really had been the moment of truth and the death certificate) but also a *wild strike against the mass media* and the puppet-headed sub-stance it secretes: public opinion. The "psychological" pressure (in reality political pressure), the repressive blackmail that the entirety of the media had exerted immediately through the dis-course on social services, usage rights, the sacralization of the "public," was immense. Here they revealed themselves clearly as a weapon par excellence of social control (and it was not necessary to believe that the government had "manipulated" them): press, radio, television exerted, spontaneously and with a beautiful unity, their real political function. Beyond the violence of the state, beyond the unions, they truly appeared as the deepest form of repression, that with which every political action should henceforth count in the first place and of which it should break the "symbolic violence." Their demagogy condensed every strategy of the neo-capitalist system: to transform every social labor relation into relations of social *service*, to set up the effective fiction of a collective responsibility, of a religious solidarity, at bottom, where all conflicts are abolished. This blackmailing of solidarity, to which the electricians ceded very quickly in 1970, also plays on the diffuse socialization of problems, on the all powerful jurisdiction of a mass (this time no longer the mass of producers and workers, to whom the union and the PC referred, but the mass of users and consumers). That this mass had no other reality than that given them by the media, who were its writers and directors, is obvious. The referenced mass is still there, like all "objective" frames of reference, only as an alibi. In its name, the journalists act like dictators, they desperately search for their social legitimacy and, under this heading, they have all become, in a few days, the CDR Vérité of the mass media. The smallest victory of the conductors should not have been enough to sell them out, to the Trade Council, setting them up in this way against the "democracy" of information, against the hypocritical and distilled temptation of all parties to "sell" their strike, to "maximize its profits" by appeasing the press and public opinion, conscious in the end that they were *also* struggling against the entire system of information, objectively in solidarity, in its contents and in its form, with the system of social domination.

3.

THIS STRIKE IS an analysis *in action* of the *present* stage of political economy. Resistant to the blackmail of use-value (the comfort of users, the moral goal of the "right to transport"), the conductors revealed the strategic position that use-value has in the system of exchange value. Use-value, in solidarity with exchange value, and on which the system acts—to the point of terrorism—to better assure the process of reproduction of exchange value.

When it comes to exchange value, one has suppressed the conductors' action, still according to the "catagorial" interpretation, in wanting to make believe that at bottom they were only aiming for a more comfortable place in the capitalist system of exchange value. They have disclaimed all that at a much more radical level by refusing to "sell out" their strike, which is to say to make it valuable in exchange value. In acceding to this trap, they effectively reentered the game. By refusing, they impeached the system of exchange value not only in the act of the strike, at the level of the sale of labor power, but beyond that, by refusing to sell their strike itself to the media. This is decisive, since it seizes the system not only according to 19th century analyses, but in its present structure: that of the generalization of the system of exchange value in exchange—sign value.

IT IS IN THIS SENSE that this strike is itself truly *general*: because it questions the system of exchange value in its *generalized* form. Generality is a regressive anti-revolutionary concept, in its acceptation of "masses," it assumes its true meaning, which is that of radicality (which attacks the system in its roots, which is to say in its general form).

Since May 1968, this is the most decisive theoretical and practical step that has been taken. That it wasn't students this time (toward whom the blackmail of the "privileged group" already delivered the base), but because it is convenient to refer to a "fraction of the working class," should not carry any proletario-centric conclusion. The displacement of politics is also the displacement of the notion of classes. Since this displacement, as a general category, returns in the topic of the system, it is condemned. No matter what particular "category" can return thereafter in the decisive place—non-place of the political act (this is true as well for ethnic and linguistic, "particularist" cultural insurrections).

One must accept this strike as a wild analysis. Which is to say that none of the models of revolutionary analysis have a grip on it.

Disconcerted, the whole world was too happy to unburden themselves of the event thanks to a superficial, "objective" analysis: the
number of conductors, the caste pride, their egoistic revendication.
It's clear: all of this is reactionary. And of course: the conductors
themselves developed nothing theoretically from what was implicated in their strike. It was opaque to them: this is another aspect
of its wild character: it is not even folded in models of analysis.
Irrecuperable for any orthodoxy, even Leftist, since it lacks the
great Subject of History, the proletariat armed with a clear conscience of its actions. Too bad for dialectical prescience and its
Office for the Study of History, if radical practice creates an event
somewhere else.

8

Requiem for the Media

Introit

THERE IS NO revolutionary theory of the media. The "revolution of the media" has to date remained empirical and mystical, as much in Marshall McLuhan as among those who stand so willfully apart from him (the intelligentsia of the Left in particular). McLuhan himself has said, with his Texo-Canadian brutality, that with the appearance of the telegraph, Marx's theory, a contemporary of the steam engine and the railroad, was already obsolete during his lifetime.[1] In his candid fashion, he is saying that Marx, in his materialist analysis of production, has almost circumscribed a privileged domain of productive forces from which language, signs and communication have been excluded. To tell the truth, Marx does not even have a theory of the railroad as a "medium," as a mode of communication: it isn't considered. All technical evolution in general is only considered under the heading of production—primary, material, infrastructural—the sole determinant of social relationships. Dedicated to an intermediary ideality and a blind social practice, the "mode of communication" has been at leisure for a century to "make its revolution" without changing anything in the theory of production.

From here, and on the condition (which is already a revolution in relation to orthodox Marxism) that the exchange of signs is not considered as a marginal, superstructural dimension among beings that the single true theory (materialist) defines irrevocably as "producers of their real life" (of goods destined to satisfy their needs), we can envision two perspectives:

1. We retain the general form of Marxist analysis (dialectical contradiction between forces of production and relations of production), but we admit that the "classical" definition of productive forces is a restricted definition, and we enlarge our analysis in terms of productive forces to the entire field thus far blind to signification and communication. This implies setting loose in all their originality the contradictions freed from this theoretical and practical extension of the field of political economy. This hypothesis is the point of departure for Enzensberger: "Monopoly capitalism develops the consciousness shaping industry more quickly and more extensively than other sectors of production; it must at the same time fetter it. A socialist media theory has to work at this contradiction."[2] But this hypothesis accomplishes little more (and, in this sense, it is also late) than to virtually extend the commodity form to every domain of social life. And in fact there already is a "classical" theory of communication, a "bourgeois" political economy of signs and their production, as there came to be one of *material* production since the 18th century. It is a class-bound theoretical discipline.[3] Until now, no fundamental critique, no logical extension of Marx's critique, has responded to it. The critique of the political economy of the sign has been rendered impossible by the relegation of this entire domain to the superstructure. Thus, at best, Enzensberger's hypothesis could only make up for the tremendous delay in classical Marxist theory.

2. This hypothesis is only radical in the eyes of orthodox Marxism, which, completely immersed in the dominant models,

and for its own survival, forbids itself even this much. But the radical alternative is elsewhere. In place of reinterpreting the crucial problem posed to revolutionary theory by the production of meanings, messages, and signs in terms of classical productive forces—which is to say of generalizing a Marxist analysis considered to be definitive and sealed with the approval of the "spokesmen of the revolution"—the alternative is to disrupt these terms in light of the irruption of this problem in the theoretical field (which no Marxist who "respects himself" would do, even as a hypothesis).

In other words, maybe the Marxist theory of production is itself irremediably partial, and cannot be generalized. Again: the theory of production (the dialectical continuity of contradictions linked to the development of productive forces) is strictly homogeneous with its object, material production, and cannot be transferred, as a postulate or theoretical framework, to contents that it was never given.[4] The dialectical form is adequate to certain contents, those of material production: it exhausts its meaning, but does not exceed, as an archetype, the definition of this object. The dialectic is in ashes because it offered itself as a system of interpretation for the *separated* order of material production.

This hypothesis is, all in all, logical. It attributes Marxist analysis with a global coherence, an internal homogeneity which forbids it from retaining such and such an element and from excluding such and such an other, according to a technique of *bricolage* of which the Althusserians are the most subtle pyrotechnicians. Conversely, we will give Marxist theory credit for a maximum of coherence, and it is for this same reason that we will say that this coherence should be broken, because it is a without response before a social process which far exceeds that of (material) production.[5]

Enzensberger: A "Socialist" Strategy

LACKING A THEORY and an offensive strategy, Enzensberger claims, the "left" remains disarmed. It contents itself with denouncing mass media culture as ideological manipulation. It dreams of taking control of the media, sometimes as a *means* of aiding the masses assumption of a revolutionary consciousness, sometimes as a *consequence* of a radical change in social structures. A contradictory impulse, which simply reflects the impossibility of integrating the media into a theory of infra- and superstructure. Lacking a conception of the media as new and gigantic, potentially productive forces (Enzensberger), the media (and one should add the entire domain of signs and of communication) remains a social mystery for the "Left": it is split between fascination and panic before this wizardry, which it cannot escape, but which it morally and intellectually reproves (this of course is the "Leftist intellectual" speaking through Enzensberger's self-criticism). This ambivalence reflects only the ambivalence of the media, without surpassing or reducing it. As a good Marxist sociologist, Enzensberger imputes the "phobia" of the Leftist intellectuals and movements to their bourgeois or petit-bourgeois origins: they defend themselves instinctively against mass culture because it shatters their cultural privilege.[6] True or false, maybe it would be better to ask what responsibility the intelligentsia of the Left have in this fascinated contempt, this tactical disarray, and this refusal of investment before the media. Precisely what responsibility Marxist prejudice, its nostalgic idealism of the infrastructure, its theoretical allegiance to everything that is not "material" production and "productive labor." "Revolutionary" doctrine has never accounted for the exchange of signs other than in functional use: information, diffusion, propaganda. And the current, new look in public relations material, the entire modernist subculture of Leftist parties is not made to break this tendency: it shows well enough how bourgeois ideology can pass elsewhere only through "social origin."

All this results, following Enzensberger, in the political schizophrenia of the Left. On one side, an entire revolutionary (subversive) faction launches itself in the apolitical exploration of the new media (subculture, underground). On another side, the "militant" political groups still live essentially with archaic modes of communication, refusing to "play the game," to exploit the gigantic virtualities of electronic media. They reproach the students of May '68 for having had recourse to traditional artist's means (Beaux-Arts) for the diffusion of their slogans, and for having occupied the Odéon, a cultural capital, rather than the ORTF.[7]

Enzensberger's thought attempts to be optimistic and offensive. The media are currently under the monopoly of the dominant classes, which turn them toward their profit. But their *structure* remains "fundamentally egalitarian" and it falls to revolutionary practice to release the virtuality inscribed in them but perverted by the capitalist order—saying the word: to liberate them, to return them to their social *vocation* of open communication and unlimited democratic exchange, to their true socialist destination.

It is clear that this is a question of the extension of the same schema forever allotted, from Marx to Marcuse, to productive forces and technology. They are the promise of human accomplishment, but capitalism blocks and confiscates them. They are liberators, but we must liberate them.[8] The media, one sees, do not escape the fantastic logic of the filigreed inscription of the revolution in things. To hand the media over to the logic of productive forces is thus no longer a critical act: it more firmly encloses them in revolutionary metaphysics.

As usual, this position is lost in contradictions. On one side, though their own (capitalist) development even assures a more and more extended socialization—even though it should be technically thinkable, there is no closed circuit television for the happy few, "because this would go against the grain of the structure" of the medium.[9] "For the first time in history, the media make possible the participation of the masses in a collective process that is social and socialized, participation in which the practical means are in the hands of the masses themselves."[10] But the "socialist movements must fight and will fight for their own wavelengths."[11] Why fight (in particular for wavelengths), if the media realize socialism on their own? If this is their structural vocation?

Énzensberger claims, following Brecht,[12] that the present order reduces the media to a simple "medium of distribution."[13] We need to make the media a veritable medium of communication (the same dream always haunts the Marxist imagination: to tear objects from exchange value and return them to their use value), and this transformation, he adds, "is not technically a problem." But:

1. It is false that the media in the current order are "purely and simply a means of distribution." Here again, this makes them the relay of an ideology which would find its determination elsewhere (in the material mode of production). In other words, the media as marketing and merchandising of the dominant ideology—in which there is the assimilation of the employer-employee relationship with that of the producer-transmitter of the media—to irresponsible receptive masses. This is not as a vehicle of contents, it is in their form and their operation even that the media induce a social relationship, and this relationship is not exploitative, it is one of abstraction, of separation, of the abolition of exchange. The media are not coefficients but conductors of ideology. Not only are they

not revolutionary in destination, they are not even, elsewhere or virtually, neutral or non-ideological (the phantasms of their "technical" status or of their social "use value"). Reciprocally, ideology no longer exists somewhere else as a discourse of the dominant class before being invested in the media. It is the same in the sphere of commodities: nowhere do they possess some other status as reality (the "use value of the product") other than the form they assume in the operation of the system of exchange value. And ideology is no longer some imaginary floating in the wake of exchange value, it is itself the operation of exchange value. After the Requiem for the Dialectic, we should sound the Requiem for the Infra- and for the Superstructure.

2. It follows that when Brecht and Enzensberger affirm that the transformation of the media into a veritable medium of communication is not technically a problem ("it is" Brecht claims, "but the natural consequence of their development"), one must understand in effect (but conversely and without playing on words) that it is not exactly a technical problem, since the ideology of the media is on the level of form, of the separation that they institute, and which is a social division.

Speech without Response

THE MASS MEDIA are characterized by being intransitive, anti-mediators, manufacturing non-communication. If one accepts the definition of communication as an *exchange*, as the reciprocal space of speech and response, and therefore of a *responsibility*; not a psychological and moral responsibility, but a personal correlation from one to another in exchange. In other words, if one defines communication as something other than the simple transmission-reception of information which could be reversed in feedback. The entirety of contemporary media architecture is founded on this definition: *the media forbid response forever*; they make every process of exchange impossible (excepting in the form of the *simulation* of a response, itself integrated into the process of transmission, which doesn't change the unilaterality of the communication in any way). This is their true abstraction. And the system of social control and power is based on this abstraction.

To clearly understand the term *response*, one must understand it in the strong sense, and for this one must refer to its equivalent in "primitive" societies: power belongs to the one who can give and *to whom one cannot respond*. To give, and to do it in such a way that one cannot respond, is to disrupt the exchange to one's profit and to institute a monopoly. The social process becomes unbalanced. Response, on the contrary, disrupts this power relationship and institutes (or restores), on the basis of an antagonistic reciprocity, the circuit of symbolic exchange. The sphere of the media is the same: it speaks and *no response can be made*. This is why the only revolution in this domain—and everywhere besides, the revolution as such—is in the restitution of the possibility of response. This simple possibility presupposes the overturning of the current structure of the media in its entirety.

No other theory or strategy is possible. Every impulse to democratize its contents, to subvert it, to restore the "transparency of the code," to control the process of information, to manage a reversibility of the circuits, or to assume power over the media, is hopeless if the monopoly of speech is not broken; and this not to offer it individually to each of us but so that it can be exchanged, given and responded to,[14] as one would a look and a smile now and then, and without ever being able to be stopped, clogged, stockpiled and redistributed to some place in the social process.[15]

For the moment, we live in non-response, in irresponsibility. "Minimal autonomous activity on the part of the spectator and voter," says Enzensberger. The first and most beautiful of the mass media is in effect the electoral system: its crowning achievement is the referendum, in which the response is implied in the question, as in polls. It is a speech which responds to itself through the simulated detour of a response, and there again, the absolutization of the speech beneath the formal mask of exchange is the definition of power. Roland Barthes points to the same non-reciprocity in literature: "Our literature is characterized by the pitiless divorce which the literary institution maintains between the producer of the text and its user, between its owner and customer, between its author and reader. This reader is thereby plunged into a kind of idleness— he is intransitive; he is, in short, *serious*: instead of functioning, instead of gaining access to the magic of the signifier, to the pleasure of writing, he is left with no more than the poor freedom either to accept or reject the text: reading is nothing more than a *referendum*."[16] Today, the status of *consumer* defines this relegation, and the general order of consumption is nothing other than that wherein it is no longer permitted to give, to respond or exchange, but only to take and to use (appropriation, individualized use value). In this sense, "consumer" goods are also a mass medium. They answer to the general form we have described. Their specific function is of little importance: the consumption of products and messages is the abstract social relation that they establish, the taboo cast on every form of response and reciprocity.

Thus it is not true, as Enzensberger affirms, that "for the first time in history, the media make possible a mass participation in a production social process," nor that "the practical means of this participation are in the hands of the masses themselves." As if owning a television or a camera inaugurated a new possibility of relation and exchange! Strictly speaking, no more than owning a refrigerator or a toaster. There is no response to a functional object: its function is there, integrated speech to which it has already responded, and which leaves no place for play, for a reciprocal gesture (except for its destruction or for turning it away from its function).[17] The functional object, like all messages made functional by the media, like the operation of the referendum, therefore controls rupture, the emergence of meaning, and censorship. At the limit, if the authorities are not also obsessed with contents and convinced by the media's force of ideological persuasion, and therefore of the necessity of controlling messages, they would offer each citizen a television without concern for its programs. It is effectively useless to fantasize about the police appropriating television for the authorities (Orwell *1984*): Television is, in its mere presence, social contract at home. It is unnecessary to conceive of it as a spy-glass of the regime into our private lives, because it is better than that: it is *the certainty that the people will no longer speak*, that they are definitively isolated before a speech without response.

Such is the structure of television as a mass medium. And, in this sense, McLuhan, whom Enzensberger contemptuously characterizes as a ventriloquist, is much closer to a theory when he says that "the medium is the message" (except that, totally blind to the social form we are discussing, he exalts the media and their planetary message with a delirious tribal optimism). "The medium is the message" is not a critical proposition, but, in its paradoxical form, it has analytical value. Enzensberger's ingenuity on the "structural nature of the media" (!),[18] such that "no power can permit the liberation of their potentiality," on the other hand and although it wants to be revolutionary, is only mysticism. The mystique of the socialist predestination of the media, inverse but complementary to the Orwellian myth of their terroristic manipulation by the authorities. Even God would approve of socialism: the Christians say so.

Subversive Strategy and "Symbolic Action"

ONE MIGHT OBJECT that the mass media played a role in May '68 by spontaneously amplifying the revolutionary movement. At one moment at least during the action, they were (involuntarily) turned against the authorities. The subversive strategy of the American Yippies (Hoffman, Rubin) is based on this necessity and this possible redirection. In worldwide revolutionary movements, a theory of "symbolic action" has been elaborated from it. Redirect the media through their ability to chain react. Use their power to generalize information instantaneously. The assumption here is that the impact of the media is reversible, that it is a variable in the class struggle that one must know how to integrate to one's profit. This must be questioned, it might be only a large strategic illusion.

May '68 can serve as an example. Everything would lead us to believe in the subversive impact of the media during that period. Suburban radio stations and newspapers echoed the student actions everywhere. If the actions were the detonator, the media were the resonator. The authorities accused them directly of "playing the revolutionary game." But this evidence was based on an absence of analysis. I would say on the contrary that the media never played their role so well and that they were, in their function of *habitual* social control, on top of the events. This was because they maintained *their* form (amid the disruption of their contents) and that this form, no matter the context, makes them inexorably in solidarity with the power structure. By diffusing the event in the *abstract universality* of public opinion, they *imposed* a sudden and inordinate development on it and, through this forced and anticipated extension, they deprived the original movement of its rhythm and its meaning—in a word: they short-circuited it.

In the traditional field of politics (Left and Right),[19] where sanctified models of canonical speech are exchanged, the media transmit without altering the meaning. They are as homogeneous to this speech as they are to the circulation of commodities. But transgression and subversion don't pass over the waves while being subtly denied as such: transformed into *models*, neutralized as *signs*, they are emptied of their meaning.[20] There is no model, prototype, or series of transgression. It is therefore still the best way to reduce them. Fatal publicity is still the best way to lessen the impact of transgression. Earlier, this operation might have led us to believe in "spectacular" results. In fact, it is equal to dismantling the movement by removing its primary impulse. The act of rupture is changed into a distant bureaucratic model—and this is what the media does.[21]

All of this is readable in the derivation, the distortion of the term "symbolic." The action of March 22nd at Nanterre was symbolic and transgressive because, at that moment in that place, it invented a radical rupture or, returning to the analysis proposed above, invented a *response* there, where the administrative and pedagogical power of the institution held forth and kept others from speaking. The broadcast and contagion of the mass media did not make this action symbolic. Today however, it is more and more this last sense (the impact of exposure) which suffices to define symbolic action. At the limit, the subversive act is no longer produced *save as a function of its reproducability.*[22] It is no longer created, it is produced directly as a model, like a gesture. The symbolic has slipped from the order of the production of meaning even (political or otherwise) to the order of its reproduction, which is always that of power. The symbolic becomes *coefficient*, pure and simple; transgression becomes exchange value.

The entirety of rationalist critical thought (Benjamin, Brecht, Enzensberger) sees decisive progress in this. The media does nothing but actualize and reinforce the "demonstrative nature of any given political act" (Enzensberger). This evidently agrees with the *didactic* conception of the revolution, and, moreover, with the "dialectic of consciousness rising," etc. This rationalist thought has not renounced the bourgeois thought of the Enlightenment, it inherits all of its conceptions of the democratic virtue (here revolutionary) of the diffusion of knowledge. In its pedagogic illusion, this thought forgets that—the political act deliberately targeting the media and expecting power from it—the media itself is deliberately targeting the political act to depoliticize it. An interesting fact might be cited here as support: the contemporary eruption of news in the political sphere (which converges with Benjamin's idea of the passage of the work of art from the political stage through its reproducability). A tidal wave in Pakistan, a black boxing match in the United States, a bistro owner shoots a youth, etc. These kinds of events, once minor and apolitical, find themselves invested with a power of diffusion which gives them social and "historic" scope. Undoubtedly the new sense that they assume, the confrontation of incidents that never before made the news, and in which the new forms of politics are crystallized, is to a large extent created by the media. These news items are unplanned "symbolic actions," which return through the same process of political signification. Doubtless, their reception can only be ambiguous, and if, thanks to the media, politics returns under the heading of minor news items, thanks to the same media, minor news items invade politics. Elsewhere the status of the news has changed with the extension of the mass media: from parallel category (related to almanacs and popular histories) it has become a social system of mythological interpretation, a tight network of models of signification from which no event escapes. This is mass mediatization. It is not a group of technologies for the diffusion of messages, it is the imposition of models. Here again is McLuhan's formula: "Medium is the message" performs a transfer of meaning in the medium itself as a technological structure. This is still technological idealism. In fact, the great *Medium* is the Model. That which is mediated is not that which passes through the press, the TV, the radio: it is that which is fulfilled by the form-sign, articulated in models, regulated by the code. Similarly, commodities are not produced industrially, they are mediated by the exchange value system of abstraction. One sees that at best what functions under the sign of the media is the formal surpassing of the categories of news and politics and of their traditional separation, so as to more easily assign them together to the same general code. It is strange that we never wanted to measure the strategic impact of this forced socialization as a system of social control. Once more, the electoral system is the first great historical example of this. And it has never lacked revolutionaries (once among the greatest, today the least significant) who believed themselves capable of "playing the game." The general strike itself, an insurrectional myth for so many generations, has become a reductive schema. That of May '68, to which the media contributed largely by exporting the strike to every corner of France, while apparently the culminating point of the crisis, was in fact the moment of its decompression, of its asphyxiation through extension, of its defeat. Of course, thousands of workers went on strike. But they didn't know what to do with this "mediatized" strike, transmitted and received as a model of action (by both the media or the unions). Abstract in a sense, it neutralized local, transversal, and spontaneous forms of action (not entirely). The Grenelle accords didn't betray it.[23] They sanctioned the passage to the generality of political action, which brought an end to the singularity of revolutionary action. Today, it has become (in the form of the calculated extension of the strike) the final weapon of the unions against wildcat strikes.

The electoral system and the general strike are thus also media of a certain kind. Playing with extensive, formal socialization, they are the subtlest and most assured institutions for filtration, dismantling, and censorship. There is no exception nor miracle.

Walls and words, silk-screen posters, and hand-printed flyers were the true revolutionary media in May, the streets where speech started and was exchanged: everything that is an *immediate* inscription, given and returned, speech and response, moving in the same time and in the same place, reciprocal and antagonistic. The street in this sense is the alternative and subversive form of all the mass media because it is not, like them, an objectified support for messages without response, a distant transit network. It is the cleared space of the symbolic exchange of ephemeral and mortal speech, speech that is not reflected on the Platonic screen of the media. Institutionalized by reproduction, spectacularized by the media, it burst.

It is therefore a strategic illusion to believe in a critical reversal [*détournement*] of the media. Today such speech passes through the *destruction* of the media such as they are, through their deconstruction as systems of non-communication. This does not imply liquidation any more than the radical critique of discourse implies the negation of language as signifying material. But this certainly implies the liquidation of their present functional and technical structure as a whole, of their operational form, if I can put it that way, which reflects their social form throughout. At the limit of course even the concept of the medium disappears, and should disappear: exchanged speech, reciprocal and symbolic exchange denies the notion and the function of the medium, of the intermediary. It can imply a technical apparatus (sound, image, waves, energy, etc.) as well as a corporeal apparatus (gestures, language, sexuality), but this no longer acts as a medium, as an autonomous system regulated by a code. Reciprocity passes through the destruction of the medium as such. "People meet their neighbors for the first time while watching their apartment houses burn down."[24]

The Theoretical Model of Communication

To summarize these diverse hypotheses:

1. McLuhan (remember): the media create, they are the revolution, independently from their contents, from their singular technological structure. After the phonetic alphabet and books, radio and cinema. After radio, television. Here and now we live in the era of instantaneous, global communication.

2. The media are controlled by power. We must tear them away from it, either by taking power ourselves, or by reversing them by raising the spectacular stakes through subversive content. Here the media are viewed only as a message. There is no question of their form (any more than there is, of course, in McLuhan, who views the medium only as a medium).

3. Enzensberger: the present form of the media induces a certain type of social relationship (assimilated into that of the capitalist mode of production). But through their structure and their development, the media possess the virtuality of a socialist and democratic mode of communication, of a rationality and a universality of information. Liberating their potential will suffice.

From the perspective of a revolutionary strategy, only Enzens-berger's (Enlightened—Marxist) hypothesis and that of the radical American left (spectacular—Leftist) interests us (we are not talking about the practice of the official Left, Marxist or not, which is confused with that of the bourgeoisie). We have analyzed these positions as strategic illusions, the cause being that both of them share with the dominant ideology implicit reference to the same *theory of communication*, a theory admitted everywhere, on the strength of received evidence and a highly "scientific" formaliza-tion by a discipline, the semio-linguistics of communication, applied to structural linguistics on one side and infomatics on the other, endorsed by the universities and mass culture (mass media professionals are its connoisseurs). The entire conceptual infrastructure of this theory is ideologically in solidarity with the dominant practice, as it was and still is to classical political econ-omy. It *is* the equivalent of that bourgeois political economy in the field of communication. And I think that if revolutionary prac-tices remain bound to the strategic illusion of the media, it is because they have never made anything more than a superficial critical analysis of it, without carrying out a radical critique of the ideological matrix of its theory of communication.

Formalized most specifically by Jakobson, its basic unity is provided by the sequence:

transmitter—message—receiver

(encoder—message—decoder)

The message itself being structured by the code and determined by the context. To each of these "concepts" corresponds a specific function: referential, poetic, phatic, etc. Each communicative process is thus vectorized in a single sense, from the transmitter to the receiver. The receiver can become a transmitter in turn, the same schema repeats itself. Communication can always be reduced to this simple unity where the two polar terms are never exchanged. This structure is offered as objective and scientific, since it follows the rules of the method: it breaks its object down into parts. In fact, it contents itself with formalizing an empirical given, abstracting the evidence and lived reality. This is to say that the ideological categories through which a certain kind of social relationship speak, precisely that wherein one speaks and the other does not, wherein one chooses the code and the other has the sole freedom to submit or abstain. This structure is based on the same arbitrariness as signification: two terms are artificially isolated and artificially reunited by an objectivized content called a message. There is no reciprocal relation nor presence of one to the other of these terms,[25] since both are determined in isolation in their relationship to the message and the code, an "intermedium" which maintains both of them in a respective situation (the code holds both of them in "respect"), distanced from one another, a distance which comes to fulfill the full and automated "value" of the message (in fact: its exchange value). This "scientific" construction institutes a *model of simulation* of communication from which reciprocity, the antagonism of the partners, or the ambivalence of their exchange is immediately excluded. What effectively circulates is information, content in the supposedly readable and univocal sense. The authority of the code guarantees this univocality, and thereby even the respective positions of the encoder and the decoder. So far so good: the formula has a formal coherence which assures it is the only *possible* schema of communication. But if one suggests an ambivalent relation, it all falls apart. Because there is no code for ambivalence. Without a code, no encoder or decoder: the extras flee the stage. No message either, since the message is defined as "sent" and "received." The entire formalization is only there to avoid this catastrophe. Therein lies its "scientificity." In fact, it establishes the terrorism of the code. In this directive schema, the code becomes the sole authority which speaks, which exchanges itself and reproduces itself through the dissociation of the two terms and the univocality (or the equivocality, or the multivocality, it hardly matters: through the non-ambivalence) of the message. (Similarly, in the economic process of exchange, people no longer exchange, the system of exchange value reproduces itself through people.) This formula at the basis of communication succeeds in offering, as a reduced model, a perfect shortcut for social exchange *as it is*, as in every case the abstraction of the code, forced rationalism, and the terrorism of separation regulate it. Such is the objectivity of science.

Separation and closure: it is already the same schema active at the level of the sign in linguistic theory. Each sign is divided into a signifier and a signified, assigned to one or the other, but in a "respective" position, and each sign on the basis of its arbitrary isolation "communicates" with all the others through a code called language. There too, the scientific taboo is cast on the terms' potentiality for symbolic exchange, beyond the signifier-signified distinction, in poetic language for example. In poetic language, as in symbolic exchange, the terms *respond* to one another beyond the code. We have indicated this response throughout this text as deconstructive to every code, every control, every power, which, inversely, is always based on the separation of terms and their abstract articulation.

Thus the theory of signification serves as a nuclear model for the theory of communication, and the arbitrariness of the sign (this theoretical schema for the repression of meaning) assumes all its political and ideological scope in the arbitrariness of the theoretical schema of communication and information.[26] Which, as we have seen, echoes not only in the dominant social practice (characterized by the virtual monopoly of the pole of the transmitter and the irresponsibility of the pole of the receiver, the discrimination between the terms of the exchange and the *diktat* of the code) but also, unconsciously, through all the velleities of a revolutionary media practice. It is clear, for example, that everyone who aims to subvert media contents can only reinforce, in its autonomy, the separated notion of the message and therefore the abstract bipolarity of the terms of communication.

The Cybernetic Illusion

SENSITIVE TO THE non-reciprocity of the current process, Enzensberger believes this can be helped by demanding that the same revolution intervene at the level of the media as that which disrupted the exact sciences and the subject/object relation of understanding, which has been engaged in a continual "dialectical" inter-reaction ever since. The media would have to take into account all the consequences of the inter-reaction, whose effect is to break the monopoly and to permit everyone's integration into an open process. "The programs of the consciousness industry must subsume into themselves their own results, the reactions and corrections that they call forth...they are therefore to be thought of not as means of consumption but as means of their own production."[27] This seductive perspective: 1. leaves the separated authority of the code and the message intact; 2. attempts, on the other hand, to break the discrimination of the two poles of communication, toward a more supple structure of the exchange of roles and feedback ("reversibility of circuits"). "In its present form, equipment like television or film does not serve communication but prevents it. It allows no reciprocal action between transmitter and receiver; technically speaking it reduces feedback to the lowest point compatible with the system."[28] There again, we fail to surpass the categories of "transmitter" and "receiver," despite the effort to mobilize them through "switching." *Reversibility* has nothing to do with reciprocity. Undoubtedly, for this profound reason, today cybernetic systems understand very well how to put this complex regulation, this feed-back, to work without changing anything about the abstraction of the process as a whole, or allowing any real "responsibility" into the exchange. This is even the systems' best defense, since it thereby integrates in advance the possibility of such a response.

One can no longer effectively conceive, as Enzensberger shows in his critique of the Orwellian myth, a mega-system of centralized control (a control system for the current telephone system would have to surpass it n times in complexity, and is therefore excluded practically). But it is a little naïve to think that censorship should be eliminated though the extension of the media. Even long term, the impossibility of police mega-structures simply signifies that the current systems integrate within themselves, through feed-back and self-regulation, these henceforth useless mega-systems of control. They know how to introduce that which denies them *as a supplementary variable*. There is censorship in their operation itself; they don't need a mega-structure. They never cease from being totalitarian: they realize in some way the ideal of what we can call a decentralized totalitarianism.

At a more practical level, the media also know very well how to put in place a formal "reversibility" of circuits (letters from readers, listener call-ins, polls, etc.), without leaving room for any response, without changing the discrimination of the roles.[29] This is the social and political form of feed-back. Enzensberger is therefore always, in his "dialecticalization" of communication so strangely proximate to cybernetic regulation, a victim, though in a more subtle way, of the ideological model we are discussing.

From the same perspective, breaking the unilaterality of communication, which translates itself at once into the monopoly of specialists and professionals and that of the class enemy over the media, Enzensberger proposes as a revolutionary solution that *each of us become a manipulator*, in the sense of an active operator, an editor, etc., in short, pass from the status of receiver to that of producer-transmitter. Therein is a kind of critical reversal [*détournement*] of the ideological concept of manipulation. But here again, because this "revolution" retains as its basis the category of "transmitter," it is content to generalize as separated, making each of us his or her own transmitter, it fails to check the mass media. If each of us possessed his or her own walkie-talkie or Kodak, and made his or her own films, we know what would result: personalized amateurism, the equivalent of Sunday *bricolage* on the periphery of the system.[30]

This is evidently not what Enzensberger wants. He is thinking of a newspaper edited, distributed, created by its own readers (as *Underground* was in part), of video networks for the use of political groups, etc.

This would be the sole means to unfreeze a blocked situation: "In the socialist movements the dialectic of discipline and spontaneity, centralism and decentralization, authoritarian leadership and antiauthoritarian disintegration has long ago reached a deadlock. Network-like communications models built on the principle of reversibility of circuits might give new indications of how to overcome the situation."[31] This is a question of restoring a dialectical practice. But can the problem continue to be posed in dialectical terms? Is the dialectic itself dead at this point? The examples he gives are interesting in that they surpass a "dialectic" of transmitter and receiver. One finds in effect a process of immediate communication, not filtered by bureaucratic models, an original form of exchange, in fact, because there are *not transmitters and receivers*, but people who *respond*. The problem of spontaneity and of organization is not surpassed dialectically here, it's terms are *transgressed*.

That is the essential difference. The other hypotheses leave the separated categories to subsist. In the first case (the private de-multiplication of the media), transmitter and receiver are simply reunited in a single person: manipulation is in some way "internalized."[32] In the other case (the "dialectic of circuits"), transmitter and receiver are simultaneously the two sides: manipulation becomes reciprocal (hermaphroditic combination). The system can act on its two tableaux at the same time as on the classical bureaucratic model, and in every possible combination of the two categories. What is essential is that these ideological categories should be saved, and with them the fundamental structure of the political economy of communication.

Once again, in the relationship of symbolic exchange, there is a simultaneous response, there is neither transmitter nor receiver for one part and another of a message, nor is there any longer a "message," a *corpus* of information to decipher in a univocal way under the auspices of the code. The symbolic consists precisely in breaking the univocality of the "message," or restoring the ambivalence of meaning, and eliminating in the same blow the authority of the code.

This can help us evaluate Umberto Eco's hypothesis. Briefly stated: changing the contents of the message changes nothing, one must modify the reading codes, impose other reading codes. The receiver (who in fact is not one) intervenes here essentially, he opposes his own code on that of the transmitter, he invents a veritable response escaping the trap of directed communication. But in what way is this reader "subversive"? Is this still reading, in the sense of deciphering, the recovery of an univocal meaning? And what is the code that he opposes? Is it a singular mini-code (ideological, but without interest) or another schema directing reading? In which case it is only a question of textual variation. An example might illustrate Eco's perspective: the reversal [*détournement*] of advertising with graffiti after May '68. It's transgressive not because it substitutes another content, another discourse, but because it responds, there, in place, and breaks the fundamental rule of all media, non-response. Does it oppose a code with another code? I don't think so: it simply breaks the code. It does not offer itself as a text to be deciphered alongside the advertising discourse. It lets itself be seen as transgression. Hence the slogan, the transgressive reversal of discourse, does not act by means of another code, as a code, it acts by means of the instantaneous deconstruction of the dominant discursive code. It volatilizes the category of the code and that of the message.

Therein lies the key to the problem: wanting to conserve (even by "dialectically surpassing") *any of the separated instances of the structural communication grid,* one forbids oneself from changing anything fundamentally, and condemns oneself to fragile manipulatory practices, that it would be dangerous to mistake for a "revolutionary strategy." In this sense, only that which radically checks the dominant form is strategic.

Requiesçant media in pace

9

DNA or the Metaphysics
of the Code

JACQUES MONOD IS the metaphysical principle of identity transferred from God and the Subject to the code and the genetic program.[1]

Sweep away teleology in favor of a teleonomic principle? Sweep away the dialectical process of evolution (with its *determined* rationality) in favor of a discontinuous indeterminism —mutation and chance? Be careful not to see revolution in what is only a metamorphosis. Finality is no longer an end, it is a beginning—but it remains written in advance. Simply the final order of the great signifieds (essential or dialectical contents) hereafter yields to the play of signifiers. This is the definitive assumption of the code, through inscription in biological nature. Ideology, or the process of the naturalization of social structures of domination, never went as far. Up to this point, it nourished itself more from an imaginary nature as origin and substance. Now it nourishes itself on an imaginary nature as code. In this sense, DNA should be cleared of scientific fascination and denounced as a phantasm, as an ideological concept, as a metaphysical sanctuary. Of this genetic and molecular transcendence, Monod is the stern theologian, Morin the ecstatic supporter (DNA = Adonai). The ethics of knowledge and the idealism of the molecule go together, and mingle their phantasms.

Given the living/non-living division, denounced as the source of all metaphysics: its abolition in favor of the non-living of bio-chemistry, grounds science in all its rigor! That is the total blindness of *sense*. Certainly, once it has raised this distinction, science can realize its totalitarian aims (its phantasm here too: the universality of a single principle, of a single law, of a single order of determinations regulating every process). Science is only ever capable of thinking the principle of identity. Contradiction, conflict, castration, ambivalence escape it. And the principle of identity is *metaphysical*. And all science works furiously around this phantasm of a universal and homogeneous corpus of signification. If this is not what has given birth to every magic and every unitary religion, which is to say pure accomplishment of desire and misrecognition of the difference which grounds sense, what is it? In this, Monod's scientism easily equals every theology. Because its finalism is never that of this or that content (whether it be God or the ideality of a social order or rediscovered nature), it is in the delirious illusion to reunify, to reconcile man and the world under the single principle, *whatever it is*, and thereby to assign it an *end*. Science is monist: it can only assure itself by neutralizing difference. It is incompatible with Apollo and Dionysus, said metaphorically, with the existence of *two* principles, irreducible, irreconcilable, eternally ambivalent... The Greeks retained something from dualist religions, "animists" that despise Monod in his monist vision.

The abolition of the living/non-living cut completes the neutralization of meaning, of contradiction, of the subject, of the dialectic, of sexuality (as desire), of the symbolic. All this is flattened in the hereditary immanence of the code. *This liquidation is objectively intended throughout the book.* And this project, ultrafinalistic without knowing it (?), has nothing properly "genetic" about it: it is a *socially and historically determined program*. What is sanctioned, hypostasized here in biochemistry, is the programmatic ideal of a social order immutably regulated by a genetic code, by a calculus, by a molecular PPBS—definitively escaping all dissension, all conflict, all ambivalence.[2] Techno-cybernetics finds its ontology herein, its "natural philosophy" as Monod says. Throughout the history of science, this reductive fascination is present in biology, in physio-chemistry. It is active in Spencerian organicism (bio-sociologism) at the level of the structures of the second and third order (to take up Jacob's classifications from *La Logique du Vivant*).[3] It is active today, in modern biochemistry, at the level of fourth order structures.

There is no question, against Monod, of resuscitating the living, the "human," transcendental subjectivity and other mirages of liberal thought. A certain idealism dies with cybernetics, the most subtle heritage of which is that of dialectical thought. Nothing is serves by wanting to save Engels from Monod (and not only in the caricature offered by the "Dialectic of Nature"—the entire dialectic is devoured by a secret finality in the genesis of meaning, due to the fact that it is undoubtedly itself only an unavowed system of interpretation and of the control of meaning, a discursive rationality which wouldn't know how to admit any other principle than itself)—save truly seeing that the cybernetic critique, which feigns speaking in the name of a pure objectivity (morally directed by the "ethics of knowledge") is still much more finalized than all the ethico-political theories that it denounces, by its social efficacy. Far from finding its end in its only object as a science, it has already found it, in fact, in the social techno-cybernetics that it nourishes and guarantees. Here ethics is, as it has never been, the shadow of programmatics and politics. There is no trace of theoretical thought in any of this. Monod shows that the *facts*, the real processes (micro-macro molecular) are not dialectical. But who, if not alas the dialecticians themselves, has ever believed that the dialectic was a business of facts or an observable reality (historical as well)?

Dialectical criticism is therefore regressive here, but it works. The neo-positivism of the code, in its total blindness to the problem of meaning, can hint that the dialectic itself has passed to the side of a certain problem of meaning, of symbolism, of articulation, or symbolic disarticulation. This problem, as it was posed, would appear to be a false alternative between the all powerful genetic code and the nostalgic defense of dialectics.

Monod also did well by mixing in his criticism of animism, finalism (metaphysical and religious), and dialectics (historical). There is a certain racism in not wanting to distinguish one black from another black. In regard to "animism," that "magical" thought which is an obstacle to science everywhere, Monod offers proof of an obsolete and ferocious ethnocentrism, that one would have believed surpassed since the progress of anthropology (but is it a "science"?). Monod describes the animism of archaic societies as a phantasm—which it is not—while conversely he never reveals his own theory as what it is: the objectivized phantasm of a social order. Reductive phantasm, from which all the actualization of symbolism is excluded, so that primitive "magic," when it is not reintegrated blindly through a racist scientificity, far from being a projection alienated from irrational forces, is a rationality in its order (maybe Monod should read Lévi-Strauss?)—but of course: it intends to and succeeds at maintaining a symbolic exchange of the living which spontaneously surpasses the living/non-living cut. Because this disjunction, on which all finalistic ideological is founded, if one thinks about it, is not abolished by Monod at all. He only generalizes and privileges one of its terms (the entire ethic of knowledge is founded on the formal negation of the living). But to privilege one or the other of the terms doesn't matter: their opposition founds metaphysics. Primitive societies don't make this cut: they aren't finalistic. Through a strange ethnocentristic twist, Monod projects precisely on them, in the term "animist," the ideological phantasms of substitution which result from *our* metaphysical configuration, from this living/non-living cut.[4]

Monod can therefore deny every idealism that precedes him in the name of a definitive rigor. In fact, he only represents a more evolved phase in the history of Western metaphysics, such that in itself techno-capitalist evolution changes. He only deconstructs all subjectivity, positivistic consciousness (the idealism of the subject, etc.), to reinstitute the absolute positivity of objectivity and of the code (the idealism of the code). Politically and historically, this signifies the substitution for social control by the *end* (and the more or less dialectical *providence,* which watches for the accomplishment of that end), by social control, by *prescience*, simulation, programmatic anticipation, indeterminate mutation commanded by the code. In place of a finalized (and rationalized) process according to its ideal development, this is a business of rationalization according to the code, of generation by a *model.* In place of a prophecy, we have a right to an "inscription." Despite appearances, there is no radical difference between the two: one transcendence pursues the other, only the schema of control change (and it must be said perfect themselves fantastically). From a "liberal" capitalist society, simply productivist, to a (neo-capitalist) cybernetic social order, which now aims toward absolute social control, even more than exploitation and profit: the biological theorization of the code has given its weapons to this gigantic mutation. But this mutation is not "indeterminate" at all. It is the result of the history of an entire system wherein God, Man, Progress, and History pass away in favor of the code, wherein transcendence passes in favor of immanence because immanence corresponds to a more advanced phase in the vertiginous manipulation of social relations.

In this sense, and in this sense only, Monod's hypermoralism, his terrorism is clarified. According to a logic that hasn't ceased since the dawn of capitalism and of western rationalism, recovered by Max Weber in *The Protestant Ethic and the Spirit of Capitalism*, Monod represents the point of convergence of an advanced neo-capitalism and a hyperpuritanism of knowledge. Formally, the whole book is perfectly contradictory, if one considers that it locates all philosophical, ethical, and political choice, all valuation to the hell of superstition, so as to exalt thereafter in all its rigor the ethical position of knowledge. What is the ethical choice of science—which is not at all chance, aleatory teleonomics, but a pure decision, and, in short, the height of self-determination? Is this choice not inscribed in the code? Is it not biological evolution itself that produced "science" to reflect it? (Morin, like Novalis at one time, in his kind of cosmic morality, goes this far.) Monod is totally illogical with himself: he basically puked up all metaphysics, all finalism, all dialectics so inflexibly only so as to restore in his crystalline Puritanism the moral ethos, moral law and its absurd wager. But this is explained very well if one admits that it is only the logical heritage of the premises of rational capitalism—of that profane /sacred cut inaugurated by the West, of this intra-worldly asceticism which grants a place to knowledge, to the ethics of knowledge... and to efficacy. Axiomatic from the value, based on detachment, separation (*askesis*)—ideological prong of the first capitalists of the sixteenth century—revived here in its radical version, definitively expurgated, by the theoreticians of neo-capitalism (consciously or not). To an infinitely more subtle and more totalitarian stage of capitalism corresponds a more pure expression of its ideology: there is nothing there but logic. That DNA and moral law, genetics without appeal and the scientific vocation collide here in the worst contradiction, owes nothing to the profound coherence of the ensemble as an ideological structure. It's useless to hold Monod's absurdity and theoretical weakness against him, the truth is elsewhere.

The problem of the status of science as a discourse, of objectivity as a discourse is posed once and for all. Good time to pose it here where this discourse absolutizes itself with such candor. "Plato, Heraclitus, Hegel, Marx: these ideological edifices, presented as *a priori*, were in reality constructions *a posteriori*, destined to justify a preconceived ethico-political theory… The only *a priori* for science is the postulate of objectivity, which forbids taking part in this debate." But this postulate itself results from an entire system of values, from a never innocent decision to make the world and the "real" objective. In fact, this postulate is that of *the coherence of a certain discourse*, and all scientificity is undoubtedly only the space of this discourse, which never offers itself as such; its objective simulacra includes political, strategic, and ideological speech. A little further still, Monod expresses arbitrariness very clearly: "One can ask oneself if all the invariances, conservations and symmetries that constitute the frame of scientific discourse are not fictions substituted for reality so as to give it an operational image… Logic founded on a potentially conventional, purely abstract, principle of identity. A convention from which meanwhile human reason seems incapable of escaping." One might be better to say that science resolves itself like a generative formula, like a model discourse, on the faith of a principle of identity that is far from being a simple "convention," which is the fundamental principle of a total reduction. Monod sends himself elsewhere to slip on the dangerous hypothesis of this principle of identity as a conventional abstraction. Better to ground it solidly, in an incontestable reality. Physics is there to testify that identity is not a principle or a postulate: it is *in things*, as the "absolute identity of two atoms with the same quantum state." Thus: convention or objective reality? The truth is that science is organized, like any other discourse, on a conventional logic, but that it demands for its justification, *like any other ideological discourse*, a "real," "objective" reference in a substantial process. If the principle of identity is "true" somewhere, even at the level of two atoms, then the whole conventional edifice of science, which inspires it, it also *true*. So it is with metaphysics. The principle of identity accounts for things previously determined and formalized so as to obey it: "objectivity" is nothing other than that, and the ethics which sanctions this objective knowledge is never more than the system of defense (and of misrecognition), which wants to preserve this vicious circle.

"Fundamentally, every hypothesis which permitted belief in a true world" as Nietzsche says.

in this case would be nothing other than a code, imposing a kind of deciphering, imposing decipherment where there is properly neither finality, cipher, or value. It is a question of a gigantic secondary elaboration which hallucinates in rational terms the predestination of man for the transformation of the world (or for the "production" of himself: humanist theme generalized today: it is not longer a question of "being" oneself but of "producing" oneself, from conscious activity to the wild "productions" of desire). Everywhere man has learned to reflect himself, to assume himself, to *direct* himself according to this schema of production, which is assigned to him as the final dimension of value and meaning. At the level of the entirety of political economy, there is something of what Jacques Lacan described in the mirror stage: across this schema of production, this *mirror* of production, the human species comes to consciousness *in the imaginary*. Production, work, value, everything through which an objective world appears and in which man recognizes himself objectively—all of this is the imaginary wherein man has embarked on the incessant decipherment of himself through his works, finalized by his shadow (his own end), reflected by this operational mirror, this kind of ideal of the productivist ego—not only in the materialized form of economic obsession with output, determined by the *system* of exchange value, but more profoundly in this *over-determination by the code*, by the mirror of political economy, in this identity that man dons in his own eyes, when he can no longer think of himself other than as something to produce, to transform, to make visible as a value. This remarkable phantasm is confused with that of representation, in which man becomes—for himself— his own *signified*, enjoys himself as *contents* of value and meaning, in a process of self-expression and self-accumulation whose form escapes him.

It is clear (despite the exegetical prowess of structuralist Marxists) that the analysis of form/representation (the status of the sign, of the language which directs all western thought)—the critical reduction of this form in its collusion with the order of production and of political economy—escaped Marx. Nothing is served by making a radical critique of the order of representation in the name of production and its revolutionary watchword. The two orders are inseparable and, as paradoxical as this seems, Marx didn't submit form/production to radical analysis any more than he did form/representation. These two great, unanalyzed forms imposed their limits on him, the limits of the imaginary of political economy. We understand this to mean that the discourse of production and the discourse of representation are the mirror wherein the system of political economy comes to be reflected in the imaginary and to reproduce itself as determinant authority.

IN ORDER TO GRASP the radicality of political economy, it does not suffice to unmask what is hidden behind the concept of consumption: the anthropology of needs and use value. We must also unmask everything that hides behind the concept of production, of the mode of production, of productive forces, of relationships of production, etc. All the concepts fundamental to Marxist analysis need to be questioned starting from even from its demand for radical critique and for the transcendence of political economy. What is axiomatic about productive forces, about the dialectical genesis of modes of production from which revolutionary theory springs? What is axiomatic about the generic wealth of man—labor power, about the motor of history, about history itself, which is only "the production by men of their material life"? "The first historical act is thus the production of the means to satisfy these needs, the production of material life itself.

And indeed this is an historical act, a fundamental condition of all history, which today, as thousands of years ago, must daily and hourly be fulfilled merely in order to sustain human life."[2]

The liberation of productive forces is confused with the liberation of man: is this a revolutionary watchword or one for political economy? Almost no one has doubted this final evidence, certainly not Marx, for whom men "begin to distinguish themselves from animals as soon as they begin to *produce* their means of subsistence"[3] (why must man's vocation always be to distinguish himself from animals? Humanism is an *idée fixe* that comes to us—it too—from political economy—leave that). But is existence itself an end for man, an end for which he must find the means? These little innocent phrases are already theoretical ultimatums; the separation of ends and means already constitutes the most ferocious and most naïve postulate about the human species. Man has needs. Does he have needs? Is he sworn to satisfy them? Is he a labor power (through which he separates himself, as means, from his own ends)? Prodigious metaphors of the system that dominates us; a fable of political economy still recounted to generations of revolutionaries, infected even in their political radicality by the conceptual virus of this same political economy.

Critique of Use Value and Labor Power

IN THE DISTINCTION between exchange value and use value, Marxism assumes its greatest force but also its weakness. The presupposition of use value, the hypothesis, beyond the abstraction of exchange value, of a concrete value, of a human finality of commodities in the moment of their direct relationship of use for a subject, we have seen that this value is only an effect of the system of exchange value, a concept produced by the system, in which the system completes itself.[4] Far from designating a beyond for political economy, use value is but the horizon of exchange value. A radical questioning of the concept of consumption begins on the level of needs and products. *But this critique assumes its full scope in its extension to that other commodity, labor power.* The concept of production then falls under radical critique.

Don't forget that according to Marx himself the revolutionary originality of his theory consists in unleashing the concept of labor power from its status as an exceptional commodity, the insertion of which, in the cycle of production *under the name of use value* carries the X element, the differential extra-value which generates surplus value and the whole process of capital. (Bourgeois economics speculates on simple "labor" as one factor of production among others in the economic process).

The history of the use value of labor power in Marx is complex. Adam Smith attacked the Physiocrats and the Exchangists with the concept of labor. Marx in turn deconstructed abstract social labor (exchange value) and concrete labor (use value) in the double concept labor power/commodity. And he insisted on the necessity of maintaining in all their force the two aspects, the articulation of which alone can aid in objectively deciphering the process of capitalist labor. To A. Wagner, who reproached him for having neglected use value, he responds: "… the *vir obscurus* overlooks the fact that even in the analysis of the commodity I do not stop at the double manner in which it is represented, but immediately go on to say that in this double being of the commodity is represented the *two-fold character of the labor* whose product it is: *useful labor* i.e., the concrete modes of the labors which create use values, and *abstract labor, labor as expenditure of labor power*, irrespective of whatever 'useful' way it is expended… that in the development of the *value form of the commodity*, in the last instance of its money form and hence of *money*, the *value* of a commodity is represented in the *use value* of the other, i.e. in the natural form of the other commodity; that surplus value itself is derived from *a 'specific' use value of labor power* exclusively pertaining to the latter, etc. etc., thus for me use value plays a far more important part than it has in economics hitherto, however, that is only ever taken into account where it springs from the analysis of a given economic constellation, not from arguing backwards and forwards about the concepts of words 'use value' and 'value'."[5]

It is clear that in this text the use value of labor, losing its "naturality," recovers a "specific" value that is much greater in the *structural* functioning of exchange value. Also, that in maintaining a kind of dialectical equilibrium between qualitative concrete labor and quantitative abstract labor, Marx—while granting logical priority to exchange value (the given economic formation), retaining, even in that structure, a kind of concrete precedence, a concrete positivity of use value—still retains something *of the apparent movement of political economy*. He does not radicalize the schema to the point of reversing this appearance and revealing use value *as produced by the play of exchange value*. We have shown this for the products of consumption, it is the same for labor power. The fact of defining objects as useful, and responding to needs, is the most complete, the most internalized expression of abstract economic exchange: its subjective closure. The fact of defining labor power as the source of "concrete" social wealth is the complete expression of the abstract manipulation of labor power: the truth of capital culminates in this "evidence" of man as producer of value. Such is the twist by which exchange value retrospectively originates and logically closes itself off in use value. In other words, here the signified "use value" is still an *effect of the code*, the final precipitate of the law of value. It does not suffice to analyze the operation of the quantitative abstraction of exchange value *starting from* use value, one must still make visible the conditions for the possibility of this operation: to understand the production of even the concept of the use value of labor power, of a specific rationality of productive man. Without this generic definition, no political economy. Therein, in the last instance, lies the foundation of political economy. It is therein as well that one must disrupt it, by unmasking this quantitative—qualitative "dialectic," behind which the definitive structural institution of the field of value is hidden.

What is Concrete about Labor: the Quantitative—Qualitative "Dialectic"

"THE QUANTITATIVE CONSIDERATION of labor could only come about once it had been universalized during the 18th century in Europe... Until then, different forms of activity were not comparable in their breadth... At first, all tasks presented themselves as diverse qualities."[6] Qualitative labor, differentiated in relation to its process, its product, and the destination of its product. Historical epoch of the artisanal mode of production. Succeeded, in the capitalist mode of production, by the double aspect under which labor is analyzed: "While labor which creates exchange values is *abstract, universal,* and *homogeneous,* labor which produces use value is concrete and special and is made up of an endless variety of kinds of labor according to the way in which and the material to which it is applied."[7] Here we rediscover the moment of use value: concrete, differentiated, incomparable. In opposition to the quantitative measure of labor power, labor use value remains a qualitative potentiality. Neither more nor less. It is specified by its own end, the material that it works, or simply because it is the energetic expenditure of a particular individual at a particular moment. The use value of labor power is the moment of its actualization, of the relation of man to the useful expenditure that he possesses—it is basically an act of (productive) *consumption*—and this moment retains, in the general process, all of its singularity. At this level, labor power is incommensurable.

There is a profound enigma in the articulation of Marx's theory: how is surplus labor born? How does the actualization of labor power, by definition qualitative, come to be "more" or "less"? If not by supposing that the "dialectical" opposition of the quantitative and the qualitative only expresses an apparent movement.

In fact, this is again a question, with the *effect* of quality and of incomparability, of the *apparent* movement of political economy. What the universalization of labor in the 18th century, and its repro-duction thereafter, produced, was not the reduction of concrete qualitative labor into abstract quantitative labor, but, from the outset, the structural articulation of both terms. On the basis of this "fork" labor is truly universalized, not only as market value but as human value. Ideology always proceeds in this way through a binary struc-tural division (or moreover by redoubling in a qualitative structural effect, which is an effect of the *code*) investing the entire field of possibility. Henceforth there can only be labor—qualitative or quantitative. The quantitative still only signifies the comparability of all forms of labor in abstract value. The qualitative, under the banner of incomparability, goes much further: it signifies *the comparability of every human practice in terms of production and labor*. Or again: the abstract and formal universality of the labor power commodity underlines the "concrete" universality of qualitative labor.

But the word "concrete" here is an abuse of sense. It seems to oppose abstraction to the interior of the fork; in fact it is the fork itself which grounds abstraction. In the play of one and the other—of abstract and concrete, of qualitative and quantitative, of exchange value and use value—the autonomization of labor is sealed. The fetishism of labor and of productivity comes to be crystallized in this structured play of signifiers.[8]

What is concrete about labor? Marx: "The indifference as to the particular kind of labor implies the existence of a highly developed aggregate of different species of concrete labor, none of which is any longer the predominant one. So do the most general abstractions commonly arise only where there is the highest concrete development, where one feature appears to be jointly possessed by many, and to be common to all."[9] But if no type of labor dominates all the others, it is because labor itself dominates all the other regimes, that it substitutes itself for all other forms of wealth and exchange. Indifference in regard to determinate labor corresponds to a much more complete determination of social wealth by labor. And what is this social wealth, placed entirely under the sign of labor, if not use value? The "richest concrete development" is the qualitative and quantitative multiplication of use values. "The greater the extent to which historic needs—needs created by production itself, social needs—needs which are themselves the offspring of social production and intercourse, are posited as *necessary*, the higher the level to which real wealth has become developed. Regarded *materially*, wealth consists only in the manifold variety of needs."[10] Is this not the program of an advanced capitalist society? Because it does not conceive of a mode of social wealth other than that founded on labor and production, Marxism no longer furnishes, long term, a real alternative to capitalism. Adopting the generic schema of production and needs, there is an astounding simplification of social exchange by the law of value. A fantastic proposition, if conceived correctly; arbitrary and fantastic in regard to the status of man in society; belied by the analysis of all primitive or archaic organizations, and by the feudal symbolic order, and even by that of our societies. It is clear that all of the perspectives opened up by the contradictions of the mode of production drive us into political economy.

The dialectic of production only redoubles the abstraction, the separation of political economy. And this leads to the radical interrogation of the Marxist theoretical discourse. Since the dialectic abstract-concrete relationship is in the final instance defined by Marx as the relationship between "scientific representation and real movement" (what Althusser will analyze precisely as the *production* of a theoretical object), it appears that this theoretical production, itself caught in the abstraction of representation can only redouble its object, in this case the logic and movement of political economy. Between the theory and the object (this goes not only for Marxism) there is effectively a dialectical relation, in the fatal sense wherein it encloses them both in a unsurpassable specularity.[11] Thought beyond the production form, beyond the representation form becomes unthinkable.

The "Generic" Double Face of Man

IN FACT, the use value of labor power is no more real than the use value of products, no more real than the autonomy of the signified and the referent. The same fiction reigns in the orders of production, consumption, and signification. Exchange value makes the use value of products appear as its anthropological horizon. The exchange value of labor power makes use value visible as the originality and concrete finality of the act of labor, as its "generic" alibi. The logic of signifiers produces "evidence" of the "reality" of the signified and of the referent. Throughout, exchange value makes

Marxist theory, radical in its *logical* analysis of capital, sustains itself with an *anthropological* consensus with Western rationalist options, in the definitive form that it assumed in the bourgeois thought of the 18th century. Science, technology, progress, history: an entire civilization understands itself as the producer of its own development and draws its dialectical momentum toward completing humanity, designated in terms of totality and happiness. Genesis, development, finality: Marx invented none of this, nor did he change anything essential, nothing of the *idea* of man *producing* himself in his infinite determination and continually surpassing himself toward his own end.

Marx translated this concept into the logic of material production and into the historical dialectic of modes of production. But to differentiate the modes of production is to render unsurpassable evidence of production as determinant instance. It is to generalize the rational mode of economics over the entire stretch of human history, as a generic mode of human becoming. It is to circumscribe the entire history of man in what is undoubtedly only a gigantic model of simulation. It is in a way to turn against the order of capital by using as an instrument of analysis the most subtle ideological phantasm that capitalism itself has elaborated. "Dialectical" reversal? Is it not the system that is leading its own dialectic here, that of its universal reduction? If one advances the hypothesis *that there never has been and that there never will be more than a single mode of production, regulated by the capitalist political economy*, this concept only makes sense in relation to the economic formation which produces it (observe the theory that analyzes this economic formation). Thus the generalization, even "dialectical," of this concept, is but the *ideological* universalization of the system's postulates.

Ethic of Labor; Aesthetics of Play

THIS LOGIC OF MATERIAL production, this dialectic of modes of production always returns, beyond history, to a generic definition of man as a dialectical being, understandable based on the sole process of the objectification of nature. This is heavy with consequences to the extent that, even through the fortunes of his history, man (whose history is also a "product") will be ruled by this clear and definitive reason, by this dialectical schema which acts like implicit philosophy. Marx developed it in the *Manuscripts of 1844*, Marcuse revives it in his critique of the economic concept of labor: "Labor is an ontological concept of human existence as such." He cites Lorenz von Stein: "Labor is...in every way the actualization of one's infinite determinations through the self-positing of the individual personality [in which the personality itself] makes the content of the external world its own and in this way forces the world to become a part of its own internal world."[15] Marx: "Labor is *man's coming-to-be for himself* within the *externalization* or as *externalized* man...[that is] the *self-creation* and self-objectification [of man]."[16] And even in *Capital*: "So far therefore as labor is a creator of use-value, is useful labor, it is a necessary condition, independent of all forms of society, for the existence of the human race; it is an external nature-imposed necessity, without which there can be no material exchanges between man and nature, and therefore no life."[17] "Labor is, in the first place, a process in which both man and nature participate, and in which man of his own accord starts, regulates, and controls the material re-actions between himself and nature. He opposes himself to nature as one of her own forces setting arms and legs, head and hands, the natural forces of his body in motion in order to appropriate nature's productions in a form adapted to his own wants."[18] The dialectical culmination of all this is the concept of nature as "the inorganic body of man": the naturalization of man and the humanization of nature.[19]

On this dialectical basis, Marxist philosophy unfolds in two directions: an ethics of labor, an aesthetics of non-labor. The first across the entirety of bourgeois and socialist ideology—the exaltation of labor as value, as an end in itself, as a categorical imperative. Labor loses its negativity here and stands as an absolute value. But is the "materialist" thesis of the generic productivity of man far from this "idealist" sanctification of labor? It is in any case dangerously vulnerable here. Marcuse: "Insofar as they take the concept of 'needs' and its satisfaction in the world of goods as the starting point, all economic theories fail to recognize the full factual content of labor... The essential factual content of labor is not grounded in the scarcity of goods, nor in a discontinuity between the world of disposable and utilizable goods and human needs, but, on the contrary, in an essential excess of human existence beyond every possible situation in which it finds itself and the world."[20] In the name of which he separates play as a secondary activity: "In the structural sense, within the totality of human existence, labor is necessarily and eternally 'earlier' than play."[21] Labor alone founds the world as objective and man as historical, only labor founds a real dialectic of transcendence and completion. It even justifies metaphysically the burdensome nature of labor. "In the final analysis, the burdensome character of labor expresses nothing other than a negativity rooted in the very essence of human existence: man can achieve his own self only by passing through otherness: by passing through 'externalization' and 'alienation'."[22] I have only cited this long passage to show how the Marxist dialectic can lead to the purest Christian ethic (and inversely of course: today we see a large

contamination of these two points of view on the basis of this transcendence of alienation and this intraworldly asceticism of effort
and of the overcoming that Weber located as the radical germ of the
capitalist spirit). And also because since the beginning this aberrant
sanctification of labor found itself to be the secret vice of Marxist
political and economic strategy. Walter Benjamin stigmatized it
violently: "Nothing has corrupted the German working class so
much as the notion that it was moving with the current. It regarded
technological developments as the fall of the stream with which it
thought it was moving. From there it was but a step to the illusion
that the factory work which was supposed to tend toward technological progress constituted a political achievement. The old
Protestant ethics of work were resurrected among German workers
in secularized form. The Gotha Program already bears traces of
this confusion, defining labor as the 'source of all wealth and all
culture.' Smelling a rat, Marx countered that '... man who possesses
no other property than his labor power' must of necessity become
'the slave of other men who have made themselves owners...'
However, the confusion spread, soon thereafter Josef Dietzgen
proclaimed, 'the savior of modern times is called work. The...
improvement...of labor constitutes the wealth which is now able
to accomplish what no redeemer has ever been able to do.'"[23] Is
this a question of a "vulgar" Marxism as Benjamin suggests? No
less "vulgar" in the case of the "strange delusion" Paul Lafargue
denounced in *The Right to be Lazy*: "A strange delusion possesses
the working classes of the nations where capitalist civilization
holds its sway."[24] Apparently orthodox Marxism preaches the liberation of productive forces under the auspices of the *negativity* of
labor. But is this not a question, faced with the gospel of labor, of
an "aristocratic" idealism? The other is positivist, and Marxism

wants to be "dialectical," but they have the hypothesis of man's productive vocation in common. If one admits that it raises the purest metaphysics,[25] then the difference between "vulgar" Marxism and the "other" would be that of a mass religion and a philosophical theory—which, as we know, is not much.

Confronted with the *absolute* idealism of labor, dialectical materialism is perhaps only a *dialectical* idealism of productive forces. We will return to this to see if the dialectic of means and ends which is at the heart of the principle of the transformation of nature does not already virtually imply the autonomization of means (the autonomization of science, of technology, and of labor, the autonomization of production as generic activity, the autonomization of the dialectic itself as general scheme of development).[26]

In the fine print of Marxist thought and against this labor ethic, the regressive character of which evidently maintains what it represses—Marx's capital discovery about the double aspect of labor (his discovery of an abstract and measurable social labor)—there is an aesthetics of play, of non-work, which is based on the dialectic of the quantitative and the qualitative. This is the perspective, beyond the capitalist mode of production and the qualitative measure of labor, of a definitive qualitative mutation in communist society: the end of alienated labor, the free objectification of man's own powers. "In fact, the realm of freedom actually begins only where labor which is determined by necessity and mundane considerations ceases; thus in the very nature of things it lies beyond the sphere of actual material production... Freedom in this field can only consist in socialized man, the associated producers, rationally regulating their interchange with Nature, bringing it under their common control, instead of being ruled by it as by the blind forces of Nature; and achieving this with the least expenditure of energy and under conditions most favorable to, and worthy of, their human nature. But it nonetheless still remains a realm of necessity. Beyond it begins that development of human energy which is an end in itself, the true realm of freedom which, however, can blossom forth, only with this realm of necessity as its basis."[27] Or again Marcuse, returning to less puritanical (less Hegelian) conceptions, though undoubtedly entirely philosophical (Schiller's aesthetic philosophy): "Play and display, as principles of civilization, imply not the transformation of labor but its complete subordination to the freely evolving potentialities of man and nature. The ideas of play and display now reveal their full distance from the values of productiveness and performance. Play is *unproductive* and *useless* precisely because it cancels the repressive and exploitative traits of labor and leisure."[28]

This *beyond* of political economy called play, non-work, or non-alienated labor, is defined as the reign of finality without end. It is in this sense that it is and remains, in the very Kantian sense of the term, an *aesthetic*. With all the bourgeois ideological connotations that this implies. And it is true that the thought of Marx, if it settled its accounts with bourgeois morality, remains defenseless against bourgeois aesthetics, the ambiguity of which is more subtle, but whose complicity with the general system of political economy is also profound. Once again, it is at the heart of its strategy, in the analytic distinction that it makes between the quantitative and the qualitative, that Marxist thought inherits from the aesthetic and humanist virus of bourgeois thought—the concept of the qualitative is burdened with all these finalities, whether the concrete finality of use value or the endless idealist and transcendental finalities. This is the defect of every notion of play, of liberty, of transparency, of disalienation, the defect of the *revolutionary imagination*—insofar as in the ideal type of play, of the free play of human faculties, we are still in the process of repressive desublimation. This sphere of play effectively defines itself as the fulfillment of human rationality, as the dialectical culmination of man's activity, of his incessant objectification of nature and control of his exchanges with it. It presupposes the full development of productive forces, it remains "mixed up with" the reality principle and the transformation of nature. It can only flourish, Marx says clearly, when based on the reign of necessity. This is to say that, wishing itself beyond labor, but in its *prolongation*, the sphere of play is never only the aesthetic sublimation of its constraints. We are still well within the typically bourgeois problematic of necessity and freedom, the double ideological expression of which has always been, since coming into existence, the institution of a reality principle (repression and sublimation: principle of labor) and its formal surpassing in an ideal transcendence.

Work and non-work. "Revolutionary" theme. Therein lies the most subtle form of the previously mentioned binary structural opposition. The end of the end of the exploitation by labor is truly this inverse fascination with non-labor, this inverse mirage of free time (obligated time—free time, full time—empty time: another paradigm that seals the hegemony of the order of time, which is always merely that of production). Non-work is still only the repressive desublimation of labor power—the antithesis that acts as an alternative. The sphere of non-work, even if one does not confuse it immediately with that of leisure and its present bureaucratic organization, wherein the desire for death and for mortification and its management by social institutions is as powerful as in the sphere of work. Even if one envisions it in a radical way that *represents it* as other than the model of a "total availability," of a "liberty" for the individual to "produce" himself as a value, to "express" himself, to "liberate" himself as authentic *content* (conscious or unconscious), in short the ideality of time and of the individual as an empty form, to be filled in the end by his freedom. The finality of value is always there. It no longer inscribes itself, as in the sphere of productive activity, in *determined* contents. It is there henceforth as *pure form*, but no less determining. Exactly as the pure institutional form of painting, of art and theater shines, emptied of its contents, in anti-painting, anti-art, anti-theater—non-work shines with the pure form of labor. The concept can therefore be fantasized as the abolition of political economy, it is bound to fall back into the sphere of political economy, as a sign— and only a sign—of its abolition. It already escapes the revolutionaries to enter into the programmatic field of the "new society."

Marx and the Hieroglyph of Value

In *Semeiotike*, Julia Kristeva writes: "From the viewpoint of social distribution and consumption (of communication), labor is always a value of use or value which it is, and not in any other way. Value is measured by the quantity of time socially necessary for production. But Marx clearly outlined another possibility: *work could be apprehended outside value*, on the side of the commodity produced and circulating in the chain of communication. Here labor no longer represents any value, meaning, or signification. It is a question only of a *body* and a *discharge*..."[29]

Marx: "The use values, coat, linen, etc., i.e., the bodies of commodities, are combinations of two elements—matter and labor... We see, then, that labor is not the only source of material wealth, of use-values produced by labor, as William Petty puts it, labor is its father and the earth its mother... Productive activity, if we leave out of sight its special form, viz. the useful character of the labor, is nothing but the expenditure of human labor-power."[30]

Is there a conception of labor in Marx different from the production of useful ends (canonical definition of labor as value in the framework of political economy and the anthropological definition of labor as human finality)? According to Kristeva, Marx's vision is radically different, centered on the body, expenditure, play, anti-value, non-utility, non-finality, etc. She would have him have read Bataille before writing, freely—forgetting it just as quickly: if there is something that Marx did not think, it is expenditure, loss, sacrifice, prodigality, play, the symbolic. Marx thought about *production* (already not bad) and he thought about it in terms of value.

There is no escape from this. Marxist labor is defined in the absolute framework of a natural necessity and of its dialectical overcoming as rational activity producing value. The social wealth that it produces is *material*. It has nothing to do with *symbolic* wealth which comes conversely from destruction, from the deconstruction of value, from transgression and expenditure, which mocks natural necessity. These two notions of wealth are irreconcilable, perhaps even exclusive of one another, and it is useless to attempt acrobatic transfers. According to Bataille, "sacrificial economy" or symbolic exchange is excluded from political economy (and from its critique, which is only its completed form). It is just to return to political economy what belongs to it: the concept of labor is consubstantial with it. For this reason, it cannot be turned to any other field of analysis, and it certainly cannot become once again the object of a science that claims to overturn political economy. The "labor of the sign," "intertextual productive space," etc. are ambiguous metaphors. There is a choice to be made between value and non-value. Labor definitively elevates the sphere of value. This is why the concept of labor in Marx (like his concepts of production and of productive force) must be submitted to a radical critique as an *ideological* concept. With all of its ambiguities, this is not the moment to generalize labor as a *revolutionary* concept.

The citations from Marx to which Kristeva refers do not in any way carry the sense she gives them. The genesis of wealth through genital combination of labor-father and earth-mother repeats well enough a "normal" productive-reproductive schema: we make love to have children, not for pleasure. The metaphor is that of reproductive genital sexuality, not at all that of an expenditure of the ecstatic body. But this is only a detail. The "expenditure" of human power that Marx speaks of is not an expenditure of pure loss, in Bataille's sense, a symbolic (pulsionary, libidinal) expenditure, it is still a productive, finalized, economic expenditure because it engenders only through coupling with this other productive force called earth (or matter). It is a useful expenditure, an investment, and not at all a festive and free volatilization of the power of the body, a game with death, the action of a desire. Moreover, this "expenditure of the body" does not have, as in play (sexual or otherwise), its response in other bodies, its echo in a nature that would play or expend itself in exchange. It is not based on symbolic exchange. What man offers of his body in labor is never *given* or *lost*, nor *rendered* by nature in a reciprocal mode. Labor intends only to "render the yield" of nature. Expenditure in this sense is therefore only an investment of value, a *making valuable*, opposed to every symbolic play, whether in a gift or an expenditure.

Kristeva poses the problem of redefining labor beyond value. In fact, for Marx, as Jean-Joseph Goux has shown, the line demarcating value passes between use value and exchange value. "If we proceed further, and compare the process of producing value with the labor-process, pure and simple, we find that the latter consists of the useful labor, the work, that produces use values. Here we contemplate the labor as producing a particular article; we view it under its qualitative aspect alone. Here it is a question merely of the time occupied by the laborer in doing the work—of the period during which the labor power is usefully expended."[31] Thus the abstraction of value begins only that of the second stage, that of exchange value. This amounts to removing use value from the sphere of the production of value, or again: the sphere of use value is confused with that which is beyond value (this is Goux's point, in extending this proposition to the use value of the sign). Here, as we have seen, there is a very serious idealization of the process of concrete, qualitative labor and, in the end, a compromise with political economy—to the extent that the entire theoretical investment and strategy crystallizes on this line of demarcation within the sphere of value, the line "external" to the closure of this sphere of political economy is left in the shadows. By positing use value beyond exchange value, we enclose all transcendence within this single internal alternative to the field of value. Qualitative production is already the reign of a rational, positive finality—the transformation of nature is already the place of its objectification as productive power, under the sign of utility (this is simultaneously true of human labor). Labor and production—before even the stage of exchange value and of the temporal equivalence of abstract social labor—already constitute an abstraction, a reduction and an unsurpassed rationalization in relation to the wealth of symbolic exchange. This "concrete" labor, with all of its values of repression, of sublimation, of objective finality, of "conformity to a goal," of the rational domestication of sexuality and of nature, this *productive eros* already represents, in relation to symbolic exchange, the real cut that Marx himself displaces and situates between abstract quantitative labor and concrete qualitative labor. The process of "valorization" begins with the process of the useful transformation of nature, with the instauration of labor as generic finality, with the stage of use value. And this real cut is not between "abstract" labor and "concrete" labor, but between symbolic exchange and labor (production, economics). The abstract social form of labor and of exchange is only the completed form, over-determined by capitalist political economy, of a scheme of rational valorization and production inaugurated long ago, breaking with every symbolic organization of exchange.[32]

Kristeva would like to escape value, but not labor or Marx. You have to choose. Labor is defined (historically and anthropologically) as what disinvests all the ambivalent and symbolic potentialities of the body and of social exchange, reducing them to a rational, positive, and unilateral investment. Productive eros pushes all alternative potentialities of meaning and exchange, in symbolic exchange, toward the process of production, accumulation, and appropriation. If we want to question this process which places us in the hands of political economy, of the terrorism of value, if we want to rethink expenditure and symbolic exchange, the concepts of production and of labor developed by Marx (not to speak of classical economics) must be resolved, analyzed as ideological concepts in solidarity with the general system of value. And if we want to find a realm beyond value (which is in effect the only revolutionary perspective), then we must shatter the *mirror of production*, in which all of Western metaphysics is reflected. Should we abandon Marx?[33]

In the Shadow of Marxist Concepts

HISTORICAL MATERIALISM, dialectics, modes of production, labor power: all these concepts by which Marxist theory seeks to shatter the abstract universality of the concepts of bourgeois thought

(Nature and Progress, Man and Reason, formal Logic, Labor, Exchange, etc.). Marxism in its turn is in the process of universalizing them according to a "critical" imperialism as ferocious as that of bourgeois thought.

The proposition according to which a concept is not only an interpretive hypothesis, but the translation of the movement of the universe, raised by pure metaphysics. Marxist concepts don't escape this lapse. Thus, by all logic, the concept of history must maintain itself as historical, turn on and clarify itself by abolishing the context that produces it. In place of this, it is transhistorisized, it is redoubled in itself and thereby universalized. Dialectics, in all rigor, should dialectically surpass and annul itself. Production and modes of production: radicalizing the concept in a given moment, Marx made a breach in the social mystery of exchange value. Thereafter the concept took all of its strategic power from its irruption, by which it deposes political economy from its imaginary universality. But it lost it's power, already in Marx's time, by offering itself as a principle of explication. It cancels its "difference" by universalizing itself, returning by the same blow to the form of the dominant code, universality, and to the strategy of political economy. It is not tautological that the concept of history should be historical, the concept of dialectics dialectical, the concept of production itself a product (which is to say judged by a kind of auto-analysis). This simply designates the present, explosive, mortal form of critical concepts. From the moment they assert themselves in the universal, they cease to be analytical: the religion of meaning commences. They become canonical and they enter into the general system's mode of theoretical reproduction. At this moment too—and this is not by chance—they assume their scientific cast (the canonization of Marxist concepts from Engels to Althusser). They set themselves up to express an "objective reality." They become signs: signifiers of a "real" signified. And if, in the best moments these concepts have been practiced as such, this is to say without taking themselves for reality, nevertheless they have fallen into the *imaginary of the sign*, which is to say into the *sphere of truth*, no longer in the sphere of interpretation, but in that of *repressive simulation*.

From here, they can only evoke one another, in an indefinite metonymic process: man is historical, history is dialectical, dialectics is the process of (material) production, production is the movement of human existence itself, history is that of modes of production, etc. Scientific and universalist, this discourse (this code) becomes immediately imperialist. All these possible societies are summoned to respond. To interrogate Marxist thought to see if societies "without history" are something other than "pre"-historic, other than a chrysalis and a larva. The dialectics of the world of production is not yet well developed, but you lose nothing by waiting—the Marxist egg is ready to hatch. The psychoanalytical egg, elsewhere, is also already ready, because everything that we have said of these Marxist concepts goes for the unconscious, repression, Oedipus, etc. This even better: the Bororos are closer to the primary processes than we are.

All of this constitutes the most surprising—and the most reactionary—theoretical aberration. There is *neither mode of production nor production itself* in primitive societies. There is *no dialectic* in primitive societies. There is *no unconscious* in primitive societies. All of these concept analyze only our societies, regulated by political economy. These concepts have only a kind of boomerang value. If psychoanalysis speaks of the unconscious in primitive societies, should we ask what psychoanalysis represses or what repression produced psychoanalysis itself? When Marxism speaks of the mode of production in primitive societies, should we ask to what extent this concept fails to account for even our historical societies—the reason we export it. And there where all of our ideologues seek to finalize, to rationalize primitive societies according to their own concepts, to encode the primitives, should we ask what obsession makes them perceive this finality, this code blowing up in their faces. In place of exporting Marxism and psychoanalysis (not to mention bourgeois ideology, though on this level there is no difference), bring all of the impact, the entire interrogation of primitive societies to bear on Marxism and psychoanalysis. Maybe then we can shatter this fascination, this auto-fetishism of Western thought, maybe we could escape from a Marxism which has become a specialist in the impasses of capitalism much more than a road to revolution, from a psychoanalysis which has become a specialist in the impasses of libidinal economy much more than in the ways of desire.

The Critique of Political Economy is Basically Completed

UNDERSTANDING ITSELF as a rationality of production superior to that of bourgeois political economy, the weapons that Marx thought he seized turn against him and make his theory the dialectical apotheosis of political economy. At a much higher level, his critique falls to his objection to Feuerbach for making a radical critique of the *contents* of religion, but for having made this critique in a religious *form*. Marx made a radical critique of political economy, but he still made it in the form of political economy. Such are the ruses of dialectics. Therein is undoubtedly the limit of every "critique," a concept born in the West at the same time as political economy, a concept which is perhaps, like the quintessence of Enlightenment rationality, only the subtle, long term expression of the system's expanded reproduction. Dialectics does not escape the destiny of critique. We will perhaps see that the return of idealist dialectics in dialectical materialism was only a metamorphosis, that it is the logic itself of political economy, of capital and of the commodity which is dialectical and that, in the guise of having produced the internal and fatal contradiction, Marx basically only offered a descriptive theory. The logic of representation, which is to say of the redoubling of its object, haunts all rational discursivity. All critical theory is haunted by this surreptitious religion, desire indexed by the construction of its object, negativity subtly haunted by the form even of what it negates.

This is why, after Feuerbach, Marx said that the critique of religion is basically completed (*Critique of Hegel's Philosophy of Right*), and that in order to overturn this ambiguous limit beyond which it cannot go (the reinversion of religious form in critique itself), it is necessary to pass resolutely to another level—precisely to the critique of political economy, which alone is radical and which can, by making the true contradictions apparent, definitively resolve the problem of religion. *Today we are at exactly the same point as Marx was.* For us, the *critique of political economy is basically completed.* Dialectical materialism has exhausted its contents by reproducing its form. The situation at this level is consequently no longer critique, it is inextricable. And according to the same revolutionary movement as Marx's, we affirm that we must move to a radically different level which permits, beyond its critique, the definitive resolution of political economy. This level is that of symbolic exchange and its theory. And as Marx thought that he should, in order to open the way to the critique of political economy, begin with a critique of the philosophy of law, we think that the preamble to this radical shift in terrain is the critique of the metaphysics of the signifier and of the code, in the entirety of its present ideological breadth—which we call, for lack of something better, the critique of the political economy of the sign.

11

Marxism and the System
of Political Economy

A Euclidean Geometry of History?

HISTORICAL MATERIALISM APPEARED in a society regulated by the capitalist mode, a stage of actualization knotted with contradictions linked to the mode of production and the final episode of the class struggle. It hopes for the decipherment of this final phase of political economy and aims for its abolition. Theoretical rationality and universal practice, the dialectic of productive forces and productive relations, a continuous logic of contradiction, a homogeneous space of positivity and negativity: all of this, and the concept of history itself, is organized according to the idea that with the capitalist mode of production this universal process reaches its truth and its end. Prior modes of production were never envisioned as autonomous or definitive. It is unthinkable that history could have stopped during one of them. The dialectic condemns them to be no more than successive phases of a revolutionary process, which is also a cumulative process of production. The capitalist mode does not escape this inexorable logic, but it nonetheless assumes an absolute privilege to the extent that the other modes of production only opened the way to the fundamental contradiction between the production of social wealth and the production of social relations, and to the possibility for men to finally resolve their social existence *in its real terms*. In the prior formations, men blindly produced the social relations at the same time as their material wealth—the capitalist mode is the moment wherein they become conscious of this double, simultaneous production and intend to rationally take control of it. No prior society posed this question to itself, not in these terms, and hence no society could resolve it. They could not have any knowledge of the end of history because they did not live historically nor through a mode of production. This is why they were prior: their truth was already beyond them, in the future concept of history, and in its contents, the determination of the social relation through material production, the concept which would appear only at the final stage of capitalism and its critique, clarifying at once the entire previous process. Capital is therefore an end, and all of history comes to be collected in the final process of its abolition. It is the only mode of production through which critique becomes possible in its real terms. This is why the revolution which puts an end to it is definitive.

Two postulates behind all of this:

— A process of historical development is already present in all prior societies (a mode of production, contradiction, a dialectic), but they do not produce a concept of historical development nor therefore of its transcendence.

— The moment the process becomes conscious (the production of the critical concept linked to the conditions of capitalist formation) is also the decisive stage of its resolution.

All of this is perfectly Hegelian, and we can ask ourselves what kind of necessity creates the fundamental contradiction, connected to the determinate instance of the economy—everything already at work "objectively" in the prior formations—becomes manifest at the same time as the discourse capable of founding it theoretically (historical materialism). As if by chance, the *reality* of the mode of production enters the events at the moment it discovers someone to create its *theory*. As if by chance, the class struggle, at the same time that it enters its open and decisive phase, finds the theory that makes it scientific and objectively accountable (whereas the blind and latent class struggles of prior societies produced only ideologies). The connection is too beautiful and irresistibly evokes the Hegelian trajectory wherein the epic of Spirit is entirely illuminated, retrospectively, so as to culminate in Hegel's own discourse.

This connection of analysis and "objective reality" ("communism is the movement of the real itself") is only the materialist variant of the pretension of our entire culture to the privilege of being closer than any other culture to the universal, closer to the end of history, closer to the truth. This rationalist eschatology, which finds its support in the irreversibility of the linear time of accumulation and unveiling, is *par excellence* that of science. The phantasm of science is double, simultaneously that of a "epistemological break," which relegates all other thought to a senseless prehistory of knowledge and of a linear accumulation of knowledge, and therefore of truth as a final totalization. This procedure permits our societies to think and live as though they were superior to all others: not only *relatively* more advanced through the fact that they succeeded the others, but *absolutely* more advanced because, possessing the *theory* of the objective finality of science and history, they are reflected *in the universal*, given as an end and therefore, retrospectively, as a principle of explication of prior formations.

The materialist theory of history does not escape this ideology: we are at the moment of objectivity, of the truth of history, the revolutionary denouement. But what authorizes the contempt of science for magic or alchemy, for example, the disjunction of a truth to come, the destiny of objective knowledge, concealed within the infantile misunderstandings of these societies? And for the "science of history": what authorizes this disjunction between a history to come and an objective finality which robs earlier societies of the determinations by which they lived, of their magic, of their difference, of the meaning that they had for themselves, to place them within the infrastructural truth of a mode of production for which we alone possess the key? The culmination which is produced by the Marxist analysis, within which it clarifies the denouement of every contradiction, is only that of the *staging of history*, which is to say of a process wherein everything is said to be resolved later, from the perspective of an accumulated truth, of a determinant instance, of an irreversible history. History could thus be, at bottom, only the equivalent of an ideal vanishing point which, in the rational and classic perspective of the Renaissance, is permitted to impose an arbitrary unitary structure on space. And historical materialism could only be the Euclidean geometry of that history.

It is only in the *mirror* of production and of history, beneath the double principle of indefinite accumulation (production) and of dialectical continuity (history), it is only through the arbitrariness of the *code* that our western culture can be reflected in the universal, as the privileged moment of truth (science) or revolution (historical materialism). Without this simulation, without this colossal reflexibility of the concave (or convex) concepts of history or production, our era loses all privilege. It would not be closer to any term (of knowledge) or to any (social) truth than to any other.

This is not a question of an ideal perspective on historical materialism. Rather it is a question of knowing if historical materialism (history made dialectical by modes of production) does not itself constitute an ideal perspective, which is to say the point of view of a reductive ideality on all social formations, even ours. This is why it is important to begin with this *mythological reduction* and to strip our culture, *including its materialist critique*, of the absolute privilege that it grants itself through the imposition of a universal code (the strategic element of this code being the conjunction, beneath the sign of truth, of theory and reality, of "critical" theory and "real" contradictions).

Returning to Marx, Althusser develops this theory of a moment of history (ours) wherein science exists in the immediate form of consciousness, wherein the truth can be read in the open book of phenomena. In opposition to all earlier modes, the capitalist mode constitutes "the exceptional, specific present in which *scientific abstractions exist in the state of empirical realities...* This historical epoch of the foundation of the science of political economy does seem here to be brought into relationship with experience itself (*Erfahrung*), i.e. with the straightforward reading of the essence in the phenomenon. Or, if you prefer, the sectional reading of the essence in the slice of the present seems to be brought into relationship with the essence of a particular epoch of human history in which the generalization of commodity production and hence of the category commodity appears simultaneously as the absolute condition of possibility and the immediate given of this direct reading from experience."[1] Marx extends this in a citation on the anatomy of the ape and in his analysis of value in Aristotle: "It requires a fully developed production of commodities before, *from experience* alone, *scientific truth* springs up."[2] If it is in the epistemological break that Marxist discourse is founded as science, this break is only possible "in a society in which the commodity form has become the general form of the produce of labor."[3] Althusser: "If the present form of capitalist production has produced scientific truth itself in its invisible reality (*Wirklichkeit, Erscheinung, Erfahrung*), in its self-consciousness, its phenomenon is therefore its own self-criticism in act (*en acte*)—then it is perfectly clear why the present's retrospection on the past is no longer ideology but true knowledge, and we can appreciate the *legitimate epistemological primacy of the present over the past.*"[4]

We can object to this Marxist scientific position in two ways:

1. We can admit that this epistemological break which, made possible by a certain historical process, makes possible in its turn a scientific analysis of this process, marks not a "critical" rupture, but a vicious circle. Made possible by the generalized commodity form, historical materialism accounts for all of the significations of our society as regulated by the generalized commodity form (either through the mode of production or through the dialectic of history. The concept by which one grasps this circularity doesn't matter. In any case, this "science," on the basis of this break, only describes the coincidence of the state of events which produced it and of the scientific model that it outlines). Dialectical? Not at all. The self-verification of a model which completes itself in the adequation of the rational (itself) and the real. In fact, this break through which Marxism prevails is equivalent, as for all "science," to the institution of a principle of rationality which is only the rationalization of its own process.

2. Instead of contesting historical materialism based on the position it grants itself (its pretension to a scientific discourse founded on a certain historical development), we can grant it that, but so as to add that, precisely from the time of Marx, the commodity form did not at all attain its generalized form, that that form had a *long history* since Marx, and therefore that it was not in a

historical position to speak scientifically, to speak the truth. In this case, another break imposes itself, which would risk making Marxism appear to be the theory of a surpassed stage of commodity production, therefore as an ideology. At least if one wanted to be scientific!

In the first case, one challenges the entire validity of Marxist concepts (history, dialectic, mode of production, etc.) as an *arbitrary* model which verifies itself, like every self-respecting model, through its circularity. One challenges historical materialism in its form, and it falls to the rank of an ideology. In the second, one preserves the fundamental *form* of the Marxist critique of political economy, but forces its *content* to break out beyond material production. In this hypothesis, one can admit that since Marx there has been such an extension of the sphere of productive forces, or again of the sphere of political economy (in which are directly integrated or are on the way to integration as productive forces; consumption as the production of signs, needs, knowledge, sexuality—in short, many things have irrupted in the "infrastructure") that the distinction between infrastructure and superstructure breaks down and that contradictions now emerge at all levels.

Something has radically changed in the capitalist sphere. Marxism no longer responds to it. It should therefore revolutionize itself in order to survive. Something it certainly hasn't done since Marx.

This hypothesis is distinguished from the first one in that it maintains that everything can still be explained in the conceptual structure of a critique of political economy (but generalized) and from the perspective of historical materialism (the instance of production), but expanded to all those domains and radically released from its economistic tendency. Go to the end of Marx. But it is not certain that this hypothesis would be tenable. It is possible that the extension of the sphere of productive forces, which equates to a radicalization of the concept, is such that the concept itself collapses. Infra-superstructure, ideology, the dialectic of productive relations, surplus value, classes and the class struggle; what becomes of all these key concepts of historical materialism, once confronted with this generalized political economy? Do they reveal such a coherence among themselves *and with the historical phase wherein they are born* that they become useless for us, even mystifying?

Perhaps political economy is inseparable from the theory of the determinant instance of *material* production. In which case, the Marxist critique of political economy is not extendable into a generalized theory.

The Third Phase of Political Economy

IN *The Poverty of Philosophy*, Marx set up a kind of genealogy of the system of exchange value:

1. Only what is superfluous to material production is exchanged (in archaic and feudal forms, for example). Vast sectors remain outside the sphere of exchange and of the commodity.

2. The entire volume of "industrial" material production is alienated in exchange (capitalist political economy).

3. Even that which was considered to be inalienable (shared, but not exchanged): virtue, love, knowledge, consciousness; all of this falls into the sphere of exchange value. This is the era of "general corruption," "the time when each object, physical or moral, is brought to market as a commodity value, to be priced at its exact value."

The schema is clear, beyond even what Marx anticipated. Between the first and second phases, the birth of capital, a decisive mutation, not only when it comes to the *extension* of the sphere of exchange, but according to its repercussions at the level of social relations. Between phases two and three, on the contrary, Marx and Marxism see only a kind of extensive effect. The "infrastructural" mutation, which locates the mode of production and contemporary social relations, is acquired in phase two. Phase three only represents the "superstructural" effect in the domain of "immaterial" values. With Marx, and against him in a way, we think that one must grant this schema all of its analytical force.

There is a decisive mutation between phase two and phase three. It is as revolutionary in relation to phase two as phase two was to phase one. To the third power of the system of political economy, another type of contradiction than that of phase two, which is properly that of capital (and of *Capital*). Anticipated by Marx, this new phase of political economy, which had not yet assumed in his time its full extent, is as quickly neutralized, drawn into the wake of phase two, in terms of the market and of "mercantile venality."

Even today, the only "Marxist" critique of culture, of consumption, of information, of ideology, of sexuality, etc., is made in terms of "capitalist prostitution," which is to say in terms of commodities, exploitation, profit, money, surplus value. These are all characteristic terms of phase two and terms about which one can say (in reserve for the moment) that they now assume their full value, but that they serve only as a *metaphoric reference* when they are transferred to analytical principles in phase three. Even the Situationists, undoubtedly the only ones who attempted to release this new radicality from political economy in the "society of the spectacle," still refer to this "infrastructural" logic of the commodity. Their fidelity to the proletariat is logical if, behind spectacular organization, the exploitation of labor power is still determinant—the spectacle being only an immense connotation of commodities—illogical if the concept of the spectacle is taken *as that of the commodity as it was by Marx in his time*, in all its radicality, as a process of generalized social abstraction of which "material" exploitation is only a particular phase. In this hypothesis, the form-spectacle is determinant, from it one sets out *as from the most developed structural phase*.[5] This overturns many perspectives on politics and revolution, the proletariat and class, but take it or leave it. Things have changed in any case. A revolution has taken place in the capitalist mode without our Marxists having wanted to apperceive it. When it comes to the objection that our society is still largely dominated by the logic of the commodity, the objection is valueless. When Marx set himself to analyze capital, capitalist industrial production was still largely in the minority. When he outlined political economy as the determinant sphere, religion was still largely dominant. The decision was never at the quantitative level, but at the level of structural critique.

This mutation concerns the passage from the commodity form to the sign form, from the abstraction of the exchange of material products under the law of the general equivalence to the operationalization of all exchanges under the law of the code. With this passage *to the political economy of the sign*, it is not a question of a simple "mercantile prostitution" of all values (the completely romantic vision of the celebrated passage from the *Communist Manifesto*, capitalism trampling all human values, art, culture, labor, etc., to make money: the *romantic critique* of profit). It is a question of the passage of all values to the value of sign exchange, under the hegemony of the code, which is to say of a structure of control and of power much more subtle and more totalitarian than that of exploitation. Because the *sign is much more than a connotation of the commodity*, than a semiological supplement to exchange value. It is an operational structure around which the quantitative mystery of surplus value appears inoffensive. The meta-ideology [*suridéologie*]

of the sign and the generalized operationalization of the signifier—
sanctioned everywhere today by the new master disciplines:
structural linguistics, semiology, information theory, and cybernetics,
which have replaced good old political economy as the theoretical
foundation of the system—this new ideological structure, which
plays on the hieroglyphs of the code, is much more illegible than
that which plays on productive energy. This manipulation, which
plays on the faculty to produce meaning and difference, is more
radical than that which acts on labor power.

The sign form should not be confused with the *function* of social
differentiation through signs, which is itself contemporaneous with
the drama of the bourgeois class, the moneyed class nostalgic for
caste values. There has long been a literature about the social psychology of distinction and prestige, linked to the consolidation of the
bourgeoisie as a class and today generalized to all the middle and
petty bourgeois classes, since the French moralists of the 17th century.
(This literature finds its philosophical resonance in the "dialectics" of
being and appearance.) But it is not a question of that. It is a question of the symbolic destruction of all social relations, not so much
of the ownership of the means of production but of the *hegemony of
the code*. This concerns a revolution in the capitalist system, equally
as important as the industrial revolution. And it would be absurd to
say that this logic of the sign concerns only the dominant class, or
the middle class "avid for distinction"—the proletariat being preserved by the materiality of its practice—as much as to say that the
theory of the commodity form was very good for the industrial and
urban classes, but that the peasants and artisans (the immense majority in the time of Marx) had nothing to do with it. This sign form
implicates the entirety of the social process. It is largely unconscious
and one must no longer confuse it with the *conscious* psychology of

prestige and the differentiation; one must not confuse the commodity form and the abstract and general structure of exchange value with the *conscious* psychology of profit and economic calculation (where classical political economy remains).

Against those who, blinded by their legendary materialism, cry Idealism from the moment that one speaks of a sign or of anything that exceeds productive manual labor, against those who have a muscular and energetic vision of exploitation, we say that if the term "materialist" has a critical meaning, and not a religious one, then we are materialists. But what's the point: happy are those who look to Marx as if he would always be there to recognize them. What we have attempted to observe here is the extent to which Marxist logic can be torn from the restricted context of political economy in which it was born, the extent to which it can account for *our* contradictions, on the condition of rendering its theoretical *curve* the flexibility that it lost long ago in favor of an instrumentalism, of a fixed linearity, on the condition of tearing it from the restricted dimensions of a Euclidean geometry of history, to offer it the possibility of becoming what it might be, a truly *general* theory. Once again, this is only an exploratory hypothesis, which postulates a dialectical continuity between the political economy of the commodity and the political economy of the sign (and therefore between the critique of one and the critique of the other). Nothing properly speaking guarantees this continuity, if not the Marxist assertion itself, which turns on the concept of modes of production. The radical hypothesis being that which can no longer even accept this fundamental concept and sees in it only the arbitrariness of a particular model. At bottom, this is the question:

— Are we still in the capitalist mode of production? If yes, continue gaily with the classical Marxist analysis.

— Are we in an *ulterior* mode, so different in its structure, in its contradictions and its mode of revolution that one must radically distinguish it from capitalism (while admitting that this is still a question of a mode of production, which is determinant as such)?

— Are we even, more simply, in a mode of production, *and have we ever been?*

ON THIS PRESENT phase of political economy, within Marxist thought we locate only the analysis centered on monopolistic capitalism. This is effectively the only point which imposes the necessity of theorizing something that Marx merely foresaw. But diverse theoreticians (Lenin, Rosa Luxembourg, etc.) did this according to the principle of the least theoretical effort, keeping as close as possible to classical concepts, and restricting the problem to its infrastructural and political givens (the end of competition, control of markets, imperialism). The monopolistic phase signifies much more than the extension of the competitive phase of capitalism. It signifies a complete restructuring and a different logic.

What happens when the system becomes monopolistic? Marx returns to a quote from Ricardo in his account (*The Poverty of Philosophy*): "Commodities which are *monopolized*, either by an individual, or by a company, vary according to the law which Lord Lauderdale has laid down: they fall in proportion as the sellers augment their quantity, and rise in proportion to the eagerness of the buyers to purchase them; their price has no necessary connection with their natural value; but the price of commodities, which are subject to competition, and whose quantity may be increased in any moderate degree, will ultimately depend, not on the state of demand and supply, but on the increased or diminished cost of their production,"[6] (and therefore of labor time). Thus when the system becomes monopolistic, labor time, the costs of production ceased to be decisive criteria (what of surplus value?). But one does not go so far with the law of supply and demand, defined by liberal thought as a *natural* equilibrium between the two terms. Their correlation is not free, any more than the market itself is free. The control of demand (Galbraith) becomes the strategic articulation. When the competitive system still acted at a contradictory and perilous level, the exploitation of labor, the monopolistic system transferred its strategy to a level where the dialectic was inactive. In the monopolistic system, there is no dialectic of supply and demand, this dialectic is short-circuited by a provisional calculation of equilibrium. The monopolistic system (the techno-structure according to Galbraith) is supported throughout by a fiction of competition;[7] throughout the hegemony of production is supported by a fiction of the dialectic of supply and demand. But there is nothing to this: in the planned cycle of the consumer demand, these new strategic forces, these new structural elements—needs, knowledge, culture, information, sexuality—are denied all of their disruptive force. In opposition to the competitive system, *consumption* was instituted in the monopolistic system as control, the abolition of demand in its contingency, socialization directed by the code (publicity, fashion, etc. are only the spectacular aspects). The contradictions do not end here: they are functionally integrated and neutralized by the process of differentiation, of redistribution (which the competitive system did not have available to it in the area of labor power). Is consumption, which characterizes the monopolistic era, anything other than the phenomenology of abundance? It signifies the passage from a mode of strategic control, of predictive anticipation, of the absorption of the dialectic and the general homeopathy of the system by its own contradictions.

Demand, which is to say needs, corresponds more and more to a model of simulation. These new productive forces no longer pose a question to the system: they are an anticipated response; the system itself controls their emergence. It can afford the luxury of contradiction and dialectic through the play of signs. It can offer itself all the signs of revolution. Since it produces all the responses, it annihilates the question at the same time. This is only possible through the imposition and the monopoly of the code. This is to say that, however one takes it, one can only respond to the system in its own terms and according to its own laws, answering it with its own signs. The passage to this stage constitutes something other than the end of competition, it signifies that, from a system of productive forces, of exploitation and profit, as in the competitive system, its logic dominated the time of social labor, we pass to a gigantic operational game of questions and responses, a gigantic combinatory wherein all values commutate and exchange according to their operational sign. The monopolistic stage signifies less the monopoly of the means of production (which is never total) than the *monopoly of the code*.

This phase is accompanied by a radical change, in the functioning of the sign, in the *mode of signification*. The goals of prestige and distinction still correspond to a traditional status of the sign, where a signifier refers to a signified, where a formal difference, a distinctive opposition (the cut of clothes, the style of an object) still refers to what we might call the use value of the sign—to a differential profit, to a lived distinction (signified value). This is still the classical era of signification, with its referential psychology (and philosophy). This is also the *competitive* era in the manipulation of signs. The sign form describes an entirely other organization: the signified and the referent are abolished to the benefit of a single game of signifiers, a generalized formalization wherein the code no longer refers to any subjective or objective "reality," but to its own logic: it becomes its own referent, and the use value of the sign disappears to the benefit of its commutation and exchange value alone. The sign no longer designates anything, it reaches its true structural limit, it only refers to other signs. The whole of reality becomes the place of a semiurgical manipulation, of a structural simulation. And since the traditional sign (in linguistic exchange as well) is the object of a conscious investment, of a rational calculation of signifieds, here the code becomes the instance of absolute reference, and at the same time the object of a perverse desire.[8]

The homology with the sphere of commodities is total. "Traditional" commodities (up through the competitive era of capitalism) are at once exchange value and real use value. The proper and final relationship of the subject with the produced object, the consumptive finality of the product still exists; just like the use value of the signified in the classical organization of the sign. There is already a general equivalence of production (the abstraction of exchange value), but not yet a general equivalence of consumption, the products retain a concrete finality. With monopolistic capitalism, the same mutation takes place as in the sphere of the sign. The final reference of products, their use value, completely disappears. Needs lose all autonomy, they are coded. Consumption no longer has an ecstatic value, it is placed under the constraint of an absolute finality, which is that of production. Production, on the contrary, is no longer assigned to other finalities than itself. This total reduction of the process to one of its terms, for which the other is no more than an alibi (use value alibi of the code), designates more than an evolution in the capitalist mode: a mutation. Through the elevation of production to total abstraction (production for production), to the power of a code *which no longer even risks being called into question by an abolished referent*, the system succeeds in neutralizing not only consumption, but production itself as a field of contradictions. Productive forces as a referent ("objective" substance of the process of production) and therefore also as revolutionary referent (motor of contradictions of the mode of production), lose their specific impact, and the dialectic between productive forces and relations of production no longer acts, just as the "dialectic" between the substance of signs and the signs themselves no longer functions.[9]

Contradiction and Subversion: the Displacement of the Political

WITH THE GENERALIZATION of political economy, it becomes more and more evident that its originary action is not where Marxist analysis grasped it, in the exploitation of labor as productive force, but rather in the imposition of a form, of a general code of rational abstraction, of which the capitalist rationalization of material production is only a particular case. The domestication of language in the code of signification, the domestication of all social and symbolic relations in the schema of representation are not only contemporaneous with political economy, *they are its process itself.* Today it betrays its form and radicalizes itself in these "superstructural" realms. The capitalist system, linked to profit and exploitation, is only the inaugural modality, the infantile phase of the system of political economy. The schema of value (exchange and use) and of general equivalence is no longer limited to "production": it invested the spheres of language, of sexuality, etc. The form has not changed. One can also speak of a political economy of the sign, a political economy of the body, *without metaphor*. But the center of gravity has been displaced. The epicenter of the contemporary system is no longer the process of material production.

Nothing says that at bottom the political economy of language, of the sign, of representation did not begin well before that of material production. If material production—the quantitative operationalization of productive forces—was able to serve, for nearly two centuries, as a fundamental reference, this is perhaps according to an apparent movement. For a much longer period, the operationalization of the code has been fundamental (division, abstraction, functional systematization and structural organization). Today the code unfolds all of its consequences. But this is not a question of changing the determinant authority or of reversing priorities: that would be a return to a naïve idealism, which privileges the contents of representation, while the naïve materialism privileges the contents of production. There is no choice between the two. The system itself does not present this problem. It doesn't bother with this materialism or idealism, whether infra- nor super-structural. It proceeds according to its form, and this form carries production and representation, signs and commodities, language and labor power at the same time. In the final instance, it is its own determination. Today this form inscribes terror and social abstraction at every level.

The properly capitalist phase of socialization forced by labor, of the intensive mobilization of productive forces has been overturned. Now we have a *desublimation of productive forces*—without the logic of the system betraying the world in the least, on the contrary, its logic of reproduction expanding in its way. Everything happens as if the industrial coercion, disciplinary concentration, the integration of larger and larger masses in the apparatus of production since the 19th century, the directed crystallization of every energy into material production, was only a provisional solution, enormous but provisional, an enterprise of rationalization and of social control, the breadth of which largely surpasses this phase. Surplus value, profit, exploitation—all of these "objective realities" of capital never do more than mask the immense social domestication, the immense directed sublimation, of which the process of production is only the *tactical* aspect. Today the system reproduces itself according to an inverse tactic: no longer a general mobilization but a techno-structural rationalization, which has the effect of corrupting whole categories or a greater and greater fraction of the productive social time of all categories. Today, contradictions appear from this "demo-bilized sphere," repressively "desublimated" in regard to production, no longer from the sphere of productivist exploitation.

Forced industrialization and direct exploitation are followed by prolonged education, studies subsidized through the student's 25th year, permanent development, recycling. All things apparently destined to multiply and differentiate social productivity. In fact, the system does not need this sophistication, this polyvalence, this real, statistically restrained, high level, permanent development. At its limit, it fulfills itself in a very mobile structure of polyvalent tech-nocrats assuming all the functions of decision, and in a mass of disqualified, unaccountable, socially irresponsible others offered this illusion of participation and personal development.[10] All of these institutions of "advanced democracy," all of these "social conquests," related to education, to culture, to personal and collective creativity, all of this is, as never before, the right to private property; the real right of some and, for the remainder, day-care, cribs, social controls wherein productive forces are deliberately neutralized. Though the system no longer needs the productivity of everyone, it needs everyone to play the game.

Hence the paradox for those who must struggle to remain within the circuit of labor and productivity, of those who have been forced or left out of that circuit, *off limits*, through the development of productive forces—the inverse of the initial situation of capitalism.[11] New contradictions are born from this. If the exploited class bore a violent contradiction, it was not on the order of an integration, a wild and forced socialization, but in a socialization nevertheless, in the structure of the general productive system. The revolt arose from the integration of labor power as a factor of production. The new categories of people, de facto dropouts, testify to the incapacity of the system to "socialize society" in its traditional strategic structure, to dynamically integrate it, even by violent contradiction at the level of production. And it is on the basis of their *total irresponsibility* that these marginal generations carry on the revolt. This revolt can remain ambiguous, if it survives in the mode of anomie and loss, if it occupies by default the margin that the system assigns it, where it is institutionalized as marginal. But it suffices that it radically adopts this forced exteriority to the system in order to call the system into question, no longer through functioning from within, but from without as a fundamental structure of society, as code, culture, interiorized social space. The entire system of production would be disinvested in this way, teetering on the social void that it has itself produced. All of its positivity would sink into this non-place, this disaffected zone, where those left to their own devices return their complete disaffection. Subversion is born here, from *elsewhere*, while contradiction works the system from *within*.[12]

Hence the major role of students, of the young, those disqualified in advance, voluntarily or not, but also of every kind of social category, of regional, ethnic, or linguistic community, once the community falls, through the process of centralization and the technocratic pyramidalization of the system, into the margin, the periphery, the zone of disaffection and irresponsibility. Excluded from the action, their revolt consequently targets the rules of the game. Desocialized, they put not only their own exploitation by the system but the social capitalist *reality principle* in check. Segregated, discriminated, satellitized, these categories are relegated bit by bit to *the position of unmarked terms* in the code that structures the system. Their revolt consequently targets the abolition of the code, of this strategy made of distinctions, of separations, of discriminations, of structural and hierarchized oppositions.

The Black revolt targets race as code, which is to say a level much more radical than economic exploitation. The Women's struggle targets the code which makes the feminine an unmarked term. That of the youth targets a process of extreme racist discrimination, in which it lacks the right to speak. And so it is with all of these categories which fall beneath the structural bar of repression, of relegation, where they lose their meaning. This position of revolt is no longer that of the economically exploited, it targets less the extortion of surplus-value than the imposition of the code in which the present strategy of social domination is written.

The more that the system is concentrated, the more it expels these entire categories. The more it hierarchizes itself according to the law of value (sign or commodity), the more it excludes those who resist that law. So it was with the confinement of the mad on the threshold of Western rationality (Michel Foucault). It is the same today for all of civil society, which has become a place of confinement, wherein quieted man is closely watched. Everywhere, behind factories and schools, suburbs and offices, museums and hospitals, asylums and ghettos are profiled as the purest form of truly rationalized society.

This terroristic rationality produces, over the centuries, the radical distinction between masculine and feminine, with its "racial" inferiorization and sexual objectification of the feminine. No culture but ours has produced this systematic abstraction, wherein all the elements of symbolic exchange between the sexes have been liquidated for the sake of a binary functionalism. And this separation, which has assumed its entire force through capitalist political economy, is not at all reabsorbed in our day: sexual hyperactivism, the "equalization" of the sexes, the "liberation of desire," in short the "Sexual Revolution" quite simply offers the illusion of symbolic destructuring under the sign of sex as a differential mark, as an index of status, and as a function of pleasure. The women's struggle (or gay liberation) targets this mark, not the democratic and rationalist revindication of equal political and sexual rights (equivalent to the salary claims of the worker), not the accession of women to power, turning the code in their favor, but the abolition of the code. Marxism has ignored this subversion of the political economy of sex, the law of value in the sexual domain, and of the phallus, of masculinity, as general sexual equivalent. Marxism "dialectically" subordinated it to economic contradictions, allowing all of its radicality to escape.

The same for racial discrimination: no other culture than ours has produced this systematic distinction between black and white. Not as afterthought, but as structural element, which is reproduced ever more intensely today, in the guise of a tottering liberal universalism. And the objectification of the blacks, to the extent that it is not that of an exploited labor power, is an objectification by the *code*. As one can clearly see, an entire arsenal of *significations*, irreducible to economic and political determination, support it. The emancipated black or the black member of the bourgeoisie remains black, just as the proletarianized immigrant remains primarily an immigrant, and the Jew remains a Jew. The code resurges with still more violence in everything that would seem to repress it.

In Marxist terms, the superstructure is imposed with more force as contradictions linked to the infrastructure are resolved, which is paradoxical to say the least. And here again the autonomization of the blacks as a principle of revolution, and even the autonomization of women as a sex or of the proletariat as a class, only renews the racial or sexual code, the game of political economy, by simply displacing the marked term.

Other discrimination: that of the youth, which is not at all a secondary effect of class domination or of economic exploitation, but the most explosive consequence of the present system: the hierarchal monopoly of the decision more and more circumscribes a zero term in social signification. The youth occupy this non-place in the most critical way, though not as an age group. If its revolt has such repercussions everywhere, this is because this non-place traverses all social categories. Today in economics, in politics, in science, in culture, irresponsibility is crucial: irresponsibility is the revolt of the dispossessed, of those who have never been able to speak.

Speech defines itself as incessant response (responsibility), wherein all social transcendence dissolves. Against it, political economy has throughout its history fomented the *discourse* in which everything that is exchanged is exchanged under the authority of the code. Alongside all of these discriminations, markings and demarkings about which we have spoken, the system produces a fundamental separation, which recuperates all of the others: that of the signifier and the signified. Thanks to it, and to the entire logic of communication that it institutes, the system has succeeded, slowly but inexorably, in neutralizing the symbolic power of speech. Binary structure, the abstraction of representational discourse, the general equivalence of the code, the foreclosure of speech.[13]

The insurrectional practice of recent years has given new life to this speech, overshadowing traditional contradictions.

These revolts lack the profile of the class struggle. But capitalism evolves, and with it its life lines. Until now buried beneath the "determinant instance" of the mode of production, they emerge according to the enlarged logic of the reproduction of the system. That of the ethnic, linguistic, repressed minorities, enslaved through the thread of history by bureaucratic centralization; that of the family, of the relegation of women, of children, of the youth, and of the aged, the entire cycle of repression and of leveling organized around the nuclear family as a structure of the reproduction of the order of production—that of non-genital, polymorphous, "perverse" sexuality, liquidated or ordered by the reality principle of genital sexuality; that of nature consigned to total spoliation as a productive force: the capitalist process crosses every network of natural, social, sexual, and cultural forces, every language and code: it needs the domination of nature, the domestication of sexuality, the rationalization of language as a *means* of communication, and the relegation of ethnic groups, of women, of the youth to genocide, ethnocide, and racial discrimination. One should not see these things, in accordance with a rigid Marxism, as simple excrescences, or even as attempts to divert the fundamental theme, which would remain and always be the "class struggle." In this doctrinairy confusion, there is a mystification of Marxist thought which, by circumscribing the fundamental determination within economics, permits these mental, sexual, cultural structures to function effectively. If capitalism, across the centuries of "superstructural" ideology, acted to disarm the contradictions at the level of economics, today's strategy is inverted: the system acts, with reference to economics (well being, consumption, but also working conditions,

salary, productivity, growth), as an alibi for the more serious subversion which threatens it in the symbolic order. Today the sphere
of economics, with its partial contradictions, acts as an ideological
factor of integration. Making itself complicit with debt, with diversion, Marxism is very simply exploited by capitalism as a
(spontaneous and benevolent) force of ideological labor. Everything
that now privileges the field of economics, salary claims or the
theorization of economics as the final authority—Séguy or Althusser
—is "objectively" idealist and reactionary.

This radical subversion—*transversal* to the extent that it trans-
verses the contradictions linked to the mode of production
—*non-dialectical* to the extent that there is no dialectical negativity
between the repressed, unmarked term, and the marked term—this
radical subversion can only transgress the line and deconstruct the
code.[14] This subversion telescopes the "traditional" contradictions.
But they do not converge because they are separated by a strategic
mutation in the system. Hence the impossible conjunction of the
working class and the students (or the idle young and the workers)
under the pious invocation of a common exploitation. The respective demands diverge, and diverge more and more, despite the
desperate efforts of the student and left movements to "politicize"
their subversion through immersion in the working class. Between
the workers obstinately defending themselves on the basis of their
salary and their integration in the industrial system, their "right
to work" and the advantages the system provides them,[15] and the
demobilized, demarcated, excluded categories (sex, age, race,
ethnicity, language, culture and knowledge; all criteria "superstructural" and surpassed according to the rationalist perspective of the
class struggle), for whom the ethics of the system collapses, the gulf
grows faster than it can be filled in. The working class is no longer

the gold standard of revolt and contradiction. It is no longer the referenced revolutionary subject. And the hope of articulating, of making dialectical, a subversive movement that challenges the system as a code, as a complete language of repression and of separation, with its class contradictions, which challenges the system as a mode of production and exploitation, this hope is also part of the dream of political will.

However, other things appear even at the level of the process of production. There as well the secret defection runs in and grows as the chancre of capitalism. Everywhere the morality of labor, the secular "instinct of workmanship," this ethic of individual and collective sublimation of the labor process (today paradoxically reactivated by the unions and the "worker's party") is dislocated. In May '68 we saw, "Never Work," but also in the Fiat strike, at Usinor, in the strike for striking, without demands, practices which deny no longer only exploitation but labor itself, as principle of reality and rationality, as *axiom*. It is no longer a question of dialectical negativity within the mode of production, but of a pure and simple refusal of production as general axiom of social relations. Undoubtedly even corporatist and salary demands hide it, transpose it in its flight from this radical denegation—meticulously asphyxiated and channeled by the parties and unions for whom, as much as for the system itself, the economic demands are the ideal instrument of control and manipulation.[16] This is what gives the New Left and the hippie movement its meaning: not the open revolt of some, but the immense latent defection, the endemic, masked resistance—the silent majorities, nostalgic for speech and violence—something in every man profoundly rejoices in seeing a burning car (the youth in this sense is only the exponential category of a process latent in the entire social expanse, without exception for age or "objective" condition). On the contrary, the New Left commits suicide if it claims a statistical significance, if it claims to be a mass "political" force. It is irremediably lost on the level of representation and of traditional political contradiction (the same thing for the American counter-culture).

Political Revolution and Cultural Revolution

CAPITALISM HAS BEEN able, during the last one hundred years, to extract political and social changes necessary to absorb its contradictions when they are posed solely at the level of material production. Contradiction only becomes radical when it deepens, as is the case today, at the total level of social relations. By enlarging the field of social abstraction to the level of consumption, of signification, of information, of knowledge, by enlarging its jurisdiction and control to the whole field of culture, daily life, the unconscious, the system has resolved the partial contradictions linked to the economic relations of production. Through this reestablishment, which has taken it a century, capitalism, by radicalizing its own logic, has also radically altered the Marxist definitions of contradiction and revolution.

The "cultural revolution," which corresponds to this radicalized logic of capital, to this "in depth" imperialism,[17] is not the developed form of the economico-political revolution. It acts on the basis of a reversal of "materialist" logic. Against the materialist postulate according to which the mode of production and of the reproduction of social relations is subordinated to the relations of material production, one can ask if it is not the *production* of social relations which determines the mode of material *reproduction* (the development of productive forces and relations of production). A genealogy of social relations makes many other criteria of domination appear than the private ownership of the means of production: species, race, sex, age, language, culture: anthropological or cultural signs. All of these criteria are criteria of *difference*, of signification and the code. That they all "descend" in the last instance from economic exploitation is a simplistic hypothesis. It is reasonable on the other hand that this hypothesis is only the rationalization of an order of domination which reproduces itself through it, which plays with economics as a tactic, a detour, or an alibi. Today, what's essential is no longer profit nor exploitation. *Perhaps it never was, even in the Golden and Iron Ages of capitalism.*

It is directly at the level of the production of social relations that capitalism is vulnerable and on the road to perdition. It catches its death, not from being unable to reproduce economico-politically, but from being unable to reproduce itself. The social symbolic relation is the unbroken cycle of giving and receiving, which, in the primitive exchange, includes the consumption of the "surplus" and the deliberated anti-production, when the accumulation (the non-exchanged thing) risks breaking this equilibrium.

At all levels, the system is sick of desublimation, of liberalization, of tolerance, of seeking to surpass itself to survive: consumption, the satisfaction of needs, sexual liberation, the rights of women, etc. It is ready for anything that will reduce social abstraction, that will get people into the game. But, it can only, here again, accomplish liberalization if it is hyper-repressive: needs, forever contingent and heterogeneous, are homogenized and definitively rationalized according to models; sexuality, ever repressed, is liberated as a game of signs, made objective as a function of the body and benefit of the pleasure principle.

Freedom of information? So that it can be better framed and modeled by the media. The pressure of political economy is accentuated everywhere. Latest avatars: anti-pollution and "job enrichment." Here too, the system seems to release its constriction and to restore the dignity of nature and work: the desublimation of productive forces in relation to traditional exploitation. But we are well aware that a symbolic relationship between man and nature and man and work will not return here. The functionality of the system will only become more flexible, be reinforced.

Coding, hyper-coding, universalization of the code, proliferating axiomatization of the capitalist system (Deleuze), and, against this triumphal abstraction, against this irreversible monopolization, the symbolic demand, the demand that nothing ever be offered without being returned, won without being lost, produced without being destroyed, spoken without response.

The Economy as Ideology and Model of Simulation

AGAINST THIS SYMBOLIC subversion, which arises everywhere to some extent under the heading of "cultural revolution," the capitalist system has every interest in "closeting" contradictions within the economy, as a diversion. Making the economy autonomous is an ideological strategy. The same thing that Bourdieu describes in *Reproduction in Education, Society and Culture* in regard to the academic and cultural system.[18] (This system theorizes itself as transcendent and offers itself as a democratic and universal virtuality—education and culture for all—the class structure relegated to the order of production.) Through this autonomizing effect and behind this simulacra of transcendence, the system fulfills its ideological function best and most effectively restores the dominant social relations. One can ask oneself if it can only reproduce them, and if this is not the location of a specific production of class domination. This implies a reversal of the terms of analysis: the economy can appear in our society as the place wherein our chances are most thoroughly equalized, wherein social relations are least conservative, etc. (Historically, since the rise of the bourgeoisie, it has always also played the role of an emancipatory spring-board over the most conservative juridical, religious, and cultural structures.) And the academic and cultural system also might play the decisive role in the *production* of social relations, the economy being only a relay, and the bias of *reproduction*.

In any case, the ideological process, extracted from Bourdieu's analysis, is unchanged and can be generalized: ideology always passes through the autonomization of a partial group—every autonomized partial group immediately assumes ideological value. So it is with the academic system in Bourdieu, but *all* partial fields—the economy in particular—can act as ideological fields once erected as an autonomous (and even determinant) authority. The automization of the economy is common to both capitalism and Marxism.

1.

EVERY AUTONOMOUS PARTIAL social field becomes in the same way the location of a universalist and egalitarian myth: religion occupied this place in its time, the academic and cultural system does so today, consumption as an isolated function of production is occupying it more and more. But the economy affirms itself, in its autonomy before religion, culture, etc., as the sphere of social *rationality*, as the *universal* authority on productivity (here again, the Marxists are indistinguishable from bourgeois economists), and therefore as the egalitarian myth: everyone has equal rights before the objective rationality of production.

2.

ECONOMICS IS SUPPORTED by science. All of the separate fields secrete, as separated fields, a myth of rigor, objectivity, and truth. Objectivity and truth are only the effect of the division of the field of knowledge, of its autonomization according to certain rules. Isolated from everything else by a perfect, partial knowledge—this is the imaginary of the exact sciences. Science's desire is never anything but a fascination with misunderstanding. Political economy, as the science of the separated, is therefore properly ideological, and the critique of this political economy (when it wants to take without giving, win without losing, produce without destruction) risks shattering this reciprocity and making power appear. It is this symbolic relation that the model of political economy (of capital), for which the only trial is that of the law of value and therefore of indefinite appropriation and accumulation, can no longer produce. It is its radical negation: that which is produced is no longer symbolically exchanged, and that which is not symbolically exchanged (the commodity) feeds a social relationship of power and exploitation.

Capitalism cannot escape the fatality of this symbolic disintegration under the sign of economic rationality. One could also say, with Cardan, that his fundamental contradiction is no longer between the development of *productive* forces and the relations of production, but in the impossibility of making people "participate"—but the term participation has too contractual and rationalist a connotation to express the symbolic—saying that the system is structurally incapable of liberating human potentialities other than as productive forces, which is to say according to an operational finality, which leaves no place for the reversion of loss, of gifts, of sacrifice, and therefore for the possibility of symbolic exchange.

The example of consumption is significant. The feudal system collapsed because it was unable to find means of rational productivity. The bourgeoisie itself had to make people work, but it too almost fell apart, in 1929, through its inability to make them consume. It was content, up to that point, with the forced socialization of work and exploitation. But the crisis of 1929 marked the point of asphyxiation: production was no longer essential, selling was. Consumption became a strategic element, the people were mobilized henceforth as consumers, their "needs" became as essential as their labor power. Through this operation, the system assures its economic survival at a fantastically enlarged level. But other things are at stake in the strategy of consumption: given the possibility of waste and consumption, organizing social redistribution (Social Security, disbursements, salaries that are no longer defined as the strict economic reproduction of labor power), advertising initiatives, human relations, etc., the system created the illusion of symbolic participation, the illusion that something of that which is valued and won is also redistributed, returned, sacrificed. In fact, all of this symbolic simulation reveals itself as leading toward profit and to a hyper-power. Despite all of its good will (that at least of capitalists conscious of the necessity of tempering the logic of the system so as to put the explosion off for a more or less short term), capitalism can only make consumption consumption, a festival, an expense, since to consume is to resume production. All that is wasted is in fact invested, nothing is ever lost. Even when coffee stocks burn and enormous wealth is devoured in war, the system cannot prevent it from enlarging production. Capitalism is caught in the fatal grip of production, of accumulation, of profitability. Its aide to developing countries returns in the form of multiple profits: even if the experts in liberalism have been denouncing the catastrophe that is awaiting them at the end of the process for twenty years, the richest countries can only, even if they lucidly wanted to, limit the gulf that separates them from the Third World to the price of its real sacrifices. And this is the same for each individual: each consumer is enclosed in the profitable manipulation of goods, of signs, to his or her own profit. He or she can no longer even really lose time in leisure.[19] He or she inexorably reproduces, at his or her own level, the entire system of political economy: the logic of appropriation, the impossibility of waste, of giving, of loss, the inexorability of the law of value.

Power consists in the monopoly on speech: speech, decision, responsibility are no longer exchanged. But this situation is explosive: those who have power know it. And we see them attempting desperately to relinquish some of it, to redistribute some of their responsibility, to avoid backlash like the kind that struck in May 1968. But they *cannot*. They would really like participation, but participation reveals itself every time as the best way to reproduce and enlarge the system. The more one offers autonomy to everyone, the more the decisions are concentrated at the summit.[20] Even in 1929, the system burst by failing to promote production, so today it fails by being unable to sell speech. Because it is a system of production, it can only reproduce itself, it can no longer recover symbolic integration (the reversibility of the process of accumulation in the festival and expenditure, the reversibility of the process of reproduction in destruction, the reversibility of the process of power in exchange and death).

Every system of "scientific" (materialist) production can only reinforce the separated abstraction of its object. There is no truth in economics, or rather we can only create that truth: it is the truth of an arbitrary authority.

3.

EVERY PARTIAL FIELD—economics included—is the field of contradictions, which are themselves partial. The place of fundamental contradiction, the place of politics today, is the line of separation between partial fields. The revolution is not the resolution of these partial contradictions, but the abolition of this line. The contradictions within the partial fields are the echo of the separation that haunts them, and which is their originary act. They are therefore ambiguous: at the same time that they manifest the obsession with non-separation, they reinforce separation by making it autonomous as an *internal* contradiction. Their resolution can never reach beyond separation. This is why it is never definitive. They resolve themselves in a flight out in front of the partial system in their obsession with separation (others would say with castration). Such is the process of political economy, such is the *imaginary* of political economy (Cardan).

The entire materialist critique of ideology, its denunciation of the autonomization of the value of understanding, of culture, of this simulation of a reality principle of ideas, this whole critique *returns integrally against materialism*, which is to say against the autonomization of economics insofar as it is a (determinant) authority.

Everywhere economics appears as the theorization of the rupture in symbolic exchange, the institution of a separated field, which then becomes the vector of a total reorganization of social life. The simulation of the universal finality of calculation and productive rationality, the simulation of a *determination*, there where symbolic exchange knows neither determination nor end. The simulation of a *reality* of this authority, of an economic reality principle, which proceeds to universalize itself on the basis of the principle of separation: this *model* has today found its finished form: the placement of operational models, the simulation of situations toward the end of foreseeability and control, operational artifacts in place of reality and the reality principle of the code.[21]

Cardon: "The rationality of modern society is purely formal: it is the syllogism of belief camouflaged in the historical 'dialectic' of the development of productive forces. But in this syllogism, the premises borrow their contents from the imaginary; and the prevalence of the syllogism as such, the obsession with the detached rationality of the rest constitutes a second degree imaginary. Modern pseudo-rationality is a form of the imaginary in history: it is arbitrary in its ultimate ends insofar as they arise without reason, and it is arbitrary when it poses itself as an end (this holds for logical reason and 'dialectical' reason). In this aspect of his existence, the modern world is prey to systematic delirium, of which the autonomization of unchecked technology (and bureaucracy) is the most immediately perceptible and menacing form…the economy exhibits in the more striking way the domination of the imaginary at all levels."

The symbolic is the abolition of this economico-political imaginary (and of all other separated fields).

In this sense, the cultural revolution no longer shackles the economico-political revolution. It traverses it as a partial revolutionary discourse, and, in a certain way, a rationalizing, mystifying discourse. Revolution targeting the totality of life and of social relations can only also and initially target the autonomization of economics, the final ("revolutionary" and materialist) avatar of which is the autonomization, in the form of a determinant authority, of the mode of production. Today the system has no better strategy than the dialectic of political economy. For this reason, the cultural revolution must target the economico-political revolution.

Marxist Theory and the Worker's Movement: The Concept of Class

MARXIST ANALYSIS in terms of class and mode of production cannot account for this revolutionary potentiality, this subversion directed against the axiomatic of productive rationality (includes its internal contradictions). It is incapable of theorizing the *total* social practice (including the most radical practice) if only so as to reflect it in the mirror of the mode of production, or to return it to the dimensions of a revolutionary "politics." At the point where we are, Marxist analysis, in its revolutionary rationality, clarifies for us neither our societies nor primitive societies.

Retrospectively, moreover, one must ask if *it has not always been like this*. If, already in Marx' day, the theory of the mode of production did not extraordinarily simplify social practice. If it no longer accounts for the current revolutionary mode, did it at least, at a given moment in history (the "classic" phase of capitalism), account for its fundamental contradictions? Have modes of production (and classes and the class struggle) had their moment of truth?

Here the sacrilegious hypothesis imposes itself, that the conjunction in the 19th century of the Marxist theory and the workers movement might not have been the miracle of History—the greatest event of History, Althusser says—*but a reciprocal process of reduction and neutralization*. The objective historical result having been the saturation of the two in the Leninist *political* mixture, later in the Stalinist bureaucracy, today in the most vulgar reformist empiricism—stages of a long term that it would be too simple to impute it to some twist in the path: the profound logic of this term brings us back before Stalin, before Lenin, etc., to the crucial point in the thought of Marx himself, to the original event, always thought to be irrevocably revolutionary, of the dialectical conjunction of his theory and the objective social practice of a class called the proletariat.

We have lived in the providential shadow of that event to such an extent that the idea of this fusion was not necessary, nor necessarily best, that it ever really be formulated. The social revolt and the theoretical movement, indexing one with the other, *verifying* one and the other through history, were universalized, under the sign of dialectical revolution, as historical reason. But they were no longer a radical difference.

Effectively, the fusion was not of a radical revolt and a radical theory, both "wild" and indeterminate (as was the case in the insurrectional movements of the 19th century, up to the Commune, and once again in May '68), but of two already distinct terms, each distorted by the other. Dialectical, if you will, but it is necessary to observe that that which is dialecticized, that upon which Marxist theory hinges, is a social "reality," specified as a class, as a conscious and objective organization, as the proletariat. In theory, the proletarian organization grasps a well-determined social critique, in terms of modes of production, of relations of production and class. Part "objective" and organized class, part rational and structured (both in its materialist content and dialectical form) theory; between these two terms, each rationalized in the image of the other, the dialectical short-circuiting of the revolution takes place. It is difficult to evaluate everything that has been repressed and eliminated in this operation, which clarified, once and for all, under the sign of materialism, of history and dialectics, the revolutionary *reality principle*. Let's say that everything brought up by the "pleasure principle" and by the radicality of revolt, everything that one can still read in the insurrections of the 19th century, in the destruction of machines, in the "pre-Marxist" libertarian, utopian discourse, in the *poètes maudits*, or in the sexual revolution, and everything that intended, well beyond material production, the symbolic configuration of the totality of life and social relations, destroyed by the abstract configuration of the political economy—it is this entire wild and radical movement that Marxist *theory* and socialist *organization*, in their miraculous conjunction, made dialectical by treating class status and "historical" content as the development of productive forces. They rationalized it in antagonistic power relations *within* the same social field, magnetized by political economy. This revolt implied something other than a *dialectic of forces*: the irruption of a radical *difference*. Something other than surplus value and the exploitation of labor power: the corruption even of all social relations by the unilateral rationality of production and universal socialization under the law of value. And the operation, if one looks closely, consisted in a "dialectical" rehabilitation of the status of producer, which tripped this revolt up, which Marxist theory put forward as the point of departure for social revolution. Even the process of destruction and repression, Marxism made a revolutionary detour and a promise of liberation. (Nietzsche was right: the workers made a cardinal value of the sign of their slavery, as the Christians did of their suffering.) And the revolution was not longer for here and now: it became a historical finality. Made positive under the sign of progress by the bourgeoisie or dialectical under the sign of revolution by Marxism, it is always in opposition to the radicality of desire which traverses every finality of its non-sense, the imposition of a meaning, the rational projection of an objective finality.

Alongside the situation created by massive industrialization, concentrationary discipline, putting generations of artisans and peasants on the clock since the beginning of the 19th century, alongside the situation of destructuration and revolt created in this way, Marxist theory and the worker's organization together accomplished a task of historic rationalization, a certain kind of *secondary elaboration*: the valorization of labor as the source of social wealth, the valorization of a process of the rational development of productive forces, this *process* was confused with the revolutionary *project* (surely according to a "dialectical" negativity, behind which the confusion of this same class with labor as the class's social ethic was irrevocably hidden).

The ethic of rational labor, originally bourgeois, which served to define the bourgeoisie historically as a class, is found to be renewed with a fantastic amplitude at the level of the working class, contributing here too to the *definition* of the working class as a class, which is to say to circumscribing that class to a status of historical representability.

Respect for the machine, safeguarding the instruments of labor, implying virtual property, (a human right of some kind, in opposition to a legal right), and the future appropriation of the means of production, institute the working class in a productivist vocation which replaces the historical vocation of the bourgeoisie. That in the revolutionary project these means of production should be placed in the hands of those who produce, under the sign of social appropriation and self-management, only describes the eternal quality of the process of production, beyond the changes of modes of production. The "class of laborers" finds itself confirmed in this way, even in its revolutionary ideal, in its idealized status as productive force: it reflects itself as the "most precious human capital," as the originary myth of social wealth.

Under cover of historical materialism, the idealism of production ends by granting a positive definition to the revolutionary class. The class thus *defines itself in the universal*, according universality to labor power: it returns to an essence to which it is in fact assigned by the bourgeoisie, which defines it in its historical being through the universality of capital. Capital and labor power thus confront one another as respective values, equally grounded in the universal.[22] In this confrontation of classes, in which each has its objective historical *reference*, the bourgeoisie always carries the day. The concept of class belongs to it, and when it succeeds in enclosing the proletariat within it, it has already won. The concept of class is a rationalist, universalist concept, born of a society of rational production, and of the calculation of productive forces: in this sense, there has never been and never will be anything but a single class: the bourgeoisie, the capitalist bourgeois class—defined not only through its ownership of the *means* of production, but by the rational *finality* of production. To make the proletariat a class is therefore already to enclose it in an order of definition (underlined by "class consciousness" as the "subject of history")[23] for which the model remains the bourgeois class. The ascension to the status of class equates a rationalization of the "worker's movement" with its revolt, draws it into line with the general rationality of the industrial order. Thus "class against class" might well signify antagonism to a level of the relationship to *means* of production, but this in no way shatters the finality of production: on the contrary, making this dialectical within this schema only infinitely extends the process of political economy.

If the class struggle has a meaning, it is not in the confrontation of one class by another. (We know that when the structure reverses itself and the proletarian class triumphs, as in the East, nothing profoundly changes in social relations). It can only be the radical refusal to let itself be enclosed in the being and consciousness of a class. This is not to deny it insofar as it is deprived of the means of production. (This is unfortunately the "objective" Marxist definition of the class.) It is to deny it insofar as it is assigned to production and to political economy. Can the proletariat define itself in terms of productive forces, of labor, of historical rationality? Evidently no. In this structure, the proletariat (or any other possible class) is condemned to enter into the rational dialectic of form and content (the class structure on one hand, and its own class values on the other, when these are not its class "interests"!) It is condemned to a *class finality* which completely encloses it in the dialectical play of capitalist society.

Better, by reinforcing itself in its being, in relation to the class struggle, it reinforces the dominant class in its being. It therefore participates, functionally, in the system of power, its degraded opposition serving the reformist impulse of the capitalist system, when it can no longer reveal itself as still conservative in the realm of values. This is where we are today.

To what can we impute the historical loss of the "revolutionary double negation" (the proletariat has truly negated the bourgeoisie, but has it not negated itself as a class)?

To Lenin, to Stalin again, to an accident of the dialectic, to a fault of the proletariat itself? Simply, the conjunction of a revolutionary theory intending the abolition of classes, clarified by Marx, with a revolutionary subject (the reality and historic class or salaried workers)—we can not even say that it should not slowly be turned against itself; it *logically* produced this substantialization of social revolt in an unsurpassable theoretical class, soon fixed in its being by the organization. Starting here, the proletarian class and Marxist theory began to *mutually justify one another*, and therefore to *neutralize* one another. And the project of changing life, which Marx demanded alongside revolutionary action, quietly became the victory of the proletariat.

The Revolution as End: History in Suspense

ALONG WITH THE mode of production, the concept of history constitutes the other wing of this dialectical rationalization. Within the social structure, it is homologous with the time of the theorization of the mode of production (once again, the imposition in the Renaissance of perspectival convergence as the reality principle of space can serve as a reference).

One can speak of a "millenarian" idea in Marx:[24] communism for a "near future," imminent revolution. This "utopian" demand dates from the *Introduction to the Critique of Hegel's Philosophy of Right*, the *1844 Manuscripts*, the *Theses on Feuerbach*, and the *Manifesto*. After the loses of 1848, reconversion: communism is not among the possibilities offered by the present situation. It can only become the order of the day much later, *at the end of a period which will have created the necessary historical conditions*.[25] With *Capital*, we pass from revolutionary utopia to a properly historical dialectic, from the immediate and radical revolt to objective consideration: capitalism must "ripen," which is to say internally attain its own negation as a social system—therefore a *historical and logical necessity*, the long march of the dialectic, wherein the negativity of the proletariat no longer immediately bears on itself as a class, but rather over the long term on the process of capital. Engaged in this long objective "detour," the proletariat begins to reflect itself as a negative term and as the subject of history.[26]

The Marxist effort diverges from its radical exigency toward the story of historical laws. The proletariat no longer leaps out of its shadow, it grows in the shadow of capital. The revolution is placed in a process of implacable evolution at the end of which the laws of history require man to liberate himself as a social creature.

The radical exigency does not abandon the Marxist perspective, but it becomes a *final* exigency. Conversion from here and now toward an asymptotic fulfillment, a *deferred expiration date*, indefinitely put off, which, under the sign of a reality principle of history (objective socialization of society created by capital—dialectical process of the maturation of "objective" revolutionary conditions) will confirm the transcendence of *ascetic* communism, communism of sublimation and of hope, which, in the name of an ever renewed beyond— beyond history, beyond the dictatorship of the proletariat, beyond capitalism and beyond socialism—over and over again demands the sacrifice of the immediate and permanent revolution. Ascetic in relation to its own revolution, communism effectively suffers profoundly from not "taking its desires for reality"[27] (this transcendent dimension, this sublimation was also that of orthodox Christianity in opposition to the millenarian sects which longed for the immediate fulfillment, here below. Sublimation, as we know, represses: it founds the power of the church).

The revolution becomes an *end*, something it definitely was not in the radical exigency that presumes, in place of referencing a final totalization, that man is *already entirely there* in his revolt. Such is the meaning of utopia, if one distinguishes it from the dreaming idealism to which the "scientists" take pleasure in reducing it, so as to bury it more completely. It refuses the schema *by diluting* the contradictions. This ideal structuration leaves a place for the "reason" of history, for a conscious and logical revolutionary organization, for the dialectical prediction of a *deferred* revolution—this dialectic falling very quickly in the pure and simple schema of ends and means: *The Revolution as "end" equals the autonomization of means.* We know what became of it: all of this having had the effect of debasing the present situation, of exorcising immediate subversion, of diluting (in the chemical sense of the term) the explosive reaction in a long term solution.

"MAN SHOULD KNOW to content himself with the perspective of his liberation. This is why 'revolutionary romanticism', 'hic et nunc' revolt will persist until the Marxist perspective ceases to be a perspective" (Kalivoda). But could it be, from the moment in which it entered into the objective play of history, the resignation to the *laws* of history and dialectics, something other than a perspective? From the moment Marx began writing, the workers broke their machines. Marx didn't write for them. He had nothing to say to them—they were even wrong in his eyes: the industrial bourgeois was revolutionary. The theoretical split explains nothing. The immanent revolt of the workers who broke their machines remained forever without explanation. Marx contented himself with the dialectic, making them babes in the woods. The entire workers movement, up until the Commune, lived by this utopian exigency of immediate socialism (Déjacque, Coeurderoy, etc.), and they *were* such even in their defeat. Because utopia was never written in their future, it is what is always already there. Marx himself speaks of the beyond, he speaks of all of this as of a surpassed phase. But from what point of view was he right in *advance*? The failure of these movements (in opposition to the "Marxist" revolutions of the 20th century) is not an argument: it appeals precisely to the "reason" of history, to an objective end which could not account for the specificity of social speech not finalized by a future dimension. Here, in the verdict of history, international communism today seeks the only proof of its truth, no longer in dialectical reason, but in the immanence of facts: at this level, history is no longer even a process, it is simply a trial that always condemns revolt.

The Radicality of Utopia

IN FACT, Marx is right, "objectively" right, but this objectivity and this being right, only came about, as in all science, at the cost of a *misunderstanding*, a misunderstanding of the radical utopia contemporary with the *Manifesto* and with *Capital*. We can't say that Marx "objectively" theorized capitalist social relations, the class struggle, the movement of history, etc. In effect, Marx "objectified" the convulsion of the social order, its present subversion, its language of life and death, liberating in the moment itself, in long term dialectical revolution, in a spiral finality which was only life without the end of political economy.[28]

Accursed poetry, non-official art, utopian writing in general, offering a current, immediate content to the liberation of man should be the speech of communism, its direct prophecy. It is only its bad conscience, precisely because in it something of humanity is realized *immediately*, because it objects with pity to the "political" dimension of the revolution, which is only the dimension of its finally postponement. This art is the linguistic equivalent of the wild social movements that were born from the symbolic situation of rupture (symbolic, which is to say non-universalized, non-dialectical, non-rationalized in the mirror of an imaginary objective history). This is why poetry (not "Art") was only fundamentally linked to the utopian social movements, "revolutionary romanticism," never with Marxism as such. The contents of liberated man are fundamentally less important than the abolition of the separation of the present and the future. The abolition of this form of time, the dimension of sublimation, forbids us from pardoning the dialectical idealists, who are, at the same time, political realists. According to them, the revolution should be distilled in history, it should reach its term, it should ripen in the sun of contradiction. Present, immediate: unthinkable for them, *insufferable*. Poetry and utopian revolt have this radical present in common, this denegation of finalities. This actualization of desire, no longer exorcised in a future liberation but demanded here, immediately, even in its death drive, in the radical compatibility of life and death. Such is its ecstasy, such is revolution. It has nothing to do with the political due date of revolution.

Contrary to Marxist analysis which poses man as dispossessed, as alienated, and relates him to a total man, to a total Other, who is there in future Reason (this is utopian in the bad sense of the term), which assigns man to a project of totalization: *utopia itself knows no concept of alienation.* Utopia believes that every man, every society is already completely present, at each social moment, in its symbolic demand. Marxism never analyzes revolt, or the social movement of society, other than in the *filigree of the revolution*, as a reality on the road to maturity. Perfect racism, in the completed stage of rationality, which returns everything else into the nothingness of the surpassed.[29] With this, Marxism remains profoundly a philosophy, in everything that remains in it, even its "scientific" stage, of its vision of alienation. The other side of critical thought, in terms of alienation, is always a total essence that haunts a divided existence. This metaphysics of totality in no way opposes the current reality of this division, it is part of its system. For the subject, the perspective at the end of history, of finding transpncy, or total "use value," is as completely religious as the reintegration of essences. "Alienation" is still the imaginary of the subject, even of the subject of history. The subject does not have to become a total man again, the subject does not have to rediscover himself; today he has lost himself. The totalization of the subject is still the end of the end of the political economy of consciousness, confirmed by the identity of the subject as political economy as by the principle of equivalence. This is what should be abolished in place of cradling men with the phantasm of their lost identity, of their future autonomy.

What absurdity to pretend that men are "others" and to seek to convince them that their most cherished desire is to become "themselves"! Each man is entirely there at each instant. Society is also there, in each instant. Coeurderoy, the Luddites, Rimbaud, the Communards, the wild strikers, those of May '68 are not the revolution in filigree: they *are* the revolution. Not concepts in transit, their speech is symbolic, and intends no essence. It is a speech before history, before politics, before truth, before separation and future totality—the only speech which, speaking the world as non-separated, is truly revolutionary.

There is no possible or impossible. Utopia is there, in every energy raised against political economy. But this utopian violence does not accumulate, it loses itself. It does not seek accumulation, as does economic value, but the abolition of death. It never wants powers. Enclosing the "exploited" in the only historic possibility of taking power has been the worst redirection of revolution that has taken place. Therein we see to what depths the axioms of political economy have undermined, invested, and redirected the revolutionary perspective. Utopia seeks speech against power, and against the reality principle, which is only the phantasm of the system and of its indefinite reproduction. It only wants speech, and only to lose itself in it.

12

Strike Story

The Class Struggle as Will and Representation

THE POLITICAL "SCENE," with its representative authorities and its delegation of power to figures (parties, unions, parliaments); dueling authorities, proletarian as well as bourgeoisie; memberships mediated by their representative authorities. This is the class struggle: mass vaudeville, the proletariat plays a choice role: its "dear delegates" have their entrances and exits on stage, their comings and goings in the wings. This staging has persisted for a century, the proletariat has lived it as a conquest of its social legitimacy, it is because of it that capital has integrated the revolution as a variable. If it hasn't been like this since the 19th century (*though this is not certain*), it is clear that today society as a group recognizes itself by the *model* of the class struggle as a relationship of forces. Prior to the spiral of the strike and negation, the International of development!

The strike justifies itself historically in a system of production, as violence organized to wrest a fraction of surplus value, if not power, from the inverse violence of capital. Today, this strike is dead:

1. Because capital is capable of letting every strike rot—this because we are no longer exactly in a system of production (maximalization of surplus value). Perish the anticipated profit

that the reproduction of the form of the social relation intended to save!

2. Because these strikes no longer change the basis of anything. Today capital itself redistributes a sensible part of surplus value, because for capital this is a question of life and death. Better, the protest strike tears away from capital something it would have eventually conceded anyway, according to its own logic of reproduction.

If therefore the productive relations, and with them the class struggle, are enlisted in social relations and are politically orchestrated, it is clear that the only thing that can cause an irruption in this cycle is something that escapes organization and class definition as *representative* historical authority and *productive* historical authority.

Only those who avoid the tourniquet of production and representation can deregulate the mechanisms and foment, from the foundation of their blind condition, a return of the "class struggle" which could find its pure and simple end as the geometric location of "politics." Here the intervention of immigrants assumes its meaning in recent strikes. But this intervention does not exclude any other group *deprived of social representation*. Women, the youth, students, homosexuals, and the "proletariat" itself, when they become "wild" or if one admits that at bottom the unions don't represent the workers at all, only themselves—we are all in this sense "immigrants." Inversely, they can cease to be. There is therefore no "immigrant as such," and they don't constitute a new historical subject, a neo-proletariat which would subsume the other.

Because millions of workers find themselves, through the mechanism of their discrimination, deprived of every representative authority, it is from them that the irruption on the Western scene of class struggle carries the crisis to the crucial level of representation. Held outside class by the whole society, including the unions (and with the racial economic complicity of their "base" on this point: for the organized proletarian "class," centered on its relation of economico-political forces with the bourgeois capitalist class, the immigrant is "objectively" a class enemy), the immigrants serve, through this social exclusion, as analysts of the relationship between workers and unions, and more generally of the relationship between the "class" and every representative authority of the "class." Deviants according to the system of political representation, they infect the entire proletariat with their deviance. The proletariat itself also learns little by little to let go of the system of representation and of every authority which pretends to speak in its name.

The situation won't last: unions and bosses have detected the danger and set about reintegrating the immigrants as "entirely separate figures" within the "class struggle." But it is too late.

Autopsy of the Unions

THE RENAULT STRIKE of March and April 1973 constitutes a kind of general repetition of this crisis. Apparent confusion, disorganized, manipulated, a retreat to certain previous strikes, and, in the final count, a failure (if not the extraordinary terminological victory which replaced the term "specialized worker," henceforth taboo, with *productive agent*"!), in reality a very beautiful struggle of unions trapped between their base and the bosses. At the beginning, it was a "wild" strike instigated by the "specialized worker" immigrants. But the CGT[1] had a standing army ready for this sort of accident: the extension of the strike to other factories or to other categories of personnel, seizing the occasion of a now ritual Springtime mass action. Even this control mechanism, which has offered its proofs since '68, and on which the unions truly could have counted to be able to support themselves for a generation, eluded them this time. Even the non-wild base (Seguin, flins, Sandouville) alternately quit and resumed work (which is also important) with regard to the council of their unions. They were constantly taken off balance. What they obtained from the managers to ratify with the workers, the workers didn't want. The concessions that they won from the workers to restart the negotiations with the managers, the managers refused and closed the factories. They appealed to the workers over the unions. In fact, they deliberately created the crisis to force the unions' entrenchment: could they control all of the workers? Their social existence, their legitimacy was at stake. This is the reason the bosses "stiffened" (as did the government at all levels). This wasn't a question of a test of strength between the organized (unionized) proletariat and the bosses, but of a *test of representation* for the union under the double pressure of the base and the bosses—and this test is the result of all the wild strikes of recent years, which is to say that the non-unionized, the unmanageable youth, the immigrants, all of those outside the class, set it off.

Reality check. Today the whole purpose of the union is to disperse the crumbs of the management of capital throughout the working class (the drive belt of development), and all that it wants in exchange is the delegation of the bosses' power over this same working "class." But the bosses, very logically, offer them this delegation of power only if they are capable of taking control. If they seem entangled in the unmanageables or the wild strikers, or to harden their resolve, as was the case at the end of March, beginning of April (even if it is, a smart tactic, to smother them), then the bosses resume the caution that they showed the union when accepting to negotiate with it,[2] when accepting to negotiate only with it, and let it go. At this moment, the management plays a dangerous game, it contributes at least as much as the leftists in discrediting the unions, which are its drive belt. But it has them against the ropes when it says: Stop, if you play this little game we will force you to go to the end, to become revolutionaries, the unions can only nod and turn against their base. Oscillating from the base to the summit, and desperately seeking the delegation of power, they are in the process of losing their credibility. Power no longer offers them a choice and the "base" refuses to be a mass in motion.

Thus, at Anvers, the police should intervene to protect the union premises against the wives of the striking dock workers, who attacked them with umbrellas. "The anger of the dock workers against their unions deepens every day. They reproach the managers of the organizations for not having *recognized* their movement. The unions, for their part, estimate that the demands of the base are exaggerated and that, in any case, they are linked through the agreements of social planning reached with the bosses."[3]

The stakes at this level are extraordinary. The entire social edifice is threatened with collapse along with the legitimacy and the representation of the union. The parliament and the other mediations weigh no more heavily. Even the police serve no purpose without the unions, if the unions are incapable of policing the factories and elsewhere. In May 1968, they were the ones who saved the government. Now their bell is sounding. Profoundly, the importance of these stakes is expressed in the confusion of the events (and this is as valuable for the actions of the students as for the Renault strike). To strike or not to strike. Where are we? No one decides anything anymore. What are the objectives? Who are our adversaries? What are we talking about? We don't know. The Geiger counters, thanks to which the unions, parties, and groups measure the combativeness of the masses are spinning. The student movement dissolved in the hands of those who wanted to structure it according to its own objectives: didn't it have objectives? In any case, it did not want *to objectify itself after the fact.* The workers resumed work without result, though they refused to work eight days previously based on sensible advantages, etc. In fact, this confusion is like that of a dream: it translates a resistance or censure which wagers the contents of the dream itself. Here, it translates a capital fact, hardly acceptable to the proletarians themselves, which is that the social struggle has been *displaced* by the traditional, external class enemy, bosses and capital, by the real, internal class enemy, the proper representative authority of the class, the party or union. The authority to which the workers delegate their power, and which turns against them in the form of the delegation of the bosses' and governmental power. Capital itself only alienates labor power and its products, it only has a monopoly on production. Parties and unions alienate the social power of the exploited, and they have a monopoly on *representation.* Their purpose is revolutionary historical progress. But this progress is dispersed with minimal clarity, minimal resolution, an apparent regression, the absence of continuity, of logic, of objectives, etc. Everything becomes uncertain, everything resists when it is a question of confronting one's own repressive authority, of chasing the unionized, delegated, the responsible, the speakers *from one's head.* But this flurry in the spring of 1973 indicates precisely that we have reached the bottom of the problem: the unions and the parties are dead, all they have left to do is die.

The Dissolution of the Proletariat

THIS CRISIS OF representation is the crucial *political* aspect of the recent social movements. Meanwhile it alone might not be fatal for the system, and one already sees its formal transcendence (its recuperation) outlined everywhere (among the unions themselves) in a generalized schema of *self-management*. No more delegation of power, everyone entirely responsible for production! The new ideological generation rises! But it will have a lot to do, because this crisis is articulated on another still deeper crisis which touches on production itself, even on the system of productivity. And here again the immigrants, undoubtedly indirectly, are in the position of analysts. In the same way that they analyzed, in the crisis of reproduction we have been discussing, the relationship of the "proletariat" to its representative authorities, they analyze the relationship of the workers to their own labor power, their relationship to themselves as productive forces (and not only of certain among them as representative authorities). And this because it was the immigrants that had been most recently torn from the non-productivist tradition. Because it was necessary to socially destructure them so as to throw them into the Western labor process, and in return, they deeply destructured the process in general and the productivist morality that dominates Western societies.

Everything happens as if the hiring of labor on the European labor market provoked a progressive dissolution of the European proletariat in relation to labor and production. This is no longer only a question of "clandestine" practices of resistance to work (braking, waste, absenteeism, etc.) which have never ceased—but this time, overtly, collectively, spontaneously, the workers stopped working, like that, suddenly, one Monday, demanding nothing, negotiating for nothing, to the great despair of the unions and the bosses, and returned to work just as spontaneously, and *as a group*, the following Monday. No loss, no victory, it was not a strike, it was a "*work stoppage.*" An euphemism of longer standing than the term strike itself: the entire discipline owed to labor falls, all the moral and practical norms that have been imposed by industrial colonization for two centuries in Europe, which disintegrate and are forgotten, without apparent effort, without "class struggle" properly speaking. Discontinuity, laxity, loose schedules, with respect to salaried *forcing*, to surplus, to promotion, accumulation, projections—we do only just what we must, then we stop, and come back later. These are exactly the behaviors that the colonists reproach the "under-developed" for: it's impossible to adapt them to labor / value, to rational and continuous schedules, to the con- cept of salaried gain, etc. It is only by overseas exploration that one comes in the end to integrate them into the labor process. And it is at this moment that the Western laborers themselves "regress" more and more toward "under-developed" behaviors. It is not the smallest revenge of colonialism and of its most advanced form (the importation of labor) to see the Western proletariat itself seized by dissolution—so much so that it might perhaps one day export itself in its turn to under-developed countries so as to relearn the historic and revolutionary value of work.

There is a direct relationship between the ultra-colonization of immigrant laborers (since the colonies were not profitable in place, we imported them) and this industrial decolonization which affects every sector of society (throughout, school, factory, one passes from the phase of *hot* investments of labor *to the cool and cynical practice of chores*). As the immigrants were the ones most recently drawn from "wild" indifference to "rational" labor, they analyze Western

society in its recent, fragile, superficial and arbitrary collectiviza-
tion, forced by labor, its collective paranoia, from which we have
drawn a morality, a culture, a myth. We have forgotten that it has
only been two centuries since this industrial discipline was
imposed, at the price of unknown efforts, even in the West; that it
never really succeeded and that it began to crack dangerously (it
hardly lasted longer than that other colonization, across the seas).

Striking for the Sake of it

STRIKING FOR the sake of it—striking for strikes—is the present
truth of the struggle. Without motivation, with objective or political
reference, it responds by opposing itself to a production which is
itself without motivation, without reference, without social use
value, without any other finality than itself—*to a production for the
sake of production*, in short to a system which is no longer anything
but a system of *reproduction*, and which turns on itself in a gigantic
tautology of the labor process. Striking for the strike is an inverse tautology, but a subversive tautology since it unveils this new form of
capital (which corresponds to the completed form of political economy: the ultimate stage of the law of value wherein all use value is
abolished to the sole profit of the reproduction of exchange value).[4]

The strike finally ceases to be a means, and only a means of
ruminating on the relationship between *political* forces and the
game of power. It becomes an end. It negates through radical
parody, on its own terrain, the kind of finality without end that
production has become (senseless, absurd, without visible objective
in terms of classical utility).

In production for the sake of production, there is no more
waste. This term, valuable in a restrained economy of use, is useless

for us. It raises an old liberal or pious criticism of the system. The Concorde, the space program, etc. is not waste. On the contrary. Because what the system, at this high point of "objective" uselessness, produces and reproduces, is *labor itself*. Elsewhere this is what everyone (workers and unions included) asks of it right away. Everything turns around employment—society is the creation of employees—so as to preserve employment, British unions are ready to transform the Concorde into a supersonic bomber—inflation or unemployment: intense inflation, etc. Labor has become, like Social Security, like consumer goods, a *good* for social redistribution. An enormous paradox if one holds to traditional or Marxist political economy: labor is less and less a productive force, it is more and more a *product*. This aspect is not the smallest characteristic of the present mutation of the system of capital, of the revolution for which it passes from the specific stage of production to that of reproduction. Less and less does it need labor power to function and grow (for a long time certain American factories functioned at 60% of their potential), and one asks of it that it furnish, that it "produce" more and more labor.

The absurd circularity of a system wherein one works to produce work corresponds to the admirable demand of a strike for strikes (today this is what results from most "demanding" strikes anyway). "Pay us for the days of the strike." This is to say, basically: pay us so that we can *reproduce* the strike for strikes. A return to the absurdity of the general system.

Another concept and reality that falls: "productive" labor. This—to which the traditional analysis opposed "non-productive" labor and waste—corresponded to a criteria of the objective utility of labor, producer of value and surplus value in the structure of a social goal of production (individual and social needs). Today, when products, *all* products, and labor itself, are beyond utility and uselessness, there is no longer productive labor, there is no longer anything but *reproductive* labor. Similarly, there is no longer "productive" consumption nor "non-productive" consumption. "Productive" labor, "non-productive" services (tertiary services, intellectual services, etc.) or leisure, all of these categories are equated in the schema of reproduction which exceeds them: leisure is as "productive" as labor, factory labor is also as "non-productive" as leisure or tertiary services—no matter which formula. *This indifference marks precisely the completed phase of political economy.* Everything is *reproductive*, which is to say everything has lost the concrete finality which could distinguish it so as to no longer serve reproduction uniformly. No one produces any more. Production is dead. Long live reproduction!

The Genealogy of (Re)production

1. We need to see where this hypothesis truly leads: if labor is no longer primarily a productive force—since it appears that this historic status (almost ontological) risks changing—history changes too: *revolution* is no longer possible through labor or the laborers. If the use value of labor power disappeared—and it disappeared in labor for the sake of labor—the mechanism of surplus value and exploitation ends. This mechanism requires, as we know, the use value of labor power, only to produce an overvalue through its insertion in the labor process.

2. *Objection*: If labor is no longer primarily a productive force, it nonetheless remains a productive force, producing surplus value. Without that where would the enlarged reproduction of the system originate (we are still in the "growth" phase).

3. *Response*: What is reproduced in an enlarged way in the present system is capital in its most rigorous Marxist definition: as a *form of social relation*, and capital in its vulgar acceptation: as money, profit and economic system. We have always understood reproduction as the enlarged reproduction of the mode of production, determined by the latter. While it should perhaps be necessary to conceive of the mode of production itself as a modality (and therefore one of the possible modalities, but not the only one) of the *mode of reproduction*. Productive forces and relations of production—in other words, the sphere of capitalist material productivity, that of labor power and exploitation—is perhaps only one of the possible situations, and therefore historically relative, of the process of reproduction. This responds to the objection: reproduction is a form which surrounds and surpasses economic exploitation from afar. The play of productive forces is therefore not the necessary condition for reproduction.

Historically, isn't the status of the "proletariat" (of the industrial salaried class) only containment, concentration and social exclusion?

Manufacturing containment is the fantastic expansion of containment in the seventeenth century, described by Foucault. Wasn't "industrial" labor (non-artisan, collective, deprived of means of production, under control) born in the first large general hospitals? In an earlier time, a society on the road to rationalism confined its unemployed, its vagabonds, its deviants, it occupied them, fixed them, imposed its rational principle of labor on them. But contamination is reciprocal, and the cut through which society instituted its principle of rationality ebbed on the world of work as a whole: confinement is a micro-model that spreads thereafter, as an industrial system, to the entire society which, under the sign of labor, of finality, became productivist, a concentration camp, a detention center, a jail.

In place of exporting the concept of the proletariat and of exploitation on top of racial, sexual oppression, etc. one must ask if it has not been the reverse. If the worker is not primarily, if his fundamental status is not, like the mad, the dead, nature, animals, children, blacks, women—not a status of *exploitation*, but a status of *excommunication*—not a status of spoliation and exploitation, but a status of demarcation and discrimination.

Labor is internment, jail, control. The factory behind the apparent ends of the production. The school behind the apparent ends of knowledge. The "objective" contents (of accumulation and production) and the historic contradiction tied up in it have less importance than its form. The form of labor as a social relationship (abstraction, division, prison and control) is generalized today while it contents (production and relations of production) lose their specificity. The labor-form is only generalized at all levels of society when its determinate contents (material production, surplus value, exploitation) disappear.[5]

The contents of production can only equal, at the limit, the alibi of this form of confinement and of discrimination. I offer the hypothesis that there has only ever been a real class struggle on the basis of this discrimination: the struggle of the sub-humans against their status as beasts, against the abjection of this caste division which condemns them to the sub-humanity of labor. If one looks closely, this is what is behind every strike, every revolt, today still undoubtedly behind most "salaried" actions: their virulence comes from this, not from the cash. That said, the workers have been promoted to the dignity of a wholly distinct human being— apparently of course, but this suffices to neutralize the class struggle at this level. The proletariat as such is a "normalized" being, under this heading it takes all of the dominant discriminations into account: it is racist, sexist, and repressive. In relation to the present deviants, to the discriminated against of all kinds, it is on the same side as the bourgeoisie: the side of the human, the normal. This is so true that the fundamental law of this society is not the law of exploitation, but the *code of normality*.

May 1968: The Illusion of Production

THE FIRST SHOCK wave of this passage from production to pure and simple reproduction was May 1968. It touched the university first, the faculties of human sciences and literature first of all, because it was there that it became more and more evident (even without a clear "political" consciousness) *that one no longer produces anything*, and that we no longer do anything but reproduce (teachers first, then knowledge and culture, which were themselves only factors in the reproduction of the general system—see Bourdieu, Passeron). Experienced as total uselessness, irresponsibility ("why sociology?"), relegation that fomented the student movement of 1968 (not the absence of outlets—there were always enough outlets *in reproduction*—what no longer exists is the places, the spaces where something is truly "produced").

This shock wave has not been arrested by the victory of the UDR. It can only spread itself to the extremities of the system, while whole sectors of society fall from the rank of *productive forces* to the pure and simple status of *reproductive forces*. If this process initially touched the cultural sectors, of knowledge, justice, family (we should analyze how the destructuration of familial ties, of parental authority is linked to this passage from the family as a unity of real production to the restricted family as pure and simple element of reproduction in the structure of the system)[6]—this is to say the "superstructural" sectors. It is clear that today it also progressively affects the entire "infrastructural" sector. A new generation of strikes since 1968—partial, wild, episodic, it hardly matters—no longer testifies to the "class struggle" of a proletariat assigned to production, but to the revolt of those who, in the factories themselves, are assigned to reproduction.

Significantly, even in this sector, the marginal categories, anomical one might say, are touched first: young OS [specialized workers] brought directly from the country to the factory, immigrants, the non-unionized, etc. For all the reasons that we have indicated, the "traditional" proletariat, organized and unionized, has effectively every chance of being the last to react, since the proletariat can maintain the illusion of "productive" labor the longest. This consciousness of being, in relation to all the other real "producers," being, even at the price of exploitation, at the source of social wealth, this "proletarian" consciousness, reinforced and sanctioned by the organization, certainly constitutes the surest *ideological* rampart against the destructuration of the present system, which, far from proletarianizing whole strata of the population, which is to say expanding the exploitation of the "productive" labor as good *Marxist theory holds,*[7] aligns everyone with the same status as reproductive laborers.

Manual "productive" laborers live, more than any others, in *the illusion of production.* Just as they live their leisure in the illusion of freedom. Labor (in the form of leisure as well) invades all of life as fundamental repression, as control, as permanent occupation in places and regulated times, according to an omnipresent code.[8] One must *fix* people everywhere, at school, at the factory, at the beach or in front of the TV, in recycling: permanent general mobilization. But this labor is no longer productive in the original sense—it is no longer anything but a mirror of society, its imaginary, its fantastic reality principle. Death drive maybe.

Insofar as things are lived as a source of wealth and satisfaction, *as use value*, the worst labor alienated and exploited, they are supportable. Insofar as one can still recognize a corresponding "production" (even imaginary) for individual or social needs (this is why the concept of need is so fundamental and so mystifying), the worst individual or historic situations are supportable. Because the illusion of production is always the illusion of making these needs coincide with their ideal use value. And today those who believe in the use value of their labor power—the proletarians—are virtually the most mystified, the least susceptible to the revolt which grips people in the depths of their total uselessness, the circular manipulation which makes pure stakes of a pointless reproduction.

Because the law of value only becomes truly insupportable when value itself disappears—the use value/exchange value "dialectic" disappearing before the pure reproduction of the exchange value—when it is no longer possible to recognize it, in the term of the process of production turning on itself like a dervish, the smallest effect of social wealth, the smallest *change in life* or social relation. This stage is that of monopolistic neo-capitalism, which is still that of a dialectic of production. The day that this process generalizes itself throughout society, May 1968 will assume the form of a general explosion, and the problem of the link between students and workers will no longer be posed: it only translates the divide which separates those who, in the present system, still believe in their own labor power from those who no longer believe in it.

The Class Struggle Stripped Bare by the Workers, Even

No CHANCE FOR a larger piece of the pie; for the "reappropriation of surplus value" or the labor process: the workers don't even want the "fruit of their labor" (nor women the "fruit of their loins"). Not only is the work ethic, and its "just" reward, finished, the strike ethic is too; it's deinvestment pure and simple, indifference to collective and individual goals. Pft! By simply stopping work, the "workers" no longer only attack the system of the reproduction of capital (of labor power as exchange value), but the reproduction of labor power as *use value*. Not only do they refuse to contribute to expanded reproduction, but they no longer even want to reproduce themselves as labor power (to which demands for salary or improved working conditions always lead, as in self-management). Finished too, the revolutionary dialectic of productive forces and relations of productions—questioned by the absurd strikers, it is *their proper destination as productive force*. This is the real revolution, because this is the only one equal to the system, the only one that subverts the system in its real terms: no longer in terms of production, but in terms of indefinite reproduction.

And, with the same blow, it brings an end to the ambiguity of the class struggle. The definition of the proletarian class is irremediably ambiguous. If the bourgeois class defines itself clearly through its ownership of the means of production, the proletariat does not define itself inversely through its total dispossession. It is the owner of the essential means of production: labor power. Strictly speaking, this suffices to make it complicit with the *system* of production (and not only a victim of the *process* of production). In the order of production, contrary to the pathetic myth of exploitation, there is not a class which possesses nothing and which has nothing to lose.[9] There is therefore a fundamental ambiguity in the concept of the class struggle to the extent that it envisions the proletariat as a productive force (and how would it define it otherwise?). There is the impossibility of radical antagonism, since it shares something of the system and of its structural givens. Its negativity cannot be total. Only the refusal of production can constitute a radical threshold. Because it alone, abolishing the positive referent of the class (ownership of labor power), signifies the abolition of the class here and now.

On this point of negativity, of defection, of "nihilism" (as the champions of positive revolution would say), what's left? The essential: knowing that social wealth, the symbolic, returns in the end to the social relationship, and is no longer founded on the quantitative imaginary of material production, nor on the political imaginary of a revolution in productive relations. Wealth ceases to be economic, accumulative, therefore absent and always future—and the refusal to work (among other practices) becomes the immediate demand for wealth, forever lost in the cycle of production. A demand presented in the loss of value—even in a strike for strikes, only in the *absolute* loss of productive time, and in the new type of exchange and of social relation which is thereby invented, outside of all finality, of all mediation, and of any revolutionary future.

13

The Dramatization of Economics

The Energy Crisis

AT THE STAGE of reproduction, which is the aesthetic stage of political economy, that of a finality without end of production, the ethical, ascetic myth of scarcity collapses, and with it the principle of mercantile exchange. Scarcity must be regenerated if the economic principle is to be reactivated. Capital, which might burst from this liquefaction of values, grows nostalgic for its grand period of *ethics*, the golden age wherein we produced for our salvation, or at least to conquer nature and to meet our fundamental needs, before everything degenerated into production for production. It was the golden age of the development of productive forces. Today, to set things right, we are going to substitute an *ethic of energy conservation*.

Where does ecology come from? This sort of benediction that constitutes the energy crisis and the raw materials for a system, reflected in the mirror of production in nothing more than an empty, panic-stricken form. The crisis will permit us to return the economic code's lost referentiality, the principle of production's absent gravity. We will recover our taste for asceticism, the emotional investment which is born from lack and privation. Make production dramatic in order to save it.

Every ecological twist and turn of recent years already engaged this process of regeneration through crisis—a crisis which is no longer that of overproduction, as in 1929, but of the involution of the system on its own bases, of the recycling of its own principles and of its own lost identity.[1] This is no longer a crisis of *production* but of *reproduction*, in which we encounter the impossibility, among others, of really grasping what is true and what is a simulacrum in this crisis. Ecology is production which resources itself under the specter of scarcity, which rediscovers a natural necessity which dips back into the law of value. But ecology is too slow. A sudden crisis, like the gas crisis, constitutes a more energetic therapy. The less gas there is, the more we will perceive production. From the moment when the place of raw materials became marked, labor power also resumed its place, and the entire mechanism of production became intelligible once again. And set off...

Hence, no panic. In the hour when capitalism has virtually completed the totality of primitive accumulation on the world scale, with the intensive mobilization of labor power, the work ethic threatened to collapse, the material energy crisis came to the point of masking the veritable catastrophic destruction of the *internal finality* of production, to displace the simple economic reality of the lack of energy and raw materials, which is never anything but an *internal contradiction*. And we know that this system lives on its contradictions.

The analogous blackmail over the cost of raw materials on the part of under-developed countries with unlimited salary demands in rich countries.

With the structural development of capital, salary ceases to be a cost of labor power, it becomes a salary-income, a salary of reproductive consumption, a bonus of participation and integration in political society (under the double form of forced presence at work and forced waste through consumption). From this moment, when the law of labor-salary equivalence[2] (even rigged) is abolished by the system itself, nothing opposes unlimited salary demands any longer.[3] Maximum salary for minimum work: such is the order of the day, and it has taken on the sense of a revolt against the status of a political summons to capitalist society that salary signifies today. Because there is a "just price" for a certain quantity of labor power, but consensus and global participation are priceless. Traditional salary demands are only negotiations about the status of the producer. A maximalist demand is an offensive form of turning salary against the system of the *reproductive* condition that is created by salary. It's a challenge. The salaried employees no longer seek to negotiate or to exchange whatever it is. They want everything, that's their way not only of deepening the economic crisis of the system but of turning the total political demand that this imposes against the system. It is not at all too much for the unions to return to the salaried employees with the notion of labor-value and equivalent salary, that capital itself has abolished. It is not at all too much for the unions to canalize this limitless salary blackmail along the routes of healthy negotiation. Without unions, the workers would immediately demand raises of 50%, 100%, 200%, *and they would obtain them.* There are examples of this kind in the United States and Japan.

This is the same phenomenon that has appeared in underdeveloped countries. Without limits on the price of raw materials from the moment when they, well beyond economics, become the sign, the gauge of the acceptation of a world political order, the planetary society of peaceful existence, wherein the underdeveloped countries find themselves socialized by force under the control of the great powers. The escalation of prices then becomes a challenge, not only to the rich of Western countries, but to the political system of peaceful coexistence, faced with the domination of the world political class—whether capitalist or communist hardly matters.

It is undoubtedly for this reason that a military war was required for the Arabs to trigger the energy crisis. Previously, they had traditional salary demands: pay for gas *at its fair value*. But the war made them discover the total political coercion that peaceful coexistence had enclosed them in (this still wasn't evident with the Six Day War, but the war of 1973 put the apparatus in plain sight). Suddenly, their demands became maximal, unlimited, and their meaning changed.[4]

As if by chance, it reached Europe first, and not the two Greats (it would benefit the United States even more precisely). But this is in order: the worker's demanding pressure also eliminates small businesses and, in this sense, reinforces in a first moment the structures of large capital. It is not unthinkable that this challenge from the workers, on the level of labor power, of the underdeveloped on the level of raw materials, proceeds once again toward a reinforcement of the general system. Too bad for the dialectic! What is essential is that the one and the other are no longer left enclosed in the order of equivalences, that they pass to a challenge, that they engage the totality of that political order, and that they thereby initiate an *other type of exchange*, because the demand is not on the order of economics, it is of a symbolic order—and it is this displacement of exchange which, even in the case of defeat and of the reinforcement of the system, constitutes a revolution in terms, in the rules of the game.

Question—Response—Objection

Question

SCARCITY FOLLOWS abundance, the specter of privation dissipates at the first glimmer of furious consumption and reproduction... Nevertheless a war of a few days and an insane increase in the price of gas will suffice to collapse the beautiful assurance of consumer society and to resurrect the perspective of the "dark years" (energy crisis, inflation, the threat of unemployment...).

How can we explain the bankruptcy of the myth of abundance? Why is it less effective than that of scarcity? Why is it a necessity for the capitalist system—which surpassed without too much trouble the stage of production so as to enter into that of reproduction—to reinvest in this moribund myth and why precisely this myth? Production for production, would unlimited development be a viable objective? A switch error (capitalism realizing that it has taken a wrong turn)? Or is something else at stake? A vast masquerade mounted by capitalism itself, which serves as a myth corresponding to a surpassed stage of its own development so as to better assure its future...

IN ENGLAND, the energy crisis (inscribing itself in an agitated social context), far from bursting the situation, has on the contrary a "positive" political effect: the Britons cut the cord, accept the restrictions without a fuss... In short, start off again like its was 1940!

The crisis appears to be a powerful means of integrating the values of the political society and of the reproductive system: it is a question of "saving" both the country and the economic system at once, a rescue which demands sacrifices and privations on everyone's part, though it hardly matters!

By playing this instrumental role of integration, scarcity enters in competition with its opposite—obligatory consumption (cf. the change in the nature of salary, a consequence of the development of capitalism). The scarcity of energy mobilizes energies in the service of capital, it obtains the participation of everyone to save capitalism, as well and even better than consumption could, because it is more dramatic, more easily dramatizable. But how can it be explained that asceticism and privation can replace waste and play exactly the same role?

For the workers, an economy of unlimited production is linked to a demand for unlimited salary increases, which places (or threatens to place) capital at risk. But we can ask ourselves if, far from running a *real* risk, the "maximalist demand" is not on the contrary triggered by capitalism itself. After all, we understand clearly that salary increases and paid vacations are not great victories obtained through difficult struggle thanks to the combativeness of the working class, but that they have been awarded by capital since it judged them to be necessary. How would this demand for an unlimited raise be more radical, more subversive than the previous ones? It is not at all impossible that this demand *too* should be provoked by the capitalist system because it needs to develop. In the same way that ecology, the quality of life, and the struggle against pollution—which is part of the *creed* of the left—are not terrains of the struggle against capital, but clearly on the contrary means of accelerating its restructuring.

IF THE CRISIS is fomented by capital, if scarcity is only a myth that it reactivates for its own greater glory, we can ask ourselves about the revolutionary potentialities of such a situation. Capitalism? Bust!... But how? It manipulates us to the core: everything that we want is wanted by it, everything that we do, it makes us do... In this way all subversion is truly impossible.

Response

THERE IS EFFECTIVELY still an illusion in thinking that the system of capital, to a certain threshold of expanded reproduction, passes irreversibly from a strategy of scarcity to a strategy of abundance. The present crisis proves that this strategy is reversible. The illusion came once again from a naïve faith in a *reality* of scarcity or in a *reality* of abundance, and therefore from the illusion of a *real* opposition between the two terms, one following the other as its opposite (as in its dialectical surpassing). In this way these two terms are quite simply *alternatives* and the strategic definition of neo-capitalism, is not to pass from the phase of abundance (of consumption, of repressive desublimation, of sexual liberation, etc.) but to the phase of the *systematic alternation* between the two: scarcity and abundance—because the two terms no longer have any reference, nor therefore any antagonistic reality, and therefore the system can jump indifferently from one to the other. This represents the completed stage of reproduction. Thus, in the political sphere, this stage is reached when, all antagonism between the Left and the Right having been neutralized, the exercise of power can play alternatives with one and then with the other.

This terminological indetermination, this abolition of all reference, this neutralization of dialectical opposition in a pure and simple structural alternation produces the characteristic effect of *uncertainty about the reality of the crisis*. Everyone would like to ward this insupportable effect of the simulacra—characteristic of everything that proceeds from *reproduction* and from the systematic functioning of the code—off in terms of conspiracy. The crisis would be fomented by "Big Capital":[5] this hypothesis is reassuring, since it restores a *real* economico-political authority and the presence of an (occult) *subject* of the crisis, and therefore a truth to history. The terror of the simulacra is lifted: all value increases —the omnipresent economico-political fatality of capital increases, provided that it had a clear truth: increased profit, increased exploitation, the *economic* atrocity of capital recognizing our situation, wherein everything is at risk and frustrated by the code. The misunderstanding of this "truth" of world domination, if it is one, is equal to the crisis which reveals it for the first time in all of its breadth.

Because the crisis of 1929 was still a "real" crisis of production, a crisis of capital measured by its rate of reinvestment, of surplus value and profit, a crisis of (over) production measured by the social goals of consumption. And the regulation of demand resolved this crisis in an endless exchange of goals between production and consumption. Henceforth (and definitively after the Second World War), one and the other cease to be opposed and eventually contradictory poles. Suddenly, the whole field of economics loses, along with even possibility of the crisis, all internal determination, even its reality principle. It no longer subsists as a referential alibi, as a process of economic simulation in the confines of a process of reproduction that entirely absorbs it. We know that the force and the process of labor itself—to take the central theme of all revolutionary dialectics—have lost their negativity, that labor now makes and consumes itself as a finished product, like any other consumer good. Better: the essential objective of production becomes the *production of labor*. At this cyclical stage of reproduction, all use value is abolished, and therefore also the "revolutionary use value" of labor in classical theory.

The era of simulation is thus opened everywhere by the commutability of once contradictory and dialectically opposed terms. Commutability of labor and of end product, of production and consumption, of scarcity and abundance—but one would recover this genesis of simulacra throughout: commutability of beautiful and ugly in fashion, of Left and Right in politics, of true and false in the media, of nature and culture at all levels of signification. Everything is undecidable. This is the characteristic effect of the domination of the code,[6] which rests everywhere on the principle of the neutralization of indifference. This process, long since operational in culture and politics, in "superstructural" realms, today extends to the economy itself, the entire so-called "infrastructural" field. The same *indetermination* reigns here from now on. And of course, with the *determination* of economics every possibility of conceiving economics as a *determinate* authority vanishes.

Use value—exchange value, productive forces—relations of production: all of these "dialectical" oppositions on which Marxism still functioned (according to the same schema as once bourgeois rationalist thought on the opposition between true and false, beautiful and ugly, appearance and reality, good and evil) have also been neutralized, and in the same way. Everything that happens on the level of political economy is also commutable, reversible, exchangeable according to the same code as in politics or in fashion or in the media. Indefinite specularity of the true and the false: we understand this in metaphysics or in morality, but indefinite specularity too of productive forces and relations of production, of capital and labor, or use value and exchange value: that is hard to support; what would we talk about? What would happen to the revolution? The law of value no longer resides in the exchangeability of all commodities under the sign of general equivalence, but in the exchangeability, otherwise more radical, of all the categories of political economy (and of its critique) according to the code. Hence the impossibility of a contradiction and of a *real* crisis at the level of economics. Hence the transference of all real risk to another level, that of the symbolic, which is to say the demolition of the code (which is to say not only the abolition of the economic law of equivalences, but of the structural law of commutations).

This is also why the essential problem of this crisis is that of its "reality" or simulacra.

Objection

Was there ever any *real* scarcity, and therefore an economic reality principle—such that today we can say that it disappears as reality and no longer functions except as a myth, and at the same time an alternative myth to that of abundance? Has there historically ever been a *use value* of scarcity, and therefore an irreducible finality of economics, such that today we can say that it has disappeared in the cycle of reproduction to the benefit of the singular sole hegemony of the code, of a regulation by the code which is a veritable sentence of life and death? We say: economics itself *produced* (and it never produced anything but itself) a need for this dialectical tension between scarcity and abundance—but the system, to reproduce itself, today has no other need than for the mythic operation of the economy.

The Naturalization of Economico-Politics

Because the entire sphere of economics is now defused, everyone can admit it in terms of economico-politics and production. Economics becomes the explicit discourse of an entire society, the vulgate to all analysis, preferably in its Marxist variant. Once, all of this was forbidden, censored, infamous, immoral. Today, the Left and the Right, all the ideologues have found their maternal language in political economy. All sociologists, human scientists, etc. turn tendencially toward Marxism, to Marxist thought as a referential discourse. Even Christians, absolutely Christians of course. The entire divine New Left comes up. Everything has become politics too, through the same operation of diffusion and ideological standardization. News is political, sports are political, art doesn't talk about it: rationality today is entirely on the side of the class struggle. The entire latent discourse of capital has become manifest, and everywhere we see a certain jubilation in this assumption, in this apparition of "truth."

May 1968 marked a decisive step in this *naturalization of political economy*. Because the shock of May 1968 undermined the entire system in the depths of its symbolic organization, it made it urgent, vital, the passage of "superstructural" ideologies (moral, cultural, etc.) to making the infrastructural itself ideological. Capital, generalizing, making the discourse of its *Marxist* contestation official, will henceforth speak the discourse of its "truth." It will redouble its power behind this legalization of economics and politics. Political economy stops the necessity of 1968, Marxist political economy, as it was the unions and the leftist parties that "negotiated" the crisis on this terrain. The hidden referent of economics and politics has been deterred so as to save a catastrophic situation, and today it continues to be diffused, generalized, desperately reproduced everywhere because the catastrophic situation opened by May 1968 has not ceased.

Hence the vanity of all economic explication ("revolutionary" or not) of the present energy crisis. Even if this crisis does not constitute, as we would like to say, a true "May 1968 of energy and raw materials," something, on a world scale, needs a moment to escape negotiation: this challenge to the symbolic order that we are talking about and through which the Arab countries, suddenly, ceased to be underdeveloped because they changed the terrain and the definition of exchange. This is the *truth* of this crisis, however infinitesimal and ephemeral. Everything else is a simulacra. And the simulacra is on top in all the economic and political interpretations that have rushed in on this crisis from all over to rationalize it, to relocate it in the logic of the dominant exchange. And that these explications were right in the end (which is to say that everything happens as if the Arabs were following the rules of the game, and therefore never really left it) only completes the circle. Based on its own axioms, economics, functioning as a code, always recovers its equilibrium, it always recovers its truth in the end. And all feudal powers and diplomats, Fayçal and Kissinger, can revive on this crap. After the primitive accumulation of *capital*, from which the intensive, colonial exploitation of raw materials arises, we enter into the primitive accumulation, on the world scene, of *consensus* on the economico-political code.

Radical dissensus, pure challenge and provocation, which is to say the non-negotiable, the beyond of economics or politics at all costs, is therefore finally to be sought elsewhere than in the crisis: in the attack in Rome, where the Palestinians burned a Pan-Am Boeing with thirty people on board. That event is inseparable from the crisis. Because if it illustrates in all its details the functioning of the equivalences on the world scene, the attack in Rome marks the absolute limit where those equivalences stop. And it hardly matters if, as in any provocation, it still profits from the international moral order, which refreshes itself in these bloody deaths exactly like the economic order refreshes itself in the scarcity of raw materials. It hardly matters: what is essential is that this is an act that cannot return to any old equivalence (moral: nothing can justify it, even the moral Jesuitism of the Left—politics: impossible to negotiate politically, certainly not in the history of Israel, such blackmail is perfectly useless)—or better, it cannot be reinscribed in any language, nor exchanged by any known laws. If not in a single language: that of desire and of fascination—and this is the language that the mass media secretly speaks, most "abject" because it is most "objective." Only *France-Soir* and the others, with photos of hundreds of people watching, with their noses to the airport windows, the bodies burning in the Boeing, the photographer bent over the body of a dying Italian police officer, taking the picture with a monstrous objectivity, and himself being photographed at the same moment, with the stories secretly salivating with horror and jubilation—only the abject media, who don't embarrass themselves with politics, know that the only *events*, the only events that impassion, that fascinate, that provoke desire, are precisely those that no one can reinscribe politically, morally, economically, those that can no longer be negotiated according to the code. These are the only ones that shatter the indifference, the neutralization of all spheres regulated by the code, because these are the only ones that, in one way or another, risk death.

14

The Banque Nationale de Paris Campaign

THIS BANQUE NATIONALE DE PARIS (BNP) poster deserves to be analyzed in the same sense as a theatricalization of economics.

"Your money interests me—Give, Give—Bring me your money, and you will profit from my bank."

1.

THIS IS THE first time that capital (through international financial capital, its lead institution) has stated so clearly, eye to eye, the law of equivalence, and said it as an *argument of advertisement*. Habitually, such things are kept quiet, commercial exchange is *immoral*, and all publicity aims at effacing it for the benefit of the service. One can therefore be certain that this sincerity is a mask of the second degree.

2.

THE APPARENT OBJECTIVE is to convince people through economics to get a good deal and bring their money to BNP. But the real strategy is parallel (like the policies). It is to convince people through this capitalist, "man to man" sincerity: cards on the table, no tugging the heart strings, the ideology of service at its end, etc. It is to seduce them through the obscenity of revealing a hidden,

immoral law of equivalence. "Virile" complicity: men share the obscene truth of capital among themselves. Hence this poster's scent of lubricity, the salacious and filthy tone of its eyes fixed on your money as if on your sex. The technique is that of perverse provocation, much more subtle than that of simplistic seduction with a smile (such would be the counter offensive theme of the *Société générale*: "The client should smile, not the banker." Seduce people through the obscenity of economics, take them to the libidinal level of perverse desire, with the perverse fascination that capital exerts on them even in its atrocity. From this angle, the slogan signifies simply: "Your ass interests me—Give, Give—Bring me your thighs and I'll fuck you." Which doesn't dissatisfy everyone.

Behind the humanist morality of exchanges, there is a profound desire for capital, a vertiginous desire for the law of value, and it is this complicity, alongside and beyond economics, that this poster attempts to grasp. In this it testifies, perhaps unknowingly, to a *political* intuition.

3.

I WOULDN'T SWEAR that the advertisers weren't playing with this "psychoanalytic" complicity with the law of commercial exchange and the resistances that it may have provoked. They cannot not have known (they weren't born yesterday, and the campaign was carefully planned) that this face—vampiric for the middle classes—this lubricious complicity, this direct attack, would forcibly trigger negative reactions. Why take this risk? Why bare the king before contestation, such that everything works with a minimum of mystification?

This is the strangest trap: because this poster was also made (even if not deliberately) to crystallize and displace resistances to the law of profit and equivalence—to awaken resistances so as to better impose the equivalence of capital and profit, of capital and economics (money, give / give) *at the moment when this is no longer true*, at the moment when capital has displaced its strategy, when it can pronounce its "law" because it is no longer its truth—the pronunciation of this law is no more than a supplementary mystification.

If the social domination of capital still fundamentally sustained itself with economics, this poster would never have been made. Through its very clarity, it is proof to the contrary.

Capital no longer lives off of the law of economics: this is why this law can become an advertisement, can fall into the sphere of the *sign* and its manipulation.

False reality principle that serves to attract capitalist suckers (Visa already did this: "Live like a capitalist!") and to refocus revolt on an indirect path.

A faculty of the system designating itself from its reality principle, risking itself as a lure and alibi.

4.

THE USER CAUGHT off balance: seduced by the bank's desire for him rather than by the bank arousing a desire in him for what it has to offer. A virile seduction, aggressive, where "normal" advertising offers a smiling, prostituted woman. This can be interpreted in two different ways:

— All libidinal registers are equivalent and equal publicists: nothing is more gratifying about one than the other, because advertisement functions at a level of play indifferent to good and evil, active and passive—which corresponds to the downward trend of the validity rates of psychoanalysis: as it is acculturated, it loses its specific traits, and its fundamental concepts no longer act as alternative signs, regulated keys of opposition.

— The real domination of capital is guaranteed at all levels and can create the economy through ideological mystification. It passes from referendum to ultimatum. Clarified, this says: "Whatever happens, your money won't get away from me, so come in on your own." This is the ultimatum big money offers small account holders and their traditional mentality. It is true that savings divert the flux of capital, to reinvest it in a closed individual economy, a little like the way the Sian people of New Guinea made Western money function in their symbolic economy. This has to stop. Everyone must be ready to make his or her money circulate, all of his or her money, and let go of nostalgia for gold. Everyone must be ready to circulate entirely, ceaselessly, to be no more than a perpetual com-muting element. This constitutes the true *law of value*, no longer in economic terms: quantitative equivalence and report, but in lin-guistic terms, in terms of value according to Saussure, which is today the true terrain of the conversion of the law of value: a term has value only through its relation and commutability with all the other terms—this strategy is well beyond the law of economic value. Today this is the operational sphere of capital and of its social dom-ination. Economics is only the quantitative theater of value. The poster says it, in its way; the money is nothing more than a pretext.

Where does the commutability of the poster itself, which can act like a general matrix for the law of value at all levels, come from?

For example:

Your unconscious interests me—give, give—Bring me your phantasms and you will profit from my analysis;

Your death interests me—give, give—Take out life insurance and I will make your family happy;

Your productivity interests me—give, give—Bring me your labor power and I will make you profit from my capital.

And on and on. This poster, speaking of money, can serve as a "general equivalent" to all present social relations, every institution-al order offers itself today as a *partnership*, as a dialogue on equal terms, as a reciprocity of services.

If the fundamental message of the poster is not that of the equivalence A=A give give (no one is fooled, and the advertisers *know it*), is it that of surplus value (that fact that the operation is balanced for the banker and for capital by the equation : $A = A + A$)? The poster barely conceals this truth, and everyone can uncover it. This is the twilight of capital, it almost unmasks itself, but this isn't serious, because what the poster really says is not on the order

"It must be determined whether such animals suffer *psychologically*... A psychiatric zoo becomes necessary. Mental frustration, which represents an obstacle to normal development."

Darkness, red lights, gadgets, tranquillizers, nothing works. A good example of the absurdity of remedies and of the senile dementia of "therapists." It's been noted that given the overpopulation, the pecking order (the hierarchy according to which, among poultry, each has access to food) makes it such that some of them cannot even get enough to eat. It's necessary to divide the pens so as to *democratize* access to food. Failure: the destruction of the symbolic order entails total confusion among the birds, and a chronic instability (therefore a deficit!). We are familiar with analogous ravages that can result in tribal societies from democratic good will.

The animals somatize! Extraordinary discovery! Cancers, gastric ulcers, myocardial infarctions in mice, pigs, chickens.

In conclusion, the liberal author claims, it truly seems like the only remedy is space: a little more space and many of the observed problems disappear. "In any case," he adds without laughing, "the fate of these animals would become less miserable."

He is therefore satisfied with this meeting. "The present preoccupations concerning the fate of livestock seem therefore to be allied, *once more*, with morality and with the sense of a clearly understood interest." "We cannot simply do whatever we want with nature" (ecology). "For healthy animals, it is henceforth also necessary to consider the *mental equilibrium of the animals*" (economics and psychiatry). And he foresees the time when we will see animals (as we have already done for men) return to the country "to restore their mental equilibrium."

"These economic conditions (decreasing production) might drive the producers to give the animals more normal living conditions." There has never been a better statement of how "humanism," "normality," and "quality of life" are only elements of profitability.

Everything that has just been described corresponds point by point to what has happened to man as a result of industrial concentration, of the scientific organization of labor, of Taylorism, of this lacerating revision by capitalist "breeders" and by contemporary innovations in "quality of life," "working conditions," and "the enrichment of tasks." The cited text is only interesting because inevitable death makes the animal example still more stunning than that of men on the assembly line. Against this industrial organization of death, animals have no other resource than collective or individual suicide. (All of the described problems or anomalies are suicidal.) No question that they escape in this way. As it is unthinkable that their death should be questioned, and as their resistance is unspeakable for rationality (not only industrial: one senses that these anomalies really shock the specialists through their *logical* rationality). We can give them piece of mind, an irrational and shattered piece of mind, devoted to liberal, humanist therapy without changing the final objective: death.

The suicidal forms of animal resistance correspond equally, point by point to human reactions to the scientific organization of labor (and rest). The golden age of the mind and of the unconscious coincides with the crisis of this rational organization. They are therefore only a symptom of this terror, and every science that reclaims itself from this state of mind and this unconscious only verifies this state of things in its consequences; these are symptomatic, "critical" sciences, parasitic sciences, irremediably invoking the middle and long term in the sense of this state of things, and redoubling it in these terms. The order has already won since it convinced the people of the mindset, since it made them believe that there is a mindset, that there is an unconscious, that it is a "dimension of man," etc.

The same dirty trick as when the bourgeoisie enclosed the proletariat in the concept of class.

FORT WORTH, Texas. 400 men and 100 women experience the nicest prison in the world. The confinement is low level and dating is permitted. A child was born there last June and they have had only two escapes in the past three years... Men and women eat their meals together and meet again in group psychology sessions... Each prisoner possesses a unique key to his or her individual room... Couples can be alone in empty rooms. To date, 35 prisoners have fled, but they have for the most part returned on their own volition without having committed any criminal act. The wife of a detainee, by her own admission, brought heroin to her husband so that he could sell it to his friends. Another detainee, having psychological trouble, which gravely affected his sexual behavior, was authorized to leave at night to attend a meeting of alcoholics anonymous; he in fact spent the night with a prostitute, but his escapade was considered "therapeutic."

1.

THE PRISONER NEEDS freedom, sex, normality to endure prison, just as animals about to be slaughtered need a certain quality of life to have a normal death. And none of this is contradictory: it is the paradox of liberalism. The worker too needs responsibility, self-management in order to better respond to the demands of production.

2.

WE DISCOVER WITH a great ingenuity and, what's more, we discover as a new *scientific* field, that animals raised in industrial breeding have a "mindset"—since they reveal themselves as maladjusted to the death that is prepared for them. Similarly, we rediscover the psychology, sociology, and sexuality of prisoners when it becomes impossible to rationally incarcerate them (we can no longer say like beasts because even beasts pose problems), but simply like stones, like the dead. Similarly, psychology, the human sciences, and psychoanalysis would never have arisen if it had been possible to miraculously reduce the worker to rational behaviors in the structure of the scientific organization of labor. All liberalism and science arises from the impossibility of working workers to death, incarcerating prisoners to death, fattening animals to death, which is to say according to the strict law of equivalences:

— this much caloric energy and machines equals this much labor power;

— this crime equals this equivalent punishment and redemption (readaptation);

— this much food equals optimal weight (and industrial death).

This no longer works, it stops itself, while giving birth to the mind, the mentality, the neurosis, the psycho-social, etc. not at all to break this deranged equation, but *to restore the compromised principle of equivalences*. The mindset is only this: a corrective to maladaptation, an adjustment to the behavioral equation, the behavioral yield. Elsewhere it is treated as such: as a variable that one can once again circumscribe with equivalences. Every therapy, including psychoanalysis, does only this. In the sense of a better yield: industrial for the worker (from the Mayo experience to job design and job enrichment)—to a better incarceration for prisoners (who no longer escape but return)—to a better death for animals (they no longer devour themselves or destroy themselves, they wait to die at the appointed time).

3.

WHAT IS THE DIFFERENCE between a liberal prison and public housing?

Forced presence? But is the labor, the habitat, the transportation, the everydayness in general anything other than forced presence in a determined succession of space-time? Even if the walls are invisible, and if the walls are signs, every moment of life has its iron curtain.

This is no longer forced incarceration; it is no longer forced labor that counts; it is the presence, the inscription in a determinate stream. And it is because all of society is today in the image of prison and the factory that it can disappear as such. They have done nothing, liberalizing these things, but spread them as models across all social space and time.

When prison loses its reference (its function), the sanction of crime according to the play of equivalences, prison comes to be modeled on society as a whole. The process is the same: the substance of the institution is lost, and its form generalized.

The same thing for the army: it loses its reference (without an enemy). Thus the entirety of everyday life passes under the sign of "defense" and "dissuasion."

16

Death Trick

THE AD SWEATS death, though not just any death: the demagogic apology for safety. Here we abjectly speak on behalf, against suicidal "heroes," of a banal man without qualities, of a normal middle class man who wants to live and drives to live—which is not even true: this is the only "myth" that runs throughout the text—the myth of the instinct for conservation (sanctioned by morality)—here we tickle, we titillate that instinct for conservation as a genital organ of the silent majorities, opposed to the stupid *machismo* of the cowboy kamikazes of the 1950s: "The true hero is he who refuses to die" (Kierkegaard, opposing the married man to the romantic hero as the true hero of modern times—and Charles Péguy). Obscene flattery of the flat being, sexualizing the platitude: "You, little one, obscure, stale, you who refuse to die, refuse to live and live a little, you're the one who is with it." James Dean is only a larva. You are the superman unburdened of myths.

Once the silent majority has been idealized (the first operation of the police base and of the political base), we enclose it in another non-mythic death: neutral and objective like technology, silent and traditional. Death "as it has never ceased to be" in the moral order of objectivity, which is to say *safety*. The text is skillful enough meanwhile to let it show through, in its hymn to "virile" and

"Tuons une certaine Glorification de la Mort."

Les années 50: Roger Nimier achève "le train bleu", Françoise Sagan conduit pieds nus pour mieux sentir le galop effréné des 300 chevaux

et les héros de "La fête" de Roger Vailland inventent le jeu de la mort au volant. C'est la fureur de vivre.

Ce romantisme d'après-guerre atteint son apogée le 30 septembre 1955, lorsque James Dean se tue au volant de sa Porsche.

Il était le héros d'une génération. La Porsche devint un mythe.

Les héros, on le sait, meurent plus facilement que les mythes.

Et pourtant, la Porsche n'est qu'un instrument. Technique donc neutre. Il n'y a pas de mythe dans un moteur à pistons, aussi raffiné soit-il.

Pas plus qu'il n'y a de héros parmi les milliers d'automobilistes qui se tuent chaque année sur les routes.

Car ce ne sont jamais les héros qui meurent comme des lapins, bêtement, faute d'appui-tête; ou qui s'empalent sur leur volant, parce qu'ils s'enorgueillissent de conduire sans ceinture.

A une époque où n'importe qui se tue au volant de n'importe quelle voiture, à n'importe quelle vitesse, le vrai héros, c'est celui qui refuse de mourir.

Alors, le conducteur de la Porsche, délivré du romantisme, retrouve ses nerfs d'acier et l'entière maîtrise de ses réflexes pour dompter cette machine de 2,7 l qui vous rive au dossier en quelques secondes pour passer de 0 à 100 km/h.

Enfin, la Porsche elle-même, débarrassée de sa légende, redevient ce qu'elle n'a jamais cessé d'être: un fabuleux objet, fabriqué d'une façon minutieuse et artisanale, d'une rare qualité, d'une rare précision, tel que l'a voulu le Dr Porsche.

Et si, aujourd'hui, la dernière-née des Porsche 911, avec son moteur 2,7 l, ses pare-chocs à soufflets, son volant plein, ses sièges porte-tête, ses ceintures de sécurité qui s'enroulent automatiquement, a tous les attributs de la sécurité, c'est qu'il faut souvent tuer les mythes. Pour que vivent les hommes.

"responsible" safety, the threat of death, violent but filtered, sifted like a shiver of death: "this machine clinches the record in a few seconds." A "little death," a little frenzy at the heart of safety.

In fact, the driver of the Porsche will no longer die in this new machine, because he is *already dead*. Mummified in his helmet, his seatbelt, his safety features, tied up in the myth of safety, he is no more than a miniscule and traditional corpse, metallic and mechanical (he has nothing more than "reflexes," nerves of steel, in place of bare feet and horses out of Françoise Sagan). He is riveted to his machine, pinned to it. This is the secret of safety, like a steak under cellophane: *bury yourself in a sarcophagus to prevent your death.*[1]

This is about repression, the worst repression. It consists in dispossessing you of your own death, even the death that dreams, in the depths of one's instinct for self-preservation, of driving the Porsche. Everywhere, in all its forms, safety is about social control, and the "forces of safety" move from life insurance and social security to seatbelts by way of the police—"Buckle up!," an advertisement for safety belts. It isn't so much the convertibility of death into capitalist profit that is at stake but the necessity of dispossessing each of us of the final possibility of killing ourselves, that last "beautiful escape" from a life surrounded by the system. Once again, the exchange-*gift*, even in this very restricted circuit, in this symbolic short circuit, is the challenge to oneself and to one's own life that is hunted down. Not because it would express the asocial revolt of an individual—the defection of an individual, or thousands of individuals, not disobeying the laws of the system in the slightest—but because it carries in itself a principle of sociality radically antagonistic to the repressive social principle that is ours. The exchange-gift must be killed by "killing a certain glorification of death." And the subtlest way is to make this death "legendary," a romantic aberration, before definitively burying it beneath the inverse myth of safety.

Kill myths? No. Kill death's demand *with* myth. So that humans can live? No. So that they will definitively die the only death authorized by the system: living separated from their death, which only exchanges the form of their survival, "the way Doctor Porsche wanted it," all risks assured.

This advertisement clearly expresses what safety is for an entire civilization: blackmail for survival. Our entire technical culture has created an artificial place of death. Not only the weapons that remain the archetype of material production, but the machines and the smallest objects that surround us constitute a horizon of death, and of a death henceforth indissoluble because crystallized and out of reach: capital fixes death, where the living labor of death is frozen, the way that labor power is frozen in fixed capital and dead labor. Or again: all material production is only a gigantic "character armor" in which space holds death in respect. Of course, death itself hangs over space and is enclosed in the armor that it thinks protects it. Here we rediscover, on the level of the civilization as a whole, the image of the automotive sarcophagus: safety armor, miniaturized death become a technological prolongation of our own body. The body made biological, the environment technological, hand in hand with the same obsessional neurosis. The technical environment is our hyper-production of obsolescent, fragile, polluting objects. Because production lives, all of its logic and strategy articulates itself in fragility and obsolescence. An economy of stable products and of good objects is unthinkable: the economy only develops by hiding danger, pollution, usury, deception, obsession. The economy only lives through the suspension of death that it maintains *through material products*—by renewing the available *stockpile of death*, even if it must arrange it by overcharging for safety: blackmail and repression. Death is definitively secularized in material production—that's where it reproduces itself in an enlarged way as capital. And even our body, which has become a biological machine, is modeled on this inorganic body, and becomes in the same moment a *bad object*, destined for sickness, accidents, and death.

Living through the production of death, capital is well prepared to produce safety: it's the same thing. *Safety is the industrial prolongation of death*, just as ecology is the industrial prolongation of pollution. A few more shrouds for the sarcophagus. This is also true of the large institutions that are the pride of our democracy: Social Security, the social prosthesis of a dead society ("Social Security is Death"—May 1968). This is to say that we previously eliminated in all its symbolic cogs, in its system of reciprocities and deep obligations, what made it that *neither the concept of security nor that of the "social" had any meaning*. The "social" begins with responsibility for death. Just as in the destroyed cultures that we resuscitate and protect as folklore.[2] The same for life insurance: this is the domestic variant of a system that everywhere requires death as axiom. Social translation of the death of the group—each materializing for the other only as social capital indexed by death.

Dissuasion of death at the price of a continual mortification: such is the paradoxical logic of safety. In a Christian context, asceticism plays the same role. The accumulation of suffering and of penitence can play the same role as character armor, as a protective sarcophagus against hell. And our obsessional compulsion for safety can be interpreted as a gigantic collective asceticism, an anticipation of death within life itself: from protection to protection, from defense to defense, the institutions, the modern material apparatus, life is no longer anything but a bleak defensive accounting, enclosing all risks in its sarcophagus. Accounting for survival, in place of a radical accounting for life and death.

Our system survives through the reproduction of death. The Porsche, like a bomb, is a sufficient example of this mortifying cycle. But look how the system pretends to manufacture safety. A reversal? Not at all: a simple twist in the cycle, rejoining both ends. Safety is only one internal reproductive condition of the system attaining a certain stage of expansion, like *feed back* is only an internal regulatory procedure of systems attaining a certain point of complexity.

That an automobile company recycles itself through safety without changing its range, objective or product (this car can move still more quickly than those that preceded it) show that safety is only a question of a substitution of terms. *Death and safety are two equivalent terms.* The proof is that the poster, far from radically opposing the two systems of value, contents itself with risking death and safety within the same myth of virility and adventure. To chose safety today is to be a superman. It's the same as surpassing the traditional *supermen* who chose death, the easy solution. The myth therefore intends to make us courageously become safe, significantly without excluding the other term. Because each of us must indifferently consume the two false teeth. But this is difficult, *because people are indifferent to safety.* They weren't interested when Ford and General Motors proposed it to them between 1955 and 1960. *It had to be imposed everywhere.* Irresponsible and blind? No. This resistance should be associated with that which everywhere historically opposed traditional groups to "rational" social progress: vaccination, medicine, safe working conditions, education, hygiene, the regulation of births, and many other things. Almost always, these resistances have been broken, and today one can reference a "natural," "eternal," "spontaneous" need for safety, and for all the good things that our civilization has produced. We have succeeded in intoxicating the people with a virus for conservation and safety, so well that they will fight to the death to obtain it. In fact, it's more complicated: they struggle for the *right* to safety, which is of a profoundly different order. When it comes to safety itself, no one gives a damn. They must be intoxicated with it for generations before they believe that they "need" it. This success is an essential aspect of domestication and "social" colonization. That whole groups preferred to collapse rather than to see themselves destructured through the terroristic intervention of medicine, of reason, of science, and to centralized power, shows that it is forgotten, suppressed behind the universal moral law of the conservative "instinct" and of the "need" for safety, which ends up imposing itself on them. It shows what nevertheless always resurges, if only among the workers who refuse to apply norms of safety in workshops: what would they want with it, if not to save a scrap of control over their own life, even at their own risk, even at the price of additional exploitation (since they produce faster)? This is not the rationality of the proletariat. But they struggle in their way, and they know that economic exploitation is less serious than this "Accursed Share," this accursed scrap that absolutely must not be torn away from them, this share of symbolic challenge, which is at the same time a denial of safety and a challenge to their own lives. The boss can exploit them to death, but he will truly dominate them only if he can make each of them identify with his individual or class interest, submit to the economic principle of calculation and conservation, make them accountable and a capitalist of their own lives. Thus he would truly be the master, and the worker the slave (etymologically: *servus*, he who, initially condemned to death, was "conserved," so as to be condemned to the slow death of work). Insofar as through this insignificant resistance to the moral order of safety, the exploited retain a choice between life and death, the exploited win, on their own terrain: the symbolic.

The driver's resistance to safety is of the same order, and it should be liquidated as immoral: as suicide was everywhere forbidden or condemned because it signifies first a challenge that society cannot relieve, and which assured therefore the preeminence of an individual over the entire social order. Still the accursed share—the little thing that each of us assumes over our own lives in defiance of the social order—the little thing that each of us assumes over our own bodies so as to *offer* it—and which can be our own death, on the condition that someone offer it—this little thing that is the whole secret of symbolic exchange, because it is offered and received, and repaid, and therefore *impregnable* through the dominant form of exchange, irreducible to its law, and fatal to it: its only adversary, in fact, the only one that it should exterminate.

17

The Failure of Prophecy

THE SOLIDITY OF INSTITUTIONS is founded on the failure of prophecy. The failure of the Left was followed by a wave of enrollments in the communist party. Militancy rests on this kind of disillusioned investment. Frustrated by a victory, by a second coming, we are going to invest a long term practice with a fierce resignation. As we know, if the Kingdom of Heaven was in this world, the church wouldn't exist. The communist party does well to circle power like a cat without ever wanting to take it. Because it only exists through the postponement of the revolution. Each failure of the revolution, each (narrowly) missed opportunity reinforces it in its being, in waiting, as a long term institution. It likes its elections, and has confidence in the silent majorities, in the right to spare it victory and the risks of power. Just less than 50% is its ideal situation. That permits it not to risk either alternation (in which case it would be eroded by the socialist party) or revolution (in which case it would be eroded by history). That permits it to remain as a reserve of the Left, of the Republic, of history, of revolution. This ghetto wherein we enclose it, and from which it makes us feel pity for it, is the only artificial space wherein it can survive. There it can exert its vocation as a great power at rest, its frozen vocation as a manager sheltered from power, its vocation as an oppositional

silent majority. Moscow and Peking deliberately chose Giscard—
nothing says that the communist party did it in secret.

As we approach alternation (or the reversibility of the Left-Right
political equation), the contents of these two terms become indifferent and aleatory. Left and Right exchange their objectives and
their politics—and even "objective" social membership no longer
matters. In the United States, Texas oil workers are democrats,
dock worker's unions are republicans. Much more than the political determination, these are the tricks of clans at stake, of organic
solidarities. As in Corsica. They have no problems: they vote for
their clan. The vote is recycled as a symbolic practice of kinship and
a ritual of recognition. The Giacommetti for Mitterrand, the
Biaggini for Giscard. Before laughing we should ask ourselves if:

— this is not a collective practice of resistance to the democratic
"rules of the game"—like the way that the Sianese recycle European
money in their tribal circuit of exchange.

— if it is not already largely but shamefully the same in supposedly "rational" electoral practices. Look at petitions in the press
(an appeal to Christians in favor of X, an appeal to intellectuals in
favor of Y, an appeal to friends of Israel in favor of both, on the front
and back of each page, appeals to researchers, sports fans, artists,
progressives with disabilities, macro-bio-geneticists of the Vaucluse,
etc.). The entire market of categorical and nominal values puts itself
in play to launch appeals to families, to "totemic" affiliations, stim-
ulants for reorganization. But these informal groups lack true
organic solidarity. They only translate the desire to reorganize
around an intermediary authority (two step flow of communication), against the total abstraction of the media at its height. At the
same time, they show that every "scene" is ripe for "production,"

that all the channels of representation intermingle and underscore one another, and that delirium over the brand image is general.

> "The France that works and thinks"
> — *L'Humanité*, 20 May 1974

A PERFECTLY REPRESSIVE and disgusting new myth of the Left was born in the last elections. The Left is the *real* society, the "vital forces of the nation." Producers, intellectuals, the youth, "workers," urban populations, etc. everything that is best, the entire future of France votes Left. On the Right, the residue, the resigned, the imbeciles, the old men, unfortunate women (the old, though there are a lot of them), dirty farmers, the *lumpen* (those with the lowest income vote on the Right), the military (except the enlightened fringe of modern officers). In short, all kinds of categories that *should no longer exist*, according to solid historical logic. At the hatch, the old. They are blocking the road of history. At bottom, all of these people lack a *social* existence, they are not fit for socialism. There is a hint of genocide in all this, of Leftist racism become officially the "social real," with the whole excuse of the sociological apportionment of categories, referring everyone else to non-existence, to dumb and mean non-existence. A new subject of history: the "vital forces," the normal against the abnormal, the effective and dynamic living being against the social wastes. The Left turns into a caste. At least the proletariat recognized the social and historical reality of the bourgeoisie, that's why they fought it. But it was only a class. Today, the Left has fashioned a historical shield out of racist and discriminatory terms. It separates everyone else as asocial and already outmoded. That prevents it from posing the question of its own non-existence.

Why doesn't everyone vote on the Left? All the reasons are gathered, all the good reasons (even capitalist ones) are on the Left. Would it be that a group of people resists somewhere, without knowing it, the latent racism of the social rationality that the Left incarnates, the *rationality* that presents itself as social *reality*, that claims the principle of the historical reality for itself, etc. Hegel and the dialectic in the service of reason, and therefore of social efficacy: such is the Left.

Are the people stupid? Can we not give them credit and think that they set themselves against this *hidden* truth of the Left, and not because they are stupid, vicious beasts? Those that the Left excludes today as "non-vital" forces because they do not vote Left can feel confirmed in their opinion.

DEMOCRACY, OR THE FREE choice of individuals, comes through in its logical functioning as an inverse situation of facts:

1. Obligatory: mobilization through the political middle, the point of alternating 50/50, equal to that of countries where the vote is obligatory. The realized democracy can surpass the constraints of the Right, it imposes a statistical, structural, and accountable constraint (polls, 50/50).

2. Aleatory: when democracy attains an advanced formal stage, it distributes itself around the middle. The vote rejoins the Brownian movement of particles and the calculation of probabilities: 50/50, it's as if everyone voted by chance. As if monkeys were voting.

50/50: EQUILIBRIUM FORCED by democracy, to the extent that it is the realization of the law of equivalence, that completes itself in the law of commutability and reversibility.

It is no longer in the name of revolution that the Left will one day inevitably attain power, but in the name of reversibility and of the indifference of present terms: alternation.

This is no longer in France exactly—due to the inertia of historical contents. The perfect equilibrium of democracy is only obtained through the total abolition of contents and references. The Left still maintains the pathos of contents (society, justice, equal opportunities, etc.)—but as lip-service. It will come to power when it is completely emptied of its contents. Mitterand is still too pathetic (even if he reeks of the role of composition). He must come to this sovereign indifference with regard to the entire social substance, so as to be able to put alternation in play. He must become *cool*. *Cool* is the fundamental quality of the gambler, for whom there is no longer any finality, but only the rules of the game. *Coolness* is the pure play of discursive equivalences, of equivalences in writing. It is the ease of those who risk the most with words and numbers, the omnipotence of operational simulation. The sophistic purity is *cool*, polls are *cool*: no longer is anything exchanged against the real. Giscard is *cool*: it is a brand without substance, without anything substantial or historical. This is its efficacy in the system of the exchange of signs in which the absolute law is the loss of all referentiality. The Left still wants to win, it still seems to want to win in the name of *what it is*—in the name of intelligence, in the name of history, in the name of revolution, in the name of economics… Naïveté: It will win when it has recognized its equivalence with the Right in the order of the political rules of the game. Besides, it will get there quickly, it's doing everything for it, the communist party first and foremost.

50/50: THE END OF the end of political representation. Everything happens as if the political class (Left and Right both complicit) had organized itself for the strictest competition, to save the stakes of democracy. This comes from the strategy of the game, through which everyone finds themselves mobilized by the simple formal constraint of the perfect competitive equation of the two parties. If the same parties reign, political disaffection, abstention is maximum. The closer we are to 50/50 the closer to total mobilization we are. Nice job. From this, it hardly matters that the present parties historically and socially express whatever they do, it is sufficient that they are almost equal. To be equal, they must *effectively* no longer represent anything. At the end of the end of political representation everything happens elsewhere. At this perfect point, "it" no longer represents anything. But the fascination of the game is much greater.

If there is only one, or several, one can abstain—choose or not choose. The constraint of choice becomes maximal when there are *two camps present*, both in competition. This is why democracy (and maybe every order in general, cf. pacified coexistence or distinctive oppositions) stabilizes itself on the two, through the bipartite structure.

The game can ramify itself, without ceasing to be henceforth fundamentally bipartite. Thus those who vote liberal in the United Kingdom in fact vote against the preponderance of the two major parties, against their factual equivalence and their dual monopoly. But of course, these liberal votes return to fatten the political class, through new alliances. (Feedback is possible.) The structure remains bipolar. (Look at Denmark, where this dominant structure in all the "advanced" Western countries burst, toward a dispersion and a plurality which is perhaps the end of the political structure itself.)

"Some will undoubtedly regret that television and prognostic betting (the polls) slowly replaced the formation of an opinion. They have understood nothing of politics."
— Bernard Chapius

TELEVISION AND POLLS are *cool media*—politics itself tends to become a cool medium.

There is a certain and necessary relationship between the passage to alternation, to the "statistical" modeling of alternation, and polls entering in as a mirror of this equivalence, a mirror of a political opinion and of its indefinite reproduction—a little like the gross national product is the imaginary mirror of productive forces, without respect for the whole in their destination, their social finality or counter-finality. The whole is what "it" reproduces. The same goes for public opinion: it must be redoubled incessantly in its own image. This is the secret of a mass representation. No one should *produce* an opinion any longer, if it confronts itself and confronts others. Everyone should *reproduce* the public opinion, in the sense that all the opinions are engulfed by this *general equivalence*, in this model of simulation, and in process once again (reproducing it, to the extent that they have it, at the singular level of individual choice). Here too, the production of opinions is over, long live the reproduction of the *medium* by the *medium*!

Public opinion is its own *medium* and its own message. Polls are the incessant imposition of the *medium* as message. To the extent that they are effectively of the same order as the electronic *media* and television (McLuhan)—television is itself finally only a daily perpetual poll, a game of questions and responses wherein public consensus measures itself against general models at each instant.

The translation of McLuhan's formula, "the medium is the message," into the sphere of politics is the principle itself of the political economy of the sign (the total loss of the objective reference of the contents and of the contents of *production* itself, the passage to the commutable game of the terms, disappearance of use value as a "dialectical" moment of one exchange value to another). This is the democratic formula of alternation, the two co-present terms at stake; their reversibility automatically eliminates their antagonistic contents.

What the medium imposes becomes the message, this is still an equivalence, but this time much more advanced, and truly general. The equivalence of public opinion to itself. Traditional universal voting already imposes a certain kind of equivalence, the kind implicated by (political) representation, but it is not truly general, because we still distinguish a representative and something represented (some class or social category, some specific opinion) and there is still the possibility of a real political antagonism between the representatives as a function of their solidarity with a certain "base" reference. In the present system, there is no longer any distance between the representative and the thing represented: its the same thing, always already a simulacra: what is essential is that, at any instant, public opinion should be *equal* to itself and not deny itself. This characterizes, beyond the representative and the thing represented, the pure form of representation, as simulation characterizes, beyond the signifier and the signified, the pure form of the political economy of the sign. Just as money and its pure accountability characterize, beyond exchange value and use value, beyond real wealth and signs of wealth, the pure form of value.

SAUSSURE PROVIDED two dimensions to the exchange of terms in language: assimilating them to money: we should be able to exchange money for a real good of some value, on the other hand, we should be able to situate it in relation to the other terms in a monetary system. In this latter aspect, it reserves, as a fact of language, the term value: the relativity, internal to the general system, of all the terms among themselves—at the independent and even perhaps exclusive limit, of the first aspect: the relativity of each term to what it signifies (or of money to what one can obtain with it through exchange). It is this stage of the total relativity of the second order at the exclusion of the first that has now been reached, as much in the monetary sphere—with buoyancy, the loss of the gold standard and systems of writing—as in the sphere of signs with the media, where all signs are simulation—they can be exchanged among themselves without exchanging anything against the real. (They can even be exchanged well, perfectly, totally among themselves on the *condition* that they are no longer exchanged elsewhere. Saussure neither saw this nor sensed it: he still articulates, almost dialectically, the two aspects of value, as concomitant and necessary, one for the other—just as Marx still dialectically articulates use value and exchange value. But this entire edifice of value, as much for words as for money or merchandise, is collapsing today, liberating the whole structural game of value for the *expenditure* of substantial aspects of value.) Similarly in the political sphere, the simulation of opposition between two parties and their system of feedback (the absorption of the majority by the minority and vice versa, the absorption of their reciprocal objectives, the reversibility of every discourse of one by the other) accompanies the loss of reference to every real, social *production* of opinion and of the only reference to the general equivalent that public opinion is.

THE POLLS MANIPULATE the *undecidable*. Have they inflected the vote? True or false? Has Giscard profited by the backlash of abstentions? True or false? The extreme sophistication in the analysis of their counts is always open, here too, to the reverse of this hypothesis. Statistics are never casuistics. The undecidable is proper to every process of simulation: the internal logic of the these procedures (statistics, probabilities, cybernetics) can be rigorous and "scientific." Nevertheless, somewhere it doesn't stick. It is a fabulous fiction whose index of refraction within reality (true or false) is non-existent. This is also what lends force to these *models*—but it is also what makes them undecidable, and leaves them no other truth than that tested by the paranoid projections of a society (or of a caste, or of a group) that dreams of a miraculous appropriateness of the real and its models, and therefore of a control and an absolute manipulation.

The only people who believe in the polls are the members of the political class (just as the only people who really believe in publicity are publicists and advertisers). This is not through some particular stupidity (it's not particular) but because the polls, as we have said, are homogeneous, in their modeling, with the current mechanisms of politics. They assume therefore, in this order, a tactical value, a "real" impact, they can act like a regulating factor of the political class. At the limit, they are an instrument that the political class offers itself to risk and reproduce according to its own rules. The class has a reason to believe in them and they do. But who else really does? The people get a taste of the burlesque spectacle of the political sphere, hyper-representative of nothing at all, through polls and the media. They *consent* to this spectacle and they vote? Certainly. Just as they think and say they will buy a particular soap based on their faith in advertising. But thus far no one has proven that this is the final word.

THE PROBLEM WITH POLLS is not their objective influence. Their objective influence, like that of propaganda, we know, is largely canceled and biased by the primary groups, by individual and collective resistance and inertia. What they do, on the other hand, when they are effective (outside of their tactical efficacy within the political class, though the two are fundamentally linked), is neutralize and absorb all public speech, every resurgence of a violent political process: they pacify, by institutionally taking charge of every virtuality of political expression. Presenting themselves as anticipated results, they short circuit every *process* of expression. Besides, we recognize the deception, the species of profound disillusion that they provoke at this level, at the same time as the jubilation proper to their *statistical contemplation.*

Universal voting has always already played the role of a neutralizing and massive interdiction, but on a scale much more partial and episodic—still corresponding to an "archaic" stage of representation and to an "organic" status of the political sign (a signifier, a signified, a referent). With these polls, the interdiction becomes perpetual feedback, it liquidates all speech through anticipation, the received word thickens the process of institutional simulation.

THE FORGETTING, the instantaneous and almost complete foreclosure that follows the scent of politics, wherein people are remobilized as never before, is interesting. Passivity or inertia? That doesn't tell us anything. Another interpretation would be to see the elections (the presidential elections above all and following the death of the president) as a *rite of inversion* (Balandier) analogous to that of primitive societies, an enormous parenthesis, almost a dream—that would explain the oblivion that all that immediately falls into. The elections, which were once a moment of political continuity, would more and more take on the cast of a programmed acting out, struck by retrospective amnesia. Seductive, but without foundation: this is still, under the flag of ethnology, social psychology.

The reason should be sought in the current structures because the mobilization is accomplished according to a pure formal constraint (50/50)—and not on contents—that falls just as quickly. Continuity, like social memory, is founded on contents, the "dialectic" of contents. This is because the mobilization happens by means of a process of the simulation of politics, that it makes itself part of this very successful simulation. For this reason too it is canceled, in the same way that one show follows another on television. They have no specific weight but an immediate intensity, due to their abstraction itself, like a game: games—a cool medium par excellence, fascination and forgetting.

This is therefore not at all a question of "inversion," as Balandier says (nothing has been inverted or subverted) but of simulation. We are in the time of simulation. This is why, as Giscard d'Estaing said so well, "we live in a time without memory."

18

Taking Hostages

It is impossible to destroy the system according to a logic of
contradiction or through a return to the relationship between
forces—in short through a direct, dialectical revolution of economic or political infrastructure. Everything that is produced by
contradiction, by the relationship between forces, by energy in
general only returns to the systems and stimulates it, in keeping
with the (dis)torsion of a Moebius strip.

We will never conquer the system with its own logic, that of
energy, of calculation, of rationality or of revolution, that of power,
of history, of the dialectic... Even the worst violence at this level,
in terms of relations of force, is without effect. What must be done
is to displace everything in the symbolic sphere, where the law is
that of defiance, of reversion, of outbidding. Such that the only
response to death is equal or greater death. In the symbolic sphere
there is no question of violence or of real force. There is only a
question of logic and defiance. The worst error, that of all our
revolutionary strategies, is believing we bring the system to an end
on the level of the *real*: that is the revolutionaries' imaginary, which
imposes the system itself on them, which lives and survives only to
ceaselessly cause those who attack it to struggle on the level of
reality, which is always its own. It's there, where everyone likes to

throw all their energies, all their imaginary violence, that an implacable logic constantly folds back on the system. The system has only to perpetrate real violence or counter-violence, it lives through symbolic violence. Not in the degraded, ideological sense wherein this formula has met its fate: a violence of signs thanks to which the system would come to be redoubled, or to "mask" its material violence, that being the only truth, in which the relationship between forces and the true stakes of social relations are bound. No, symbolic violence in itself has no more to do with signs than it has to do with the relationship between forces. It is derived from the split within symbolic logic and consists in the abolition of the reversion of the counter-gift and in the unilateral practice of the gift.

The true domination is elsewhere: it's symbolic. And therefore the only chance at subversion is also symbolic. If domination comes from what the system has assumed everywhere, the exclusivity of the gift, the gift of labor to which one can only respond with destruction, with sacrifice, if not in the consumption which is only another spiral of the endless system of gratification, therefore another spiral of domination—a gift of the media and of messages, to which through the monopoly of the code and its models, nothing is permitted to respond—gift, everywhere and at every instant, of the *social*, of the authority of protection, of security, of gratification and of the solicitation of the social to which nothing is permitted to escape any longer. Thus the only solution is to return the process, to turn the very principle of the system's power against it: *challenge the system with a gift to which it cannot respond—other than with its own death and decline*. Nothing, not the power system itself, under any circumstances, escapes symbolic obligation, and the only chance of catastrophe rests in this symbolic trap. This gift, this challenge to which the system has been summoned to respond under the threat of losing face and declining, this can evidently only be that of death. *The system must kill itself in response to the double challenge of death and suicide.*

On the symbolic level, which is that of sacrifice, and from which every moral consideration of the innocence of the victims is excluded, the hostage is the substitute, the *alter ego* of the terrorist, and his death is there for the terrorist's own death—they are often linked in the same sacrificial act. A deliberate death for death without possible negotiation is always at stake. The system of negotiation attempts to show itself. Behind every exchange scenario, of negotiation in terms of equivalence calculated between the "terrorists" and power (the life of hostages "against" such and such ransom, such and such liberation or compensation, against the sole prestige of the operation, to "make themselves known") that's the scenario and in accordance with it, taking hostages is not at all original. It simply creates an unforeseen, timely relationship between forces, soluble through traditional violence or negotiation. It's a tactical action and perhaps it falls rapidly into effect in this well-known dimension. The terrorists themselves seem to want to enter into the game. But we have already seen what happened at La Haye, through ten days of incredible and surrealistic negotiations, no one knew any longer what to negotiate, no one even agreed on the terms of the negotiation, nor only the possible equivalences of the exchange. Moreover, if they came to be formulated, the terrorist's demands were such that they equaled a radical denial of negotiation. In any case, the stakes posed from their side—their own death and or that of the hostages, had no equivalent accountable system. (Every death is easily accountable within the system, even wartime butcheries, because they open onto a higher bid, inexpiable other than through an equivalent death). No other response to death than death. The end of the economic order of equivalences. *They are backed into suicide on their return*, which happens manifestly, if episodically, through the flagrant proof of default. The enormous apparatus of power is liquefied in this situation, infinitesimal in terms of the relationship between forces, but in which all derision turns against it. The police, the army, all the assembled institutions and the mobilized violence of power can do nothing against the insignificant but symbolic death of one or more individuals. The system cannot die in exchange, disarticulate itself, unravel itself to raise to the challenge. This defection, this impotence of the system (it can choose to physically liquidate the terrorists—Munich—, but we know this only translates the same impotence into another compulsive and contagious form, everyone knows that power only entangles itself in its own violence, and *without truly responding* to the challenge posed to it). It's own impotence, its death in this moment, is on the contrary a symbolic response, but one in which it comes apart. The challenge is effectively murderous. Every society except for ours knows this or would know it. Our society is about to rediscover it. The true paths of a new politics are those of symbolic efficacy. Hence the ascetic who mortifies himself challenges God to make him forever equivalent. God does everything he can to make him "a hundredfold" in the form of prestige, of spiritual power, in worldly hegemony. But the secret dream of the ascetic is to reach such a point of mortification that even God can no longer meet the challenge nor expunge the debt. Then he would will have triumphed over God himself and he would be God. This is why the ascetic is eminently heretical and sacrilegious, and as such is condemned by the church, which is there only to protect God from this symbolic face to face, from this challenge in which death is at stake, where God is forced to die, to literally sacrifice himself to meet the challenge of the mortified. At all times, the church will have been necessary to avoid this kind of catastrophic clash (against itself first) and to substitute a regimented exchange of penitence and gratification, a system of equivalences between God and humankind, the church being there to regulate the modalities of exchange.

Everything happens in exactly the same way in our relationship to the system of power. All institutions, mediations, etc., all society, economics, politics, psychology, etc., are there so that no one will ever have the occasion for this symbolic challenge, this mortal challenge, of this irreversible gift that, just as the absolute mortification of the ascetic triumphed over God himself, now over all power, however omnipotent the authority should be. It is no longer necessary that this direct possibility for symbolic confrontation never took place, everything must be negotiated. And this is the source of our profound anxiety.

This is why taking hostages resuscitates something fascinating, in contrast to all the highest worldly negotiations in accordance with the rules of the game, which can only succeed. This act is not at all terroristic—suppress to suppress human life, liquidate to liquidate—no, it targets negotiation, but in impossible terms, it abolishes a universal order of negotiation. From afar, the paralysis of power doesn't come from the stakes of human life (everyone is caught, and first of all, there has never been a contradiction on this level). The entire scenario of respect for human life is only there to camouflage the true capitulation of the system; it's total impotence to respond to some intervention or symbolic challenge, however insignificant it might be.

Desperate attempt of the system to limit the damages by responding to the challenge with a mortal struggle limited by its share: volunteers offer to take the place of the hostages. But this evidently changes nothing about the problem. The innocence of the hostages is a variable of absolutely no importance, and the system finds itself responsible and unable to respond to the eventual death of its own "delegates." Only its death permits it to respond.

The attacks in Italy, in Madrid, in Los Angeles: did they come from the Left or the Right? It doesn't matter. No historical or political "determination." The system itself destabilized political rationality, that for which it is henceforth disarmed before undecipherable, illegible acts. Every interpretation is stylistically retrograde—provocation from the Right... but also: revolutionary anarchism, armed insurrection—doesn't hold. The historical role of violence? A false problem, and perfectly insoluble as we know. Revolutionary violence, reactionary violence... Nonsense! But a challenge to the system of knowing how to respond on the same "self-destructive" level, not violently offensive actions, but symbolically suicidal ones—suicide being the only thing forbidden by the system. These actions are at once an exorbitant mirror of the system's own repressive violence and the model of a symbolic violence that the system forbids itself, of the only violence that it can exert: that of its own death.

A significant hypothesis—again Moebian: what if, through its actions, the system administrated its own death, but in homeopathic doses?

Death to Savages

ETHNOLOGY IS INEXORABLY drawn to universality. The universality of the gaze leaves its object no chance—but it also bursts through repercussion. Today it is attempting to escape from this harrowing and paradoxical phase, this insoluble crisis, by suicide. It is seeking to abolish itself as ethnology so as to resurrect the Indian in his "difference." In its death, ethnology intends to resemble the object that it kills. The phantasm of a subject of knowledge that wants, through self-sacrifice, to resurrect itself as the basis of this Indian that escapes it. Contemporary neo-colonialist, anti-ethnography (whereas triumphant ethnography was brought by colonialism) is only the end of the end of ethnography, thanks to the luxury that it offers itself in the simulacrum of its own death.

Thus we will have seen Jaulin, Castaneda, and so many others, become initiates, prostrate themselves before the wisdom of sorcerers, exalt Indians as alternative models, subverting the Western order. Thus already Lévi-Strauss attributed "equal" mental structures to them, and Clastres a strategy of political dissuasion superior to ours. Thus anthropologists from the Philippines have left the Tasady to their virgin forest and renounced their object of study so as to preserve their authenticity. Everywhere ethnology is searching to move out from under its shadow, to pass to the other side of the mirror. A sacrifice of the hopeless intellect, about which we can demonstrate at each moment that it is through a surplus of universality, through a surplus of the critical gaze, which is only another spiral of ethnocentrism, that these pious souls question their Western privilege.[1] But what would this demonstration serve? We only surmount a still less subtle step in this infinite analytic regression. We can only add to the homeopathic suicide of the science which reinforces it in its being. A ruse of analytical reasoning, through which it reproduces itself endlessly.

This critical ethnology, this hypercriticism of ethnology is therefore absolutely vain, *as vain henceforth as the critique of political economy.* What must be understood is that ethnology is dead, truly and irresistibly dead, but for other reasons—the entire internal problematic of ethnology is only an effort to escape this definitive death.

Ethnology is dead because the Great Revenge, the Great reversion has already taken place, the one that brought us the Savage, rather than holding the savage at a healthy ethnographic distance (even as an ideal model), which brought the Savage to the center of white cities. The movement of the expansion of universal reason has already reversed. (It began to do so from the moment that a colonist or a missionary set foot on savage coasts. But this return in flames, this agonizing return to the Western world, this immense symbolic process of reversal and of death has taken two or three centuries to be completed). Not this time as feedback for the Western system, but in the form of the total collapse of it and of white legitimacy, in the form of the accelerated blackening of cities.

This is not a question of the banal and inoffensive ethnological dream: the savage himself becoming an ethnologist of the West. Of course, it is the same critical gaze, the same universal model that can only be inverted (that said, it is also possible that a future ethnology will belong to the old colonists, who will deepen their negritude by becoming no longer objects but subjects of knowledge).

The blackening is no longer in the statistical invasion of the cities by thousands of blacks or immigrants—nor in the Black Panthers or liberation movements. All of this negritude on the path to liberation does nothing more than borrow the paths spawned by white consciousness. No, the true negrification, the true absolute revenge, is in the savage's infection of the city and of conscience. The right to the city is black. One has to see blacks in America, their nonchalance, their profound indifference to capital. Impotence is at the center of cities—the Moluquois board a train, pestering the Dutch countryside. White legitimacy is dead—Idi Amin Dada had himself brought before English diplomats by palanquin and the Pope received him—an extraordinary historical moment! The savage was no longer an object, the savage no longer a model. The end of the other, the end of the same. The death of the object entails the death of the subject, and the incessant reversion of both entails the impossibility of any analytic gaze. The whites disappeared. "Ethnology...this exegetical form ceased to furnish the modern West with the means to articulate its identity in relation to the past or the future, to the foreign or to nature"(Michel de Certeau). This ethnology is finished, and every return to it is a regression because this is a radically new situation: we are all Indians, all blacks, all savages. Savagery is neither the origin nor the end—savagery is immediate. Something else is at stake.

It's useless to go looking for a strategy for the abolition of power among sixteenth century Indians (the way Pierre Clastres did). Here, even within the sphere of capital, is where powerlessness exerts its ravages today, and this ravaging is nothing other than the dead Indian, the one that we are—not the model Indian, not the retro Indian—but the dead Indian rotting in the heart of our culture. Rot and decomposition are fundamental symbolic processes—along with catastrophe. They are ours today. The whole space of capital is surreptitiously dismantled, deconstructed, emptied of its rationality, of its ends. The savage surgery has only just begun, but from this moment we are all entirely delivered to raw symbolic reversion, where there is no longer either a subject, an object, history, or capital. Contrary to the ethnological vision and its distinction between an Indian and a white, today we are taking hostages everywhere, where there is no difference between the hostage and the terrorist, between the "victim" and the "executioner" (besides, the public order liquidates both together, when it is logical with itself—they are as dangerous, one and the other, they always end up more or less in a pact and the link that unites them, the risk of death, is so much stronger than the institutional order: the link has the right to be destroyed at any cost). Morality only endures insofar as there is a possible distinction between the victim and the executioner. Science only endures insofar as there is a possible distinction between an object and a subject. Ethnology only endures insofar as there is a possible distinction between the savage and the white.

This is why ethnography's internal controversies are pathetic —the final convulsions of a metalanguage in agony, since white universality is devoured *in place* by the death that it sowed in the four corners of the globe.

20

Stereo Porn

"Take me to your room and fuck me.

There is something indefinable in your vocabulary, something left to be desired."

— Philip Dick, *The Schizos' Ball*

CONTRARY TO THE *trompe-l'oeil*, which simulates a three dimensional universe in two dimensions and thus passes into the fourth dimension, that of the imaginary that justly lacks the orthogonal and realist space of the Renaissance, porn in some way simulates in three dimensions what only has two, and thereby makes eroticism and sexuality a one-dimensional universe.

It's useless to seek the phantasms that pass through porn (aggravated, infantile research of the primal scene, and other nonsense). Porn is precisely that which, through a surplus of "reality," of sexual realism, which is at the same time a hyperrepresentation, a hyperallegory of sexuality, an organic oversignification, an extraordinary setting of the stage (the "obscenity" of porn)—it's more real than real, seen from up close, you finally see what you've never seen, your sex, you've never *seen* it function, not from so close, with every hair, not in general, happily for you all of this is absolutely unreal, because more true than real, a little too true, too exact, too minute, too close, too obscene. This "too" is what fascinates, and the only phantasm at stake herein is therefore that of reality, of the real, about which no one knows where it begins or where it ends. It's a little like hyperrealist painting, where you see the grain of the skin on a ten meter face, when you don't even see that on faces you normally caress. It's even already true about the color of film or television, when we almost never see the world in color but in black and white. But that "makes" it more true—color gives you more. And precisely, in giving you too much, it secures that much for you. It gives you so much, color, contrast, high fidelity sex with all the depth and sharpness, all the life, that you no longer have anything to hide, to suggest, to produce in response. It did everything for you, and that's repression.

An obscene memory, outrageous, carceral, more obscene and unreal than any porn: the memory of Japanese quadrophonics—an absolutely ideally conditioned room—fantastic technique—music in four dimensions, in three of ambient space and more in visceral interior space—technical delirium of the perfect restitution of music (Bach, Monteverdi, who knows?) *that has never existed*, that no one has ever listened to in this way, and that wasn't made to be listened to in this way. Besides, it's no longer audible, it's something else, the distance that makes what we hear music (at a concert or elsewhere) is eliminated, instantly one is invested on all sides, there is no longer even any musical space, it's a simulation of total ambiance that in fact dispossesses you of any location, of any minimal analytic critical perception that creates the *real* charm of the music. The Japanese simply confused (in good technological faith) the "real" with the most dimensions possible. If they could make hexaphonics, they would do it. The fourth dimension that they added to music is precisely that which castrates your imagination and musical pleasure. Something else is fascinating: the "rendering," the perfect technique of the "rendering," the "fidelity" (another version, just as obsessional, with scientific objectivity, and puritan virtue). Precision: you will never be able to offer anything in return for that which has been "rendered" so well for you—no more investment is possible, it's set up in advance—absolute frustration. The same thing for fans of Hi-Fi.

Porn is the quadrophonics of sex. It adds a third and fourth track to the sexual act. It's so much that it secures it in the imagination. The hallucination of detail reigns. Science already presented us with microscopics, with this excess of the real in its microscopic detail, with this voyeurism of exactitude, a close-up of the invisible structures of the cell, with this notion of an inexorable truth that no longer measures itself in any way against the play of appearances, that only the sophistication of a *technical apparatus* can reveal.

What else does porn do, in its sham vision, but want to reveal this inexorable and microscopic truth of sex to us? It is directly descended from a metaphysics that only exists through the phantasm of a hidden truth and of its revelation, in the phantasm of a liberation of the "truth" or of the repressed "energy" and its *production* on the scene of the real—the obscene scene of the real. Hence the absolute hedging of revolutionary and liberal thought on the question: should one censor porn and choose a well-tempered repression? Insoluble. Porn has reason on its side. It is part of the ravages of the real and of its "objective" liberation. We cannot want to "liberate" sex in its raw functionality. Both are obscene. Only a Jesuit morality—that of the left—can make the distinction.

The realist corruption of sex or the productivist corruption of labor—same symptom, same fight. The Japanese vaginal cyclorama is the equivalent of the worker on the assembly line. It's more extraordinary than any strip-tease—girls on the edge of a platform, legs spread, Japanese workers in their shirt-sleeves—it's a popular spectacle—permitted to shove their noses, their eyes almost, up into the girls' vaginas, to see, to see better—but what? Clambering over each other to get in, to see inside the girls, this one speaking gently the whole time, or rebuking them for the sake of form. The rest of the spectacle—flagellations, reciprocal masturbation, traditional, even violent, strip-tease, pales before this moment of absolute obscenity, of visual voracity that far surpasses sexual possession, at the same time as representation and the traditional scene, with its coded distance. Sublime porn: If they could, the guys would be entirely swallowed by the girl—the exaltation of death? Perhaps, but at the same time, they comment and compare the respective vaginas, and this without ever trying to touch them, other than as part of the game. No lewdness, an extremely serious and childish act, an indistinct fascination in the mirror of the female sexual organ like Narcissus before his own image. Far beyond the conventional idealism of the strip-tease. And what makes us think of the possibility (as in Reiser's drawings) of enlarging the register of obscenity *within* the body, in the domain of the visceral—why stop at nudity, at the vaginal or the genital: if obscenity is on the order of representation and not of properly sexual *contents*, it should extend itself to the prostitution of the interior of the body and of the viscera—who knows what profound pleasure is to be found in the visual dismemberment of mucous membranes and smooth muscles. Sexuality in its limited definition is undoubtedly still only a poor production. Obscenity still has an unlimited future.

But look, what can be analyzed as a deepening of the drive is undoubtedly also—we will never know—only an orgy of realism. Rage is also undoubtedly a drive, that eventually substitutes itself for all the others (the other forms of desire for the code): the rage to make everything *comparable*, to bring everything into the visible jurisdiction of signs. That everything should be explored and brought into the artificial light of the sign, that everything should be liberated and translated into visible energy. That every word should be liberated and befit desire. We wallow in a liberalization that is only the growing process of obscenity. Everything that is hidden, that still enjoys being forbidden, will be unearthed, rendered unto the word and into evidence. The real grows, the real enlarges, one day the entire universe will be on the order of the real, and when the real becomes universal, that will be death.

In contrast (though it really isn't one) with clothes, nudity is never more than an extra sign. Insofar as nudity is hidden by clothes, it does not function as a sign, but as a hidden, ambivalent referent. Then this referent itself becomes a sign, it surfaces as a sign and returns to the circulation of signs: design nudity. The same operation to the second power with hard core or blue porn. The sexual organ, gaping, erect, or in action, is still only an extra sign, a extra gadget in the hypersexual panoply. Design phallus. The more one supposedly advances into the absolute veracity of sex, into its unveiling operation, the more one sinks into the accumulation of signs, the more one encloses oneself in the tangle of signs and over-signification— the disenchantment of accumulation and the lure of the real.

HEGEL: "Just as when speaking of the exterior of the human body, we have said that its entire surface, in opposition to that of the animal world, reveals the presence and the pulsation of the heart, we say of art that it has the task of creating in such a way that at every point of its surface the phenomenal, the apparent becomes the eye, seat of the soul, rendering itself visible to the spirit."

Here Hegel says nothing other than the Indian when he responds to the white who asked him why he is naked: "For me, all face." The body itself in a non-fetishistic culture (that doesn't fetishize nudity as the objective truth of the body), the body is the visage, which is to say (etymologically) that it looks at you. The body is not opposed to the face, singularly rich in expression, singularly bright and meaningful, as it is in our culture. But this dismantling of meaning to the exclusive profit of the face is still only an intermediary phase. A bit more and the inexpressive and functional nudity of the body will efface every visage: erotic models or porn actors are by definition faceless—they should not be pretty or ugly or expressive or have meaning or a gaze—it's incompatible. The spectacular nudity of the body is there to kill meaning and the gaze. In porn, the reductive process is completed: not only the face, but the rest of the body is abolished in the same spectacularization of sex as organ. Some porn films are no more than visceral sound effects over a coital close-up: even the body has disappeared—when a face or a body appear, they have the air of displaced, inconvenient, surrealistic accessories. They risk creating meaning where everything else intends to neutralize it, to abolish it in the exacerbated dizziness of the reality of sex.

A culture of the desublimation of meaning—where everything comes to be, to be materialized in the most "objective" way. A porn culture par excellence that everywhere and always intends the operation of the real. An imaginary culture par excellence that this ideology of the concrete, of facticity, of use, of the preeminence of use value, of the material infrastructure of things. A one-dimensional culture where everything exalts itself in the concreteness of production or in the concreteness of pleasure—labor or unlimited mechanical copulation—the same dimension of productivity. Only that which can be produced, shown and proven, stripped and set up, accounted for and accumulated, exists. The obscenity of our functional world is that nothing is left to chance. It's the same as that of a sexualized doll, rigged with genitals, that pisses, that speaks. The reaction of the little girl: "My little sister, she knows how to do that too, couldn't you give me a real one?" Everywhere the same process of grotesque simulation (the "grotesque" art of gardens doing the same thing, topped with rocky nature) consists in adding organs, functions, or factory work.

All porn turns on the female sex. Incessant devouring, gaping voracity at the horizon of which one always senses the fragility, the uniqueness, the disfunction of the male sex. The inverse of the traditional social myth, where the phallus is offensive, where rape is always a male act. Through this switch (always phallocratic of course, the same sex changes poles), porn nevertheless makes it apparent that if, as a myth, masculinity, machismo is inexhaustible, as merchandize, available on the sex market, it is always lacking. This is what everyone is lacking, men and women in a rarified and reified sexual representation—the equivalent of creating value in the economic sphere. The erection is never certain. The female sex is always credible, it suffices as an opening. No zero position.

In the utopian universe of porn, that of the realized profusion of sex, the absolute advantage is therefore on the female side. Men play a role of derisory figuration and besides, flaccid or erect, the masculine sex is unimportant. The irruption of hard core changes nothing. Porn remains the expression of female sexual revenge— narcissistic or devouring, or homosexual, or masturbatory—the phallus is never more than a dildo (this is perhaps also the revenge of the Western, the reign of masculine homosexuality). Historical revenge, after so many centuries of repression of feminine frigidity.

We'll see. The feminine was powerful in its repression. We are about to lock it in the eager, demanding sex—the extortion of sex as a labor power. Why has the masculine sign + active, become the sign—passive? Why privilege the feminine? Something other than sexual difference is at stake—perhaps an end to the determinate representation of sex and to sexual difference itself? The feminine would bear the indeterminate, and therefore the imaginary.

The masculine is no longer interested because it is too determined—the phallus the canonical sign of the sex. The privilege of the feminine is perhaps conjugated with the system's passage to indetermination—feminine sexuality floating and diffuse, in opposition to the masculine sex, and its axis on the genital determination.

For a long time we have been able to believe that the feminine sex was tolerated and tolerable because it was not the marked sexual term—the masculine sex taboo and foreclosed on the contrary for that same reason. If it really was marked, it would know how to act and to be represented (not more than the real phantasm—vaginal devouring—it would know how to be presented in an image— Gillette publicity: the woman's mouth on the razor blade). Its appearance on the horizon of porn is therefore a sign of an exhaustion of the sexual mark. Disinvestment that accompanies an aggravated demand and an obsessive overdetermination of all things through sex.

"In Japan, sex is in sexuality, and nowhere else. In the United States, sex is everywhere except in sexuality."
—Roland Barthes, *The Empire of Signs*

THIS IS ONLY the logical paradox of a society of abundance, an "affluent society." Its imperative, its utopia is the certainty of production, of the absolute availability of all goods. It would know how to tolerate the rarity of sexual goods. It should provide sex just like everything else. Everything will be sexualized, but in the feminine mode, that of waiting, of languor, of demands—because only the feminine sex can be produced discretely, it alone has an unlimited availability. At the same time, this society proves its own incapacity to deliver without restriction the most precious sexual goods (in its myth about itself), the only thing that fails and will always fail: the erect phallus. Every erotic spectacle and all porn turns around the masculine sexual malfunction (alongside the lack of presence and the feminine sexual demand). This pet theme is undoubtedly impregnated with puritan obsession: the more profoundly it recovers the despair of a society in which, in its profusion, something slips away, the only thing that cannot be produced industrially—a malfunction that it conjures, by default, in erection, ascendance, growth, the schemas of verticality, of productivism, etc. Thus porn and sex in general are nothing but an effect of fashion or of commercial calculation: in them, and in their fundamental obsession, the drama of scarcity is played out for all of society in its total fragility, behind the desperate and mechanical objectification of the signs of sex.

21

The Spiraling Cadaver

THE UNIVERSITY IS in decay: nonfunctional on the social plane of the market and employment, lacking cultural substance or a point to its knowledge.

There is no longer even any power, strictly speaking, it too is in decay. Hence the impossibility of returning to the flames of 1968: a return to questioning knowledge against power itself—an explosive contradiction of knowledge and power (or a revelation of their collusion, which is the same thing) in the university and, at the same time, through symbolic (more so than political) contagion in the entire institutional and social order. *Why sociologists?* marked this twist: the impasse of knowledge, the dizziness of nonknowledge (which is to say at once the absurdity and the impossibility of accumulating value in the order of knowledge) returns as an absolute weapon against power itself, to dismantle it according to the same vertiginous scenario of dispossession. This is the effect of May 1968. Today it is impossible since power, following knowledge, has fled the field, has become ungraspable, has dispossessed itself. In an henceforth floating institution, without knowledge content, without a power structure (except for an archaic feudalism that administers a mechanical simulacra whose destination eludes it and whose survival is as artificial as that of barracks and theaters), the offensive irruption is impossible. Having no more sense than that which precipitates rot, accentuating the parodic, simulacral side of dying games of knowledge and power.

A strike does exactly the opposite. It regenerates the ideal of a possible university, the fiction of universal access to a culture (now unlocatable and meaningless). This ideal substitutes itself as a critical alternative, as therapy for the functioning of the university. It still dreams of a substance and a democracy of knowledge. Besides, everywhere today the Left plays this role: the justice of the Left reinjects an *idea* of justice, a demand made by logic and social morality into a rotting, unraveling apparatus, which is losing all conscience of its legitimacy and renouncing its function almost on its own. The Left secretes and desperately reproduces power, because it wants power, and it believes in it, and revives it where the system puts an end to it. The system eliminating its axioms and its institutions one by one, and realizing one by one all of the objectives of the historical and revolutionary Left, it sees itself constrained to revive all the mechanisms of capital to be able to reverse them one day: from private property to small enterprise, from the army to national grandeur, from puritan morality to petit-bourgeois culture, from justice to the university—everything must be saved from disappearance, from what the system itself, in its atrocity, certainly, but in its irreversible drive, has liquidated.

Hence the paradoxical but necessary inversion of all the terms of political analysis.

POWER (or what takes its place) no longer believes in the university. It fundamentally knows that the university is only a zone for the shelter and surveillance of a whole class of a certain age, it need only select them—it will find its elite elsewhere, otherwise. Diplomas mean nothing: why would it refuse to offer them, it's ready to give them to everyone, so what's the point of this provocative politics, if not to crystallize energies around fictive stakes (selection, labor, diplomas, etc.), on an already dead and rotting referent?

By rotting, the university can do still more damage (rot is a *symbolic* apparatus—not political but symbolic, and therefore subversive for us). But for that it must set aside rot itself and give up the dream of resurrection. It must transform rot into a violent process, into a violent death, through derision, defiance, through a multiple simulation that would offer ritual death to the university as a model of the whole society rotting, a contagious model of disaffection of an entire social structure, where in the end death would make its ravages, that the strike desperately attempts to ward off, in complicity with the system, and succeeds on top it all only in sloughing the university off to a slow death, a delay that is not even a possible site of a subversion, of an offensive reversion.

This is the effect of May 1968. At a less advanced moment of the process of the liquefaction of the university and of culture, an irreversibly suffered process of dismantling, of disinvestment, of the deterritorialization of the institution (its substance and goals), the students, far from wanting to save the furniture, to rebel at once in a progressive and regressive way (to revive the lost object, or on the road of perdition, in an ideal mode) retorted by challenging power with the threat of the total, immediate death of the institution, the challenge of a far more intense deterritorialization than the one that came from the system, and summoning the power to respond to that complete unmooring of the institution of knowledge, to this total lack of a need to accumulate in a given place, to this death desired at the limit—not the *crisis* of the university, that is not a challenge, on the contrary, it is the play of the system, but the *death* of the university—power can only respond to that with its own return dissolution (for only an instant perhaps, but we've seen it).

THE BARRICADES OF May 10th seemed defensive and to be defending a *territory*: the Latin Quarter, that old boutique. But this isn't true: behind the appearance, the dead university, the dead culture hurled the challenge to power, and to their own eventual death at the same time—transformation into *immediate sacrifice* of what was only the *long term* operation of the system: the liquidation of culture and knowledge. They weren't there to save the Sorbonne, but to brandish the cadaver in everyone's face, just as the blacks in Watts and Detroit brandished the ruins of their own neighborhoods that they had themselves burned.

What can one brandish today? No longer even the ruins of knowledge, of culture—the ruins themselves are defunct. We know what we have done during the seven years of mourning at Nanterre. 1968 is dead, repeatable only as a phantasm of mourning. The equivalent in symbolic violence (beyond politics) would be the same operation that caused nonknowledge, the decay of knowledge against power—no longer recovering this fabulous energy on the same level at all, but in a superior spiral: causing nonpower, power rotting to clash against—against what exactly? That's the problem. It is perhaps insoluble. Power loses itself, power is lost. There is no longer anything around us other than mannequins of power, but the mechanical illusion of power still administers the social order, behind which the absent, illegible terror grows, the terror of control, of a definitive code, of which we are all insignificant terminals.

ATTACKING REPRESENTATION no longer has much meaning either. One clearly senses that all the student conflicts (the same as, more broadly, at the level of global society) over representation, over the delegation of power, for the same reason, are no longer anything other than phantom scenes that nevertheless suffice, through despair, to occupy the forefront of the stage. Through I don't know what Moebius effect, representation has turned against itself, and the whole logical universe of politics dissolved in the same instant, ceding its place to a transfinite universe of simulation, where from the outset no one is represented any longer nor does anyone represent anything, where everything that accumulates disperses at the same time, where even the axial, directive, and helpful phantasm of power has disappeared. A universe that is still incomprehensible, unrecognizable for us. A universe of a sinister cast that our coordinates, orthogonal and used to the infinite linearity of history and critique, violently resist. It is nevertheless there that one must struggle, if that still has any meaning. We are simulators, simulacra (not in the classical sense of "appearance"), concave mirrors radiated by the social, a radiation without a luminous source, power without origin, without distance. And it is in this tactical universe of simulacra that one must struggle—without hope, hope is a weak value, but in defiance and fascination. One must not refuse the intense fascination that emanates from the liquidation of every authority, of every axis of value, of every axiology, politics included. This spectacle, which is at once that of the agony and of the apogee of capital, far surpasses that of commodities described by the Situationists. This spectacle is our essential force. We are no longer in a relationship of uncertain or victorious forces, but politically, toward capital, this is the phantasm of revolution. We are in a relationship with defiance, with seduction, and with death toward this universe that is no longer one, since precisely every axiality escapes it (*universum*). We will not slip into the symbolic. The defiance that we hurl at capital in its delirium—shamelessly liquidating the law of profit, of surplus value, productive ends, power structures, and rediscovering at the limit of its process the profound immortality (but also the seduction) of primitive rituals of destruction. This defiance must be raised in an insane high bid. Capital is irresponsible, irreversible, ineluctable as value. To value alone can it offer a fantastic spectacle of its decomposition—only the phantom of value still floats over the desert of the classical structures of capital, like the phantom of religion floats over a long disenchanted world, just as the phantom of knowledge floats over the university. It is left for us to become the nomads of this desert, but disengaged from the mechanical illusion of value. We will live in this world, which for us has all the disquieting strangeness of the desert and of simulacra, with all the veracity of living phantoms, of errant and simulating animals that capital, that *the death of capital* has made of us—because the desert of towns is equal to the desert of sands— the jungle of signs is equal to that of forests—the dizziness of simulacra is equal to that of nature—only the vertiginous seduction of a dying system remains, in which labor buries labor, value buries value—leaving a virgin space, fearful, without clearings, continuous as Bataille wanted it, where only the wind lifts the sand, where only the wind watches over the sand.

What is political about this? Very little.

But we also have to struggle against the profound fascination exerted on us by the death throes of capital, against capital's staging of its own death, where we are the ones in real agony. To let capital initiate its own death is to grant it all the privileges of the revolution. Surrounded by the *simulacra* of value and by the *phantom* of capital and of power, we are much more disarmed and impotent than surrounded by the *law* of value and of commodities, since the system has revealed itself to be capable of integrating its own death, and since we are relieved of responsibility for this death, and therefore of the wager of our own life. The supreme ruse of the system, that of the simulacra of its death, through which it keeps us alive, having liquidated through absorption every possible negativity, only a superior ruse can forestall it. Defiance or imaginary science, only a *pataphysics of simulacra* can deliver us from the system's strategy of simulation and from the impasse of death wherein it encloses us.

Here again a paradoxical but total reversion of the terms of "political" analysis is imposed.

May 1st, 1976[1]

22

Labor Story

Publicity Campaign (from the Minister of Labor)
"Whoever gives the best of himself also has the right to an equitable
share"... Priority to manual labor
"Whoever builds, etc.
"Whoever has a responsibility, no matter what it is, etc.".....

The first notable advertisement since BNP, and for the same reason, through a provocative and direct implication in the "social
relations of production" (whereas advertisement usually acts on
the product and on the level of individual consumption). Where-
from one can deduce (because the advertisement *cannot* pass to the
side of production) that the social relations of production have
well and truly become an object of consumption, a theme of mass
consumption—the social is orchestrated like any other economic
or commercial theme.

Thus, in the BNP advertisement, even the circuit of value
and of equivalence became a leitmotif of collective consumption.
Capital offers itself to be seen as a *commodity*, as an use value,
making the social relation and the structure of production equivalent to a bar of soap or a finished product. A very beautiful
strategy of dissuasion.

Similarly this time with labor. All the negativity of labor as a contradictory and hidden social relation must be removed, and it must be praised as the most beautiful, finished, social product.

A reversal of the sign of production: from shameful stigma and foul process that every ad up till now used to hush up, production and labor became advertising arguments (a little like cast concrete or the structures that are apparently now the glory of design: unobscured material as a *sign*—the truth of social or manual labor, the obscenity of production as a supplementary sign of prestige). The labor principle, the virtue of labor regenerates itself in this way, but more than anything for what it was in the moral or historical order—no: labor, labor time, labor power as an *attribute* of the finished object, as surplus value of sign and prestige. So goes consumption, absorbing even production in the meanders of its code. (See the television sequence with the father and son: henceforth, the car is beautiful because it is "produced," the fruit of social labor, etc.—an extraordinary demagogical return—a ruse of desublimation. Like sex and repression, and everywhere today the unconscious, the production that becomes the most beautiful argument for consumption, sex becomes the most beautiful argument for the body, etc.)

Production as *aesthetic*. Manual labor as an aesthetics of simulation.

All of us, moralists that we are, evidence a healthy indignation before the abject prostitution of labor in aesthetics and advertisement's manipulation on one side, in condescension otherwise full of contempt, worthy of the worst mentality of charitable ladies. But looking more closely, this indignation is entirely retro and testifies only to our moral and political archaism. Because *labor is truly dead*, dignity, virtue, the value of labor, its historical status as fundamental source of social wealth—all that is dead, and everyone knows it, the workers themselves undoubtedly experience it, and this advertising campaign *proves* it by seeking—*on the contrary*—to regenerate it in the very eyes of those who no longer believe in it. Behind its moral hypocrisy, this poster says the objective truth of this society where the final pathetic and sacred possibility, the final myth, that of production and labor, has itself been desanctified. This poster is therefore right, and the indignation that it provokes is *naïve*. It still comes from a belief in the historical dignity of the proletariat, in our profound respect, much more profound than we think, for the value of labor and the political virtue infused in exploited labor.

Fundamentally, our reaction is this: agreement with the advertisement when it speculates on commodities, but watch out! when it touches on the values of the infrastructure, lower your paws before labor and exploitation, because that, that's serious, and that brings up the revolution (which must be left to the revolutionaries).

This campaign is abject in effect, in that it openly doesn't care about the world (in the same way that the BNP poster didn't, with that particular salaciousness, proper to the media in general, which must flatter the people to fuck them), but it is also beneficially abject in that it wounds our moral and referential system of defense, which would still like to believe in labor and its value. An archaic nostalgia in relation to which this poster is a length ahead.

It is fundamentally a museum piece, an ethnological document on the death of labor. Labor deposited in the Museum of Popular Arts and Traditions. This poster is only possible because no one "gives the best of themselves"—such performance, dangerous for the social order, is consequently forbidden. There's no question of enjoying your job—the *instinct of workmanship* is condemned.

If this poster was taken literally, it would be lacerated immediately, it would scream. This is why no one believes in labor any more.

Or again: it is because no one believes in advertising. The two myths fall to the bottom simultaneously through indifference. That would be the truth of this poster and of the indifference that it encompasses: the only person who still believes in labor is the Minister of Labor, as a professional necessity. He started this campaign just like other Ministers finance research projects on other things. No profitability, no operational finality, but to do it *as if it functioned*, as if in search (to find!), as if there were stakes or an objective. Because that's essential: to make an obstacle to the drift of references and investments. Where we rediscover simulation fully, and the artificial resurrection of all ends in bulk on the market of the sign (here, even desire plays its role and simulation is felt, the final imaginary solution for the social order: to convince the people of their desire, of the urgency of fulfillment, of "giving the best of themselves"—the final end without end: the operational aesthetics of desire). As here the operational aesthetics of labor: one acts *as if* it worked, as if one were taking care of people, as if they had no other objective than a "equitable share," as if the indignity of labor was unbearable, when it is labor itself that is—or better, when dignity and indignity have long since disappeared along with the meaning of labor (hence the naiveté of an objection like that of *Le Monde*: "If you believe that an advertising campaign will suffice to revalorize manual labor— you would be better off redistributing your advertising budget to the workers themselves.") Nonsense. From neo-social advertising, to archaic out-bidding, to *supersocial* "politics"; each seems to be taking the other literally, according to the rules of the game of truth.

Of course, the unions themselves would react just the same, because here they are beaten on the terrain of the lure on which they live. Their inertia could signify that they don't believe in this advertisement or they disdain it too much to react. In fact, they are too worn out to do it. Better: they are paralyzed, they would pro-foundly have liked to take the initiative on such a campaign. They have been doubled by the Ministerial demagogy: they can only distinguish themselves from it through a minor point of marketing (now they are trying to regain it).

Up till now, the manipulation of the myth of labor was left to the forces of the Left, the parties and the unions. Political manip-ulation no less abject than the spectacular manipulation of advertisement. To canonize labor as a productive and revolutionary force would certainly be no better than playing with it as a sign. One myth follows the other, simulation follows production, and exploited labor is now projected on the screen of the city like any other spectacle[2]—what's the scandal? That labor and production *also* happen entirely in the spectacular mode must delight every logical mind and without precluding idealism: the radicality of the spectacle and of simulation is unlimited, so much the better—if there is a revolution at the end, it will at least be radical!

Or again: the poster attempts to rehabilitate manual labor as if it was a sin, attempts to redeem it as if it was a defect. The abject ideology of the patroness? But *isn't it*? Would it be better to under-stand productive labor as a defect than to praise it as a historical right and to praise the exploited, *as such*, as the subject of history?

LIKE SEX, labor is strong only when repressed—negated, misunder-stood, unaware of its power. When it is revived in a complementary representation, the panegyric of publicity, it is emptied of its final contradictions or split energies. Obscene and pacified, it becomes a model of accomplishment—again like sex. In the end, socialism changes labor as such: the object of need itself and the perfect alibi of the social.

23

Value's Last Tango

"Where nothing is in its place, there's disorder
Where there's nothing in a desired place, there's order"
— Brecht

THE PROFESSORS PANIC at the idea that we are going to award diplomas without counterpart in "real" work, without an equivalent in knowledge. This panic is not that of political subversion, it is that of seeing value disassociate itself from its contents and functioning all alone, in the same form. The values of the university (diplomas, etc.) are going to proliferate and continue to circulate, a little like floating capital or Eurodollars, they will swirl without referential criteria, completely devalorized in the end, but this is unimportant: their circulation alone suffices to create a social horizon of value, and the mania of the phantom value will be only more grand, even though its reference (its use value, its exchange value, the "labor power" of the university that it recovers) is lost. The terror of value with equivalence.

This situation only appears to be new. It is new for those who still think that the university develops a real process of work, and who invest their life, their neurosis, their raison d'être therein. The exchange of signs (of knowledge, of culture) in the university, between "teachers" and "students" has already for some time been nothing but a doubled collusion of bitterness and indifference (the indifference of signs that brings with it the disaffection of social and human relations), a doubled simulacra of a psychodrama (that of a demand hot with shame, presence, oedipal exchange, with a *pedagogical incest* that seeks to substitute itself for the lost exchange of labor and knowledge). In this sense, the university remains the place of a *desperate initiation in a form void of value*, and those who have lived there for some time recognize this strange labor, the true hopelessness of non-labor, of non-knowledge. Because the current generations still dream of reading, of learning, of competing, but their heart is no longer in it—as a whole, the ascetic cultural mentality has run body and belongings together. This is why the strike no longer means *anything*.[1]

This is nevertheless also why we have been trapped, we have trapped ourselves, after 1968, by granting diplomas to everyone. Subversion? Not at all. Once again, we were the promoters of the advanced form, of the pure form of value: diplomas without work. The system wanted no more of it, but it wanted that—values functioning in the void—and we started it, with the illusion of the opposite.

The student distress at seeing diplomas conferred without work is equal and complementary to that of the teachers. It is more hidden and insidious than the traditional anguish of failure or of obtaining worthless diplomas. Insuring the diploma against all risks, which empties the contents from all the vicissitudes of knowledge and its selection, is hard to bear. Also it must be complicated by either a benefit-alibi, simulacrum of work exchanged against a simulacrum of a diploma, or by a form of aggression (the teacher summoned to teach, or treated as the automatic distributor) or of rancor, so that at least something will still happen with a "real" relation. But nothing does. Even the house-cleaning scenes between teachers and students, that are now a large part of their exchanges, are no longer anything but recollections, like the nostalgia for violence or for a complicity that once opposed them or united them around a stake of knowledge or a political stake.

The "hard law of value," the "law set in stone"—when it abandons us, what sadness, what panic! This is why there are still good days for fascist and authoritarian methods, because these methods revive some of the violence that is necessary for life—undergone or inflicted, it hardly matters. The violence of ritual, the violence of work, the violence of knowledge, the violence of blood, the violence of power and of politics... oh how wonderful! It's clear, it's luminous, the power relations, the contradictions, the exploitation, the repression! It's missing today and the need for it makes itself felt. The teacher's reinvestment of his or her power through "free speech," the self-determination of the group and other modern foolishness—it's all a game in the university (but the entire political sphere is articulated in the same way). No one is fooled. Simply in order to escape profound deception, in the strong sense, the catastrophe that entails the loss of roles, of statutes, of responsibilities and the incredible demagoguery that is deployed through them, one must recreate the professor either as a mannequin of power and knowledge or as a bearer of a scrap of ultra-Leftist legitimacy—if not, the situation is intolerable for everyone. It is on this compromise—the artificial figuration of the teacher, the equivocal complicity of the student—it is on this phantom scenario of pedagogy that things continue and this time can last indefinitely. Because there is an end to value and to labor, there is no end to the simulacrum of value and of labor. The universe of the simulation is transreal and transfinite: no test of reality will come to put an end to it—except total collapse and the slippage of terrain, which remains our most foolish hope.

24

The Magic Struggle or
the Final Flute

A SPECTER HAUNTS the spheres of power: communism. But a
specter haunts the communists themselves: power.

Everything is faked in the current political scene, regulated by
a simulacrum of revolutionary tension and the seizure of power by
the communists (and the Left in general); in fact, behind every
stage where the communists continue to devote themselves to form
a front against the Right and thereby to preserve the whole edifice,
a negative obsession with power is at work, giving them an ever
renewed force of inertia: the shame of revolution stimulates them.
They are not alone in this case, because politics eludes everyone,
and the Right itself has no vitality. But it discovered that the communists have always appeared historically, from the Leninist
perspective to which everyone adheres (and to which they believe
themselves to be faithful), as politicos, as professionals in the
seizure of power. Political failure and decay is more flagrant for
them. Fear of the power that weakens even the perspective opened
by Sanguinetti in *The Real Report on the Last Chance to Save Capitalism in Italy*,[1] of seeing the communists take over for the
dominant class in the exercise of power and the *political* management of capital (the last Italian elections unmasked the *utopia* still
nourished by the old cynical idealism of the class struggle).

Where does this impotence, this castration come from? Who knotted their needle? What magic always causes their failure so close to their goal and not through defiance, like a long-distance runner who in his solitude chooses to lose and to thereby deny the rules of the game—no, why irresistibly fail to take power, why do they desperately put the brakes on, like in a cartoon, at the sight of the abyss of power?

ENRICO BERLINGUER[2] declares: "There is nothing to fear in seeing the communists take power in Italy." An ideally ambiguous formula, since it signifies:

— that there is nothing to fear since the communists, if they come to power, will change nothing in its fundamentally capitalist mechanism,

— that there is no risk that they will *ever* come to power (because they don't want to),

— but also, that in fact power, real power no longer exists—there is no power—and therefore no risk that someone will take it or retake it,

— and again. I (me, Berlinguer) have no fear of seeing the communists take power in Italy—which can appear logical, even evident, but at bottom not really, since,

— it can mean to say the opposite (we don't need psychoanalysis for that): "I'm afraid" of seeing the communists take power in Italy (and there are good reasons for that, for a communist).

All of this is simultaneously true. This is the secret of a discourse whose ambiguity translates the drift of power. The impossibility of a determinate position of power. A degree zero of political will. All the parties bear the cost of this liquidation, but the communists testify most cruelly to this abolition of political will to power.

THE AFFAIR OF THE "false" document, the circular from Moscow to the Portuguese Communist Party about the most effective means of taking power. The incredible naiveté of all these vaudeville actors. It had to be the opposing Left that launched this hoax in order to resuscitate the political energy that the communists had long since lost. In the shadow of the flowering communist parties, for a long time, there has only been a virgin Left waiting to be raped by the Right. Was the document real or fake? It doesn't matter, since evidently the inverse is true: knowing that the communists have long since been *programmed* not to take power. Besides, it was the most beautiful example of false inversion as offensive simulation: "Directives from Moscow to worldwide communist parties on the most effective methods of never taking power."

Against all the faking of the political sphere, which turns around the idea of the subversion of the current order by the communist party, against the lure of seeing the whole world as complicit, this destructive simulation had to be introduced, a falsehood that seizes the entire model of current political simulation in reverse.

They themselves (because everything happens as if they knew it) advance all kinds of good realistic reasons, in terms of relations of force, of "objective" situation, etc.: one doesn't take power in a period of crisis (which would equal managing the crisis of capital; one knows that capital is only waiting for that administrative relief, see Sanguinetti). But of course this is absurd since the resolved crisis leaves no chance for a revolutionary "relief."

Another explanation, tactical once again, but more complex: if the party takes power, it finds itself in the dilemma of falling into total reformism so as to preserve its electorate. And from this perspective, it loses before the socialists (more generally, from the reformist perspective, the Left loses before the Right, which does that better)—or rather it is summoned to assure its revolutionary perspectives, and it is immediately brushed aside. Caught between these two poles, the party has no other choice than maintaining itself just on this side of the line of power, where it can appear to have a triumphant calling and thereby save its image, without at the same time doing anything to escape this shadow, in the test of the reality of power, where it loses without reprieve. At the same time, it permits the Right to continually play on the imminence of a communist victory so as to maintain power through inertia. The political tourniquet works like this, an endless scenario where the bets are placed and where the same cards are redistributed instantly.

Nevertheless, this does not always explain why the communists are incapable of politics, which is to say of politically assuming a dissociation of means and ends—the political principle where power is the end and the means don't matter—they are obsessed by the means and have lost sight of all the ends, they are obsessed by progressive results, the slow progress of the masses, the rising of historical consciousness, etc. They no longer believe in all that, and through force of will, and good super-Kantian ethics, homogenize the means and the ends, through force of making the fact of power itself a means, they have lost the scope to take it. They have divested themselves of all political violence—because of this, they are everywhere and always the victims, and no longer entertain anything other than this sad myth of the masses dominated by an exploitative power. This is the only substance of their discourse: a lamentable and plaintive recrimination addressed to what piety, to what judicial authority, to which god who will avenge them against capital?

The communists have perhaps never really had the taste for power.[3] *Insofar as they are communists*, they undoubtedly never had a taste for *bureaucratic* domination—which is different from political activity, and is only its caricature.

Nevertheless, Stalinism is still charged with political violence, because it exceeded the pure and simple *use value* of history, of the masses, of labor and of society. It still possesses something of an absurd imperium, unleashed beyond the rational finality of society (André Glucksmann's error about the terroristic logic of Stalin's camps, "labor" camps as opposed to death camps, which would be the most accomplished model of domination). This is perhaps the secret of the communists' failure, of their complex political impotence. Since Stalin and his death, they *aligned themselves more and more with use value*, with a naïve faith in the possible transparency of history, of the social—through the elimination of every other dimension but that of a sane management of things, through which they have fallen into a *morality* unsurpassed since the glory days of Christianity. Having lost what was immoderate and immoral about capital itself and therefore also about the idea of a revolution that should have challenged capital on the terrain of its virulence (and not on that of its supposed rationality)—it is a pretty poor revolution that can only take over when capital is too weak to manage public works. In its "savage" ethic, capital itself didn't concern itself with use value, or with the social good—it was the unlimited, deranged business of abolishing the symbolic universe in an always greater indifference and an always accelerated circulation of value. That's capital: the unlimited reign of exchange value. In the symbolic and ritual order, it is not true that capital opposes a rational order of interest, of profit, of production and labor, in short an order of positive ends. It imposes a disconnection, a deterritorialization of all things, an excessive extension of value, an entirely irrational order of investment *at any cost* (the opposite of rational calculation according the Max Weber). The rationality of capital is bullshit: capital is a challenge to the natural order of value. This challenge knows no limits. It intends the triumph of (exchange) value at all costs, and its axiom is investment, not production. Everything should be gambled, put in play. The true capitalist does not thesaurize, enjoy or consume. His productivity is an endless spiral. It reverses all production in an ulterior productivity—without respect for needs, for human and social ends. At least that is the capitalism, unlimited and immoral, that dominated from the 18th century to the beginning of the 20th.

Marxism is only its degraded form. Socialism is not the superior dialectical form of capital. It is only the degraded, banal form of the social, moralized by political economy (reduced by Marx to the *critical* dimension, and having thereby lost the irrational, ascetic, sacrificial, immoral, and prodigious dimension that Weber again pointed out in this *Protestant Ethic*) and the political economy itself entirely *moralized by use value*.

All good *political* conscience (and not only economic) sought refuge in use value. The process must be redone in a light that is still more cruel than at the level of objects and commodities. Because this time the use value of the social is at stake, *society as use value*.

The dialectical rainbow that has long shined over the Marxist notion and over the sacred horizon of value has dissolved, and today, in its broken fragments, we can see what it is: not only is use value nothing, it functions as the codpiece for political economy (what Marx, it must be said, discreetly observed, but which no one who speaks for him has observed since, that all socialism, the whole idea of revolution and of the end of political economy is regulated by the triumph of use value over exchange value—and the end of commodity alienation, the universe is transfigured by use value, that of objects to that of its own sexual body and to that, more generally, in the end, of the entire society, returning to each of us the image of his or her own proper "needs"). But it is worse than that: *it is the degraded form of exchange value*. It is the completely disenchanted form of the economy, the neutral, abolished, useless phase that comes to close the delirious, endless process of commodity exchange, of the instantiations of all things in the sublime space of money (a process that, as we know, impassions *everyone*, and collectively, when use, function, need, etc. only "interest" each of us in isolation, in a mode of eternal resignation). When an object, a being, an idea has found its use value (its function, etc.), it's finished, that's complete entropy. Use value is like heat in the second law of thermodynamics: *the lowest form of energy*.

The communists believe in the use value of labor, of society, of matter (their materialism), of history. They believe in the "reality" of society, of struggles, of classes, who knows what else? They believe in everything, they want to believe in everything. That is their profound morality.

It takes away all of their capacity for politics.

They no longer believe in the sacred horizon of appearances—the revolution wants to put an end to appearances—but only in the limited horizon of reality. They believe in the administration of things and in an empirical revolution that will follow the thread of time. They believe in the coherence and in the continuity of time. Everything about politics that is excessive and immoral escapes them, all simulation, all seduction. This is what makes them stupid, profoundly stupid, profoundly riveted to their bureaucratic mentality. This is what, more concretely, makes them ill-suited to take or maintain power. They became the administrators of the use value of life, with a certain municipal smile and with the provincial swell of middle class technicians (the "middle-classes" result from the historic domestication and dumbing down by use value). The "proletariat" fought at the level of the atrocity of exchange value and of its generalized system, which is to say at the revolutionary level of capital, risking the life of their own inhumanity of exchange value against it. Whereas today everything takes the form of infantile pleas for ever greater use value, and that it is the ideology of the middle class, and socialism and communism are the expression of this degradation of the dominant values of capital and of the collapse of the political game.

In order to become pure and simple theoreticians and practitioners of the *good use of society* through the good use of political economy, the communists have fallen farther even than capital, capable only of presiding over the management of the most degraded form of the law of value.

THIS IS THE DEFINITIVE end of the dialectic. The end of the great Marxist promise.

> "The condition of the liberation of the working class is the liquidation of all class, just as the liberation of the Third Estate (of the bourgeois order) was the liquidation of all states."

THIS IS FALSE because the dialectic is over—or rather, this is the infantile malady of Marxist theory—it has never ceased to be on the side of capitalism. And what becomes clear through the impossibility of the communists taking power, through their phobia about power, is the historic incapacity of the proletariat to accomplish that which the bourgeoisie knew how to do in its time: a revolution.

When the bourgeoisie put an end to the feudal order, it truly subverted an order and a total code of social relations (birth, honor, hierarchy) in order to substitute another (production, economy, rationality, progress). And this is because it existed as a *class* (not as an *order* or an *estate*: "Third Estate" is the term that we assign to it), which is to say as something radically new, a radically new conception of the social relation, that it could disrupt the order of the *caste*.

The proletariat does not possess anything to radically oppose to the order of a class society. Contrary to the bourgeoisie which played its part (the economy) by imposing its code, the proletariat (the "theory of the proletariat") pretends to liberate itself in the name of production, which is to say that the terms in the name of which the bourgeoisie *liberated* itself as a class would be the same as those in the name of which the proletariat would *negate* itself as a class. Misdeeds of the dialectic, with which the bourgeoisie infected the proletariat. The bourgeoisie did not "dialectically" "surpass" the feudal order, it annihilated it, it substituted an unprecedented order of value for it—economy, production, class as an antagonistic code without common measure with the feudal code. And its true strategy is to trap the proletariat in the class *status*, in the class struggle —why not?—because the class is a code, and the bourgeoisie has a monopoly on the code. The bourgeoisie is the only class in the world—if it succeeded in leading the proletariat to see itself as a class, *even if it was to negate itself as such, it won.*

The true relief that would assure (that already sometimes assures) the communists and the Left is not that announced for denunciation by Sanguinetti in his *Real Report*. It is much darker and more subtle: *the communists will one day take power to hide the fact that it no longer exists.* It will not be a question of the subversion of capital, nor of a revolution of capital on itself, but quite simply of a political involution, of a reabsorption of the political and of all political violence into a society delivered only to games of mass simulation.

25

Castrated Before Marriage

THE LEFT IS POULIDOR. It pedals vigorously toward power, the crowds cheer, and, at the moment of triumph, it falls into second place, in the shadows, in the niche of the opposition. Or, the Left is Eurydice: from the moment power turns to grasp it, it returns to hell, virgin and martyr sharing the shadows with tyrants.

A truce of piss politics. Was the deception of September 23rd that of a political failure, or was it due to the fact that we robbed ourselves of everything we were really due? Even the disorder of the Right is an interesting symptom, its incapacity to exploit what could be a victory for it, but which is not one, because what is at stake in this anticipated scenario of the victory and decomposition of the Left, is precisely *anticipation*, the precession from the scenario of the historical date due and this is as fatal for the Right as for the Left, because it is the end of every strategic perspective. The whole political class is dismayed by this reversion of politics into simulation, at which neither the presiding forces nor the silent masses can do anything, but none can be said to master the process of simulation (perhaps other things take place at the level of the "silent masses").

Each of the them accuses the other of apparent divisiveness in order to reconcile the coming moment themselves, which is to say to have a strategy. But this is only a lure to amuse the crowds. In reality, the Right and the Left taken *together* act together in the work of difference, work *together* to preserve the model of political simulation, and this collusion dominates their respective strategies from afar. There are no strategies elsewhere in this system of simulated dissension, of dissuasion (which is also that of pacified coexistence at the world level) but a kind of destiny that absorbs us all, destiny of the inescapable production of the social, and of dissuasion *by* the social. (This production of the social invests us all as an irreversible ideal, if only to struggle against.) In this system of the tactical division of labor, the defection of one of the parties (today the Left) is a kind of betrayal, a low blow, an *acte manqué*, because it brings about the withdrawal of political investment, and there is so much energy that escapes the social sphere of absorption, and this is a defeat for everyone. Clearly, the Left behaves badly. It rewards itself with the fantasy of tearing itself apart over nothing, so that its true role, that which it cannot escape, is of being a trustworthy, solid *partner* in the suspenseful political balancing act with the Right, a good pole in the transmission of social electricity (here we rediscover the conjunction of the Soviets and electricity in the definition of socialism, like that of an umbrella and a sewing machine on an operating table).

But on the other hand, one can say (and the funny thing in this story is that all these hypothesis are simultaneously possible, and today this is precisely what defines the political (or the end of the political): the succession, as in weightlessness, of every hypothesis, in which none annuls the others, the cyclical interference and overlaying of all models—but this is precisely *anti-gravity*, this indeterminate effect that is electrifying, because it puts an end to every strategy and every political rationality), that if the problem of transferring power to the Left is posed all around the world, like a kind of universal epidermal turn toward "socialism," it is not or it is no longer the traditional vicissitudes of the Right that— being used to the exercise of power, transfers it to the Left for a time, so that the Left serves as a relief and a momentary trans- mission belt for the "dominant class." The Left as a historical prosthesis of the Right (which is not false either). This is a hypothesis that is also at the center of Sanguinetti's book on the best means to save capitalism in Italy.

But if one admits that the fundamental question today is no longer that of capital, but that of the social, and that the only tactic for the regeneration of the social, of the accelerated production of the social, is that of the discourse of crisis, then one must think that the Left, because it is born of and nourished by *critical* thought, it will impose itself on power as the most credible spokesperson, the most coherent effigy, the most faithful mirror of the crisis. Power will be assigned to it not to resolve the real crisis (there isn't one) but to manage the *discourse* of the crisis, the critical phase of capital that will not end, since it is that of the social.

If something of Marx must be retained, it will be this: capital produces the social, the social is its essential product, it is its "historical function." And the grand phases of the social, the convulsions and revolutions, coincide with the ascendant phase of capital. When the objective determinations of capital wane, the social surpasses it in a dialectical stride, it collapses too, in the same way that a bloodless imaginary corresponds to a moribund reality. What we are witnessing today: the Left dying the same death as power.

But one can also say (another "reversible" hypothesis): the Right always risks, at the limit of a certain lapse in power, being brought to stagnation, to an involution of the social (of the partic-ipation of the masses, etc.). Sole solution: a reinjection, an overdose of political simulation in the dying social body. A revolution in homeopathic doses, distilled by the Left, that thereby functions as a relay in the production of the social, just as the unions asserted themselves by assuring the relief of capital during the definitive socialization of labor. Did they come from anything else?

The paradox of this advent of socialism and of the Left, it that it came *too late*, when the process of socialization, after the violent and ascendant phase of capitalist socialization, was already in decline, when the social began the work of mourning. The Left never attains "power" except to manage the social work of mourning, the slow disintegration, reabsorption, involution, and implosion of the social—that is what we call socialism. Thus the unions gain uncontested management of the sphere of labor only when the process of labor, generalizing itself, loses its historic viru-lence and sinks into the scene of its own representation.

But is this socialism even capable of resolving the work of mourning? Certainly not. It can only multiply the signs of the social and simulate the social to death. In which case, as at the end of every failed mourning, one must foresee that it will fall into melancholy.

THE MOST INTERESTING thing about the current events is the pre-cession of the scenario of the real. A kind of precocious ejaculation (everything is played out and plays itself out six months before the elections) that equals a castration in time, a rupture in the scansion of the event, which always underlies an unforeseeable conjunction and a minimal moment of uncertainty. Thus May 1968, having a high degree of factuality, was neither foreseen nor a model of future events. Now, it is completely the opposite: turn abouts, surprises, ruptures, all this is a Punchinello story, deliberately directed, by old politicos, from a false, premature event taken from what was already a pseudo-event: the elections, whatever political suspense they still had. Such is the effect of a system of calculated programming and deprogramming, of a system of dissuasion where even the real will no long have the occasion to produce itself.

Independently of the motives and machinations proper to each of the actors in this vaudeville, this effacement of a few chances, of whatever small charm that was still attached to the real, to the reality principle of the event, disgusts us, without us being able to do anything about it. The real will never have taken place, the power relations that could have unleashed it were still-born, only the phantom of the silent majorities still floats over this desert, bowing in advance before the term of the ballot boxes, henceforth still more indifferent than to an episode from a past life, since the curtain has already fallen.

And despite everything the communist party will be said to be most responsible in this affair (even though the ravages of simulation far surpass it) because the communist party contributed the most to the secularization of this indifference, to making the taste for politics pass to the whole world, to the benefit of a disciplined management, an economic vision and a pure transparency of the social. In its rage to bring the social about as a pure element, as a pure abstraction and degree zero of political energy, in its rage for pure and simple social management, the communist party had every opportunity, because it is the only "homogeneous" social apparatus. But precisely this homogeneity might also be nothing more than an effect of the apparatus, and the social, because reduced to the zero degree, might simply implode brusquely under its ass.

THE ABSURDITY OF a "government pact," as if power was only the means of applying a program! There is such a contempt for power here, such a misunderstanding of politics—against which politics takes its revenge elsewhere in some way, since the inappropriateness to political sovereignty expands in relation to the impoverished conception of power as use value. By dint of analyzing the state as an executive cog wheel of the "dominant class," the communists have castrated themselves, denying the energy required to take it over (to say nothing of abolishing it). Power as *form*, whose contents are unforeseeable, and whose stakes can be reversed, the logic of politics can lead the man or the class in power to devour its own bases and to burn its own objectives—this is what must be avoided at all costs. For that, a single solution: programming. Politics must be neutralized in advance through economic and social rationality. The form must obey only its prior content, just as the real event must be no more than the echo of a calculated scenario. Same dissuasion, same contraception, came deception.

This is what the masses, who still undoubtedly possess an incurable capacity for political hallucination, have hoped for a "victory of the Left": unexpected tomorrows. And this is what must be discouraged before it is too late, and they are bound by a programmatic logic. Every program is dissuasive, because it arms itself against the future. Moreover it offers the possibility of making and unmaking situations before they have taken place. One can update them indefinitely with the danger that they will become real. One can expend foolish energy that would be threatening elsewhere.

This is the model raised to the power of preventative jurisdiction over all of society. The blackmail of the program can be substituted for every repression. Between the hard technologies of persuasion and forced socialization and the soft technologies of pure dissuasion, the program represents the bastard form of modern social bureaucracies.

The panic at the Central Committee must have been profound toward the beginning of the summer, anticipating a complete victory. But one can think that the dissuasion operation has been ready since the presidential elections, when it was clear that the critical threshold of fifty/fifty was going to be surpassed, and the investiture inevitable. From there, the great burst of hope as a prelude to the baptism of power—but *too early*, much too early, the way one sells a bear's fur out of the *fear* of killing it, the way one imagines the devil in order to make him retreat—and simultaneously, updating the scenario for dissuasion, demobilization, deception. But that is the whole history of the communist party: an equal energy is employed in mobilizing the "masses" then in demobilizing them, resulting in a zero sum game—this is the grand game of the social, cycling and recycling the masses, accelerating and braking the cycle, reinflation and inertia. This was the orbit of the cultural revolution in China—with a strong moment: that of dissuasion (1945: disarming, 1948: knowing how to end a strike, 1968: general strike and elections, this time breaking with the union of the Left). We will never overestimate the historical role of the communist party as a machine of dissuasion, a machine of useless combustion and a cycle of energies: what's left? Precisely the social, the social as a cumulative waste, as a growing dejection, as the remains of all the failed revolutions, as fallen, as inert mass, that recovers everything, according to an abstraction in the end fully realized in socialism. The famous social conquests, that created the entire ideology of the Left for a century, are only the phases of this growing neutralization.

The funniest thing is that the communist party and Marchais still take themselves for historical specters, proclaiming in a false way: "But yes, we want power!" They who have spent twenty years innocently protesting "No, we don't want power!" so as to be accepted in the political concert. The irony is that they should be suspected of not wanting it. Never have we seen a more beautiful example of an apparatus become the effective sign of its own derision. But everyone fundamentally applauds this role, because everyone needs the communist party as it has become with its political emasculation, strutting, arrogant, buffoonish, chauvinist, managerial—incarnating the visible face of the revolution, the ever visible face of a revolution gravitating endlessly in the orbit of capital.

But all the other parties, and us too inwardly, undoubtedly, magnify it well out of measure, in the disarray of imagining its disappearance. It is still that last grand vestige of a revolutionary era in politics. And in blackmail and nostalgia that is its strength. And that is its current triumph in blocking the situation with an archaic problematic (nationalizations, nation security, the working classes' standard of living) in which, in its best moments, it does not itself believe. The communist party only made sense from the perspective of the dictatorship of the proletariat. Today, it finds itself in front of the inertia of the masses, their force of inertia which undoubtedly conceals a new violence—but before this dissolution of the social, this diffuse and unintelligible solution that the social, like the political, has become, the communist party, like so many others, is without resources.

Nevertheless, we must try to understand it. It is not easy, in a society in a complete revolution toward soft technologies (including those of power), to maintain a hard apparatus and ideology. Monopoly, centralization, programming, bureaucracy, nuclear defense—the communist party remains the last great adversary of a supple, cool, self-managed, ecological, contactual (not contractual) society. Against "psych" society, porn, libido, and schizo incorporated, the party is on the side of the asylum, of discipline, that of containment and of the apparatus, still entirely within a panoptic space—Stalinist therefore by destination, but without the political violence of Stalinism—a Stalinism on a cruise, decked out with a *new look* that gives it the air of a drag queen of modern history.

Of course, the fluid and tactile, tactical and psychedelic society toward which we are dragging ourselves, the era of soft technologies is no less ferocious than that of hard technologies, and, confronted with the disquieting strangeness of simulation, we might even come to miss the clear and vigorous concept of the dictatorship of the proletariat (even if it was a dictatorship exercised *over* the proletariat, this too is unimportant for the utopian transparency of the concept— even in the ambiguity of its genitive, it was a strong concept). Today there is no longer even a proletariat forcing a violent dictatorship on itself through a despot—this is still the wager and the political resource of the totalitarian state, the risk of extermination of which the camps were the extreme form, with the despot's mad dream of *bringing an end to his own people* (Hitler in 1945 condemning the German people to death)—there is no more than the fluid and silent masses, the variable equations of the polls, perpetual test objects that, like an acid, dissolve them. To test, survey, contact, solicit, inform— this is a bacterial tactic, a virulent tactic where the social ends through infinitesimal dissuasion, where it no longer even has time to crystallize. Once violence crystallized the social, forcefully giving birth to an antagonistic social energy. That is still the demiurge of Stalinism. Today, soft semiurgy guides us.

The question of a possible resistance to this invasive tactility, of a possible reversal of simulation on the basis of the death of the social, remains posed. The problem of a "desocialized" nebula and of the new processes of implosion that it produces. But to soft technologies, the communist party opposes only the artificial maintenance of a "mass" social apparatus and of an archaic ideology of "mobilization" such that everything is already much more mobile than it thinks, circulating with an uncontrollable mobility, *including the communist party itself,* entering, like everyone else, and despite itself, in a tactical movement, henceforth without a strategy, with real social or historical reference, long since recycled, but desperately affecting the contrary: solid infrastructures, irreducible finalities. But this archaic resistance serves once more as a functional specter for a society of tolerance, and as an ideological sanctuary for the conservation of the masses.

THE COMMUNIST PARTY has an idea of the masses, of economy, of politics, and of the revolution exactly as backward as the ideas it has had about culture, which it has always conceived of as bourgeois decorative realism and Leftist scientific objectivism. It is the doctrine of the figurative social, which is to say the equivalent in politics of figurative realism in painting. All the revolutions that have taken place since the nineteenth century in form, in space, in color have remained dead letters in politics, and singularly in revolutionary politics, which struggles with its vocation for the "historical" principle of truth, reality, and rationality. Not only can nothing be imagined that equals the deconstruction of the object in painting, abstraction (a deconstruction of political space, of the subject of history, of class reference?), but the new spiral that brought hyperrealism, a game reduced to representation *en abyme*, to the hypersimulation of the real, has had no equivalent in the political sphere until our day. Is there somewhere an idea, a hint, in the heads of politicians, that all their energies and their discussions can become something like the hyperrealist performances, hyper-representatives of an undiscoverable reality?

A table is always what it is, but there is no longer any reason to represent it "as it is."

A commodity is always what it is (though Marx already showed that it was already more than it was) but there is no longer any reason to speak of its use value, nor undoubtedly of its exchange value, which still arises from a space which represents the commodity.

The real itself is always what it is, but there is no longer any reason to think or to reflect on it as such.

The communist party itself, like the real, like the social, is always what it is, but it is undoubtedly precisely more than that: which is to say exhausted in its own resemblance. Hyper.

Because fundamentally the same labor (which is not even a work of mourning because it still has a melancholic reference, and it still bears, as in transference, a resolution; the death implicated in the work of mourning is still a *real* psychological event, and part of a history) the same labor of deconstruction, of abstraction, and of hyperrealisation that took place in the domain of visual representation and in sensorial perception undoubtedly has also taken place, undoubtedly without anyone's help, in the political, economic, and social spheres—and the still greater pregnancy of the social has long since no longer been that of a dead sociality, or hyperreal, like the still greater pregnancy of labor is no longer that of dead labor, of obsessive signs of defunct labor processes, like that of sex is only that of the sexual model hyperrealized in the omnipresent signs of liberation, in the inevitable scenario of pleasure, in the endless end of desire.

We are light years from everything said and done in this world, immersed, Left and Right, in its political realism. But perhaps this realist blindness only touches what one must call the "political class," alone in believing in politics and political representation, the way that advertisers are alone in their faith in advertisement.

The social, the idea of the social, the political, the idea of politics, have undoubtedly always been carried by only a minority faction. In place of conceiving of the social as a kind of original condition, a state of things that encompasses all the rest, an *a priori* transcendental given, like time and space (but precisely, time and space have long since been made relative as a code, while the social has never been—it is on the contrary reinforced as natural evidence: everything has become social, we swim in it as in a womb, socialism has even come to crown this by inscribing it as a future ideality—and everyone does sociology to death, we explore the smallest events, the smallest nuances of the social which question the axiom of the social itself). In place of this we need to ask who produced the social, who regulates this discourse, who deployed this code, fomented this universal simulation? Was it not a certain cultural, technical, rationalizing, humanist intelligentsia that found the means to conceive of everything else and to structure it in a universal concept (the only one perhaps) which was little by little found to be a grand reference: the silent masses, from whom the essence seemed to emerge, radiating the inextinguishable energy of the social. But have we reflected that most of the time neither these famous masses nor individuals live socially, which is to say in the perspectival, rationalist, panoptic space where the social and its discourse are reflected?

There are societies without the social, just as there are societies without writing. This seems absurd only because the terms themselves are absurd—if they are no more than societies, what are they? Groups, ethnicities, categories: we fall back into the same terminology—the distortion between hypothesis and discourse is irreparable. Referencing other "societies," how do we designate, here and now, that which, in the "masses" (who are supposed to incarnate the indistinction and generality of the social) lives beneath, or beyond, or outside of the social, and what is woven at this level? How do we designate this nonsense, the unnamable remains? This isn't about anarchy, about desocialization, but a profound, radical indifference in the *relationship to* and *determination of* the social as code, as *a priori* hegemonic system. This is not about a lapse, a gap, an accident of the social, nor about those who resist it through their singularity (madmen, drug addicts, homosexuals)—they are in fact the lead categories of the social and will one day be assigned their place in a fully comprehensive sociality. This is about something else, which is not really a remainder, an excess, or an exception, but something massive, banal, and indistinct, more powerful than the social, which does not transgress it, but which simply does not know its laws or its principles. Something that eludes representation, since the social and the political are the domain of representation and the law. What do we know of this massive, but not pervasive indifference, of this defiance through inertia even at the center of manipulation, what do we know of this zone where the social, which is meaning, has perhaps never been?

26

Our Theater of Cruelty

Mogadishu

IN THE TERRORIST ACT there is a simultaneous power of death and simulation which is intolerable to see confused with the "morbid taste of death," and with the frenzy of the "morbid" and the "spectacular." Living or dead, terrorism wins out elsewhere. At least by this single fact: it alone creates the event, and thus returns the whole "political" order to its nullity. And the media, all the while orchestrating the victory of order, only causes the evidence for the opposite to reverberate: to wit, that terrorism is burying the political order.

The media are terrorists in their own fashion, continually working to produce (good) sense, but, at the same time, violently defeating it by arousing everywhere a fascination without scruples, that is to say, a paralysis of meaning, to the profit of a single scenario.

Terrorism is not violent in itself; only the spectacle it unleashes is truly violent. It is our Theater of Cruelty, the only one that remains to us, perhaps equal in every respect to that of Artaud or to that of the Renaissance, and extraordinary in that it brings together *the spectacular and the challenge at their highest points*. It is at the same time a model of simulation, a micro-model flashing with a minimally real event and a maximal echo chamber, like a crystal thrown into an unstable solution or an experimental matrix, an insoluble equation which makes all the variables appear suddenly. Not a real event, but a condensed narrative, a flash, a scenario—that is to say, that which opposes to every event said to be real the purest form of the spectacular—and a ritual, or that which, of all possible events, opposes to the political and historical model or order the purest symbolic form of challenge.

A strange mixture of the symbolic and the spectacular, of challenge and simulation. This paradoxical configuration is the only original form of our time, and subversive because insoluble. There is neither victory nor defeat: no sense can be made of an event which is irremediably spectacular, or irremediably symbolic. Everything in terrorism is ambivalent and reversible: death, the media, violence, victory. Which plays into the other's hands? Death itself is undefinable: the death of the terrorists is equivalent to that of the hostages; they are substitutable. In spite of all the efforts to set them into radical opposition, fascination allows no distinction to be made, and rightly so, for the power finally does not make any either, but settles its accounts with everyone, and buries Baader and Schleyer together in Stuttgart in its incapacity to unravel the deaths and rediscover the fine dividing line, the distinctive and valid oppositions, which are the secret of law and order. Nor it is possible to reclaim a positive use for the media, or a transparency of repression: the repressive act traverses the same unforeseeable spiral as the terrorist act; no one knows where it will stop, nor all the setbacks and reversals that will ensue. No distinction is possible between the spectacular and the symbolic, no distinction between "crime" and "repression." *It is this uncontrollable eruption of reversibility that is the true victory of terrorism.*

This victory lies not at all in the fact of imposing a negotiation and forcing a government to capitulate. Besides, the objective—most of the time to liberate imprisoned comrades—is typically a zero-sum equation. The stakes are elsewhere. And if power wins out at the objective level, it loses at the level of real stakes. It loses its political definition, and is forced to accept, all the while trying to thwart the reversibility of all the actors in the same process. Terrorists, killers, hostages, leaders, spectators, public opinion—there is no innocence in a system which has no meaning. No tragedy either (in spite of the ideology of the Baader group itself, and the pedagogy of the terrorist model on a worldwide scale). The force of the terrorists comes to them precisely from the fact that they have no logic. The orders do: it is quick, effective, flawless, without scruples; it is why they 'win'. If the terrorists had one, they would no longer be terrorists. To demand that they be at the same time illogical, which gives them their power, and logical tacticians, which would make them successful, is absurd—again a fantasy of synthesis, and of defense on our part, which allow us to recuperate ourselves in the fury of defeat.

Hence the stupidity and the obscenity of all that is reported about the terrorists: everywhere the wish to palm off meaning on them, to exterminate them with meaning, which is more effective than bullets of specialized commandos (and all the while subjecting them elsewhere, in the prisons, to sensory deprivation). This rage for meaning still makes us, with the best will in the world, treat them like idiots incapable of going all the way and blowing up the airplane and the passengers, which makes us want them not to have "won."

Not only have they not won, but they have inordinately encouraged the sacred union of all the world forces of repression;

they have reinforced the political order, etc.—let's go all the way—they have killed their Stammheim comrades, since if they had not launched and then botched this operation, the others would still be alive. But all this participates in the same conspiracy of meaning, which amounts to setting an action in contradiction with itself (here to ends that were not desired, or according to a logic which was not its own). Strangulation.

Stammheim

THE INSOLUBLE POLEMIC on the manner in which Baader and his comrades died is itself obscene, and for the same reason: there is an equal obscenity in wanting to forcibly impose meaning on the hijackers' act and in wanting to restore Baader's death to the order of factual reality. Principle of meaning as principle of truth: there you have the real lifeblood of State terrorism.

It is to believe that the German government's strategy attains perfection in a single blow: not only does it link together in an almost improvised manner the bungled taking of hostages with the immediately subsequent liquidation of the prisoners who disturbed it, but it does so in such a way (coarse, equivocal, incoherent) that it traps everyone in the hysterical search for truth, which is the best way to abolish the symbolic futility of this death.

The hijackers made so many errors at Mogadishu that one can only think that they were done "on purpose." They have finally attained their objective obliquely, which was the challenge of their own death, the latter summing up the virtual one of all the hostages, and more radically, still, that of the power which kills them. For it absolutely must be repeated that the stakes are not to beat power on its own ground, but to oppose another political order of force. One knows nothing about terrorism if one does not see that it is not a question of real violence, nor of opposing one violence to another (which, owing to their disproportion, is absurd, and besides, all *real* violence, like real order in general, is always on the side of power), but to oppose to the *full* violence and to the *full* order a clearly superior model of extermination and virulence operating through emptiness.

The secret is to oppose the order of the real with an absolutely imaginary realm, absolutely ineffectual at the level of reality, but whose implosive energy absorbs everything real and all the violence of real power which founders there. Such a model is no longer of the order of transgression: repression and transgression are of the older order of the law, that is to say, of the order of a real *system* in expansion. In such a system, all that comes into contradiction with it, including the violence of its opposite, only makes the expansion accelerate. Here, the virulence comes from the implosion—and the death of the terrorists (or of the hostages) is of this implosive order: the abolition of value, of meaning, of the real, at a determined point. This point can be infinitesimal, and yet provokes a suction, an absorption, a gigantic convection, as could be seen at Mogadishu. Around this tiny point, the whole system of the real condenses, it tetanized, and launches all its anti-bodies. It becomes so dense that it goes beyond its own laws of equilibrium and involutes in it own over-effectiveness. At bottom, the profound tactic of simulation (for it's very much a matter of simulation in the terrorist model, and not of real death) is to provoke an excess of reality, and *to make the system collapse under it.*

If it is possible, then, to think that the hijackers have acted purposefully in order to meet their death, this kind of paradoxical death which shines intensely for a moment before falling back into the real, it is possible inversely to think that the German government itself did not commit so many errors in the Baader affairs except toward a well-defined end (even without desiring it). It was able to stage Baader's death neatly—he did not do it. Far from seeing therein a secondary episode, it must be seen as the *key* to the situation. By sowing this doubt, this deliberate ambiguity concerning the facts, it ensured that the truth about this death, and the death itself, became fascinating. Everyone exhausted himself in argument and in attempts at clarification—clarifications reinforced by the theatricality of the event which acts as a gigantic dissuasion of the terrorists' execution—everyone, and above all the revolutionaries who really wanted Baader to have been "assassinated." They too were vultures of the truth. What's the bloody difference anyway—suicides or victims of liquidation? The difference, of course, is that if they were liquidated and it can be proven, then the masses, guided by the truth of the facts, would know that the German State is fascist, and would mobilize in order to wreak revenge. What a load of rubbish. A death is romantic or it is not. And in the latter case, there is no need for revenge; it is of the imaginary order. What nonsense to fall back in the reality of a contract of revenge and equivalence! The avengers equal the moralists: always evaluate the price, and have the just price paid. It matters little that the "reality" of this death (the truth about…) is stolen from you, since it is not of the order of the real, and therein lies its force. You are the one you depreciates it by wanting to institute it as a fact, as capital with the value of death, and to exhaust it in death, whereas death at full price, not liquidated in the equivalence of meaning, and vengeance, opens a cycle of vertigo in which the system itself can only come to be implicated in the end, or brutally, through its own death. Such is the inspired maneuver of the German government, which consists in delivering through its "calculated" errors an unfinished product, an irrecoverable truth. Thus everyone will exhaust himself finishing the work, and going to the end of the truth. A subtle incitement to self-management. It is content to produce an event involving death; others will put the finishing touches on the job. The truth. Even among the very ones who revolt at Baader's death, no one sees through this trap, and all function with the same automatism on the fringe of open complicity which all intelligent power contrives to spread around its decisions.

Far from harming Baader, the flaws of Stammhaim stem from a strategy of simulation by the German State which alone would merit analysis and denunciation. A strategy of sacred union, and not at all moral, against the terrorist violence, but, much more profoundly, *a sacred union in the production of truth*, of the facts, of the real. Even if this truth explodes (if in fifteen years it is finally established that Baader was coldly liquidated), it will hardly be a scandal. No power will be frightened by it; if necessary, the crew of leaders will be changed. The price of the truth for power is superficial. On the other hand, the benefits of general mobilization, dissuasion, pacification, and mental socialization obtained through this crystallization of the truth are immense. A smart operation, under which Baader's death threatens to be buried indefinitely.

— Translated by John Johnston and Stuart Kendall

Notes

1. On *Utopie*, an interview with Jean Baudrillard

1. [Founder and figurehead of the National Front, an extreme right wing party that made news with its ascension during Mitterrand's two terms. From 1983 to 1998, Le Pen was in the news and collected, in certain elections, more than fifteen percent of the votes before his influence lessened after a split in his party at the beginning of 1999. When Baudrillard gave this interview, he had just published "De l'exorcisme en politique ou la conjuration des imbeciles" in *Libération* (May 7, 1997), wherein he asked: "Why has everything that is moral, faithful, and conformist, that was traditionally on the right, passed to the left?" This article was reprinted, the same month, by Éditions Sens&Tonka under the same title (in 2002, it would be republished with a second article, also on Le Pen, under the title, *Au royaume des aveugles...* also by Éditions Sens&Tonka). It was also reprinted in a collection of Baudrillard's "responses" from *Libération*, *Screened Out* (Verso, 2002).]

2. [The "Movement of March 22nd" was started at Nanterre, two months before the "events" of May 1968. So as to reduce the overcrowding that was threatening the walls of the old Sorbonne, an entirely new university was built in 1965 at Nanterre-la-Folie. Surrounded by slums, this university was of course frequented by rather well off students from Western Paris. The social contrast was sharp between the students and the residents of the city. The leftist militants rapidly took root and diverse strikes and demonstrations followed. In March 1967, an initial occupation of a girls dorm at the university—in the name of free circulation—sanctioned twenty nine expulsions. In November 1967, a massive strike ensued against the selection. In January 1968, Daniel Cohn-Bendit, still a student, heckled François Missoffe, the Minister of Youth and Sports—who had come to inaugurate the university pool—about the absence of accounting for questions of sexuality in youth politics. The same month, Dean Pierre Grappin called the police against the group that was already known as the "*enragés.*" Simultaneously, the struggle crystallized around the role of the human sciences and in particular of sociology in the capitalist system. When the news was filled with worker's strikes and the anti-war movement against Vietnam, militants

attacked the American Express Bank, on the Boulevard Saint-Germain in Paris on March 22nd. Several students from Nanterre were arrested. Demanding the liberation of their comrades, one hundred forty two students occupied the administration building at the university and wrote the manifesto of the "March 22nd Movement." General assemblies followed and their radicalization accompanied mounting tensions on campus prior to May. "March 22" was characterized by its relative "ecumenism" (the "movement" linked and mixed all the factions, anarchists, Trotskyists, Maoists... It unfolded outside of the groups) and its iconoclastic and heretical methods. On this "movement" see Jean Pierre Duteuil, *Nanterre, 1965–66–67–68, vers le mouvement du 22 mars* (Acratie, 1988).]

3. [An international congress on design was held in Aspen in 1970, organized by Rayner Banham among others. The French delegation was composed of Jean Aubert, Jean Baudrillard, François Barré (director of CGI), Gilles de Bure, Henri Ciriani, Claude (a designer, teaching at the *Institut de l'environnement*) and Françoise Braunstein, Roger (designer, teaching at ENSAD) and Nicole Tallon, Éric Le Comte (industrial designer), Odile Hanappe (economist, teaching at the Institut de l'environnement), Alain Fischer (geographer).]

4. [Hubert Tonka, ed. *Parc Ville Villette (Vaisseau de pierres)* (Princeton Architectural Press, 1988). *Trans.*]

5. [*Unités pédagogiques* was created in January 1969. These new architecture schools replaced the old "architecture" section of the *École nationale supérieure des beaux-arts*, the dismantling of which was decided at the end of the month of August 1968. Initially, eighteen *Unités pédagogiques* were created (thirteen in the provinces, five [then six in January 1969, then eight by the end of July 1969, and finally nine by 1974] in Paris). This marked the end of the singular *École nationale supérieure des beaux-arts*, maintained under the tutelage of the regional schools. The protesters on all sides assembled at first in UP 6. Several months later, Bernard Huet and his team left that effervescent "hive" to found UP 8. During this time, the students close to the communist party founded their school, UP 1. On another side, the "conservative" teachers, nostalgic for the old school, gathered essentially within UP 4. A split would intervene several years later resulting in the creation of UP 9. Today, these two schools are still strongly marked by the conservative style of the teachers who started them. UP 3 was founded at Verseilles. Initially conceived as rather conservative, the school has been profoundly renewed through the 1970s around the instructional team assembled by Louis Arretche, by the acts of a fringe of research-educators that strongly contributed, in France, to the renewal of urbanism. The UP became *Écoles d'architecture* [EA] with Duport's reforms in 1984.]

3. The Ephemeral

1. [*Utopie* (1967–1969) contrived a "critical column" wherein a member of the group could express themselves in counterpoint or disagreement with the group. This "note" appeared alongside Jean Aubert's article "Devenir suranné, considérations sur l'obsolescence du 'construit dans la ville'."]

4. Play and the Police

1. [CRS. Compagnie républicaine de sécurité. A state police force. *Trans.*]

2. In his recent work *La Révolte contre le Père* (Payot, IMS), Gérard Mendal also came to the conclusion that social Power in industrial society represents a confusion of the two parents in the collective soul.

3. I am not afraid to reference my own work: see *The System of Objects* (1968).

4. It is in this double sense that we understand "consumption": culpability at once savors itself in an object which satisfies delectation and this shared pleasure founds a collective value, in complicity with the group and with cultural privilege.

5. Herbert Marcuse, *Fin de l'Utopie* (Éditions de Minuit) 10.

6. It is perhaps a law that affinity was in the same air of the civilization, therefore in the same symbolic field, collusion between order and disorder, between Law and subversion. A disavowal of the regressive type perhaps corresponds to a society with a regressive tendency, a pure transgression, and no longer an historical and politically conscious "revolution."

5. Technics as Social Practice

1. The socialist countries have elevated the power of technical culture. However, it seems that at the end of a period, the scale of traditional values, in a hurried moment, tends to reconstitute itself, benefiting cultural values. In any case, the profound changes in cultural habitus can only appear over the long term.

2. See Edgar Morin, *Cinema, or Imaginary Man* trans. Lorraine Mortimer (Minneapolis: University of Minnesota Press, 2005).

3. This does not exclude the real changes that technology engenders every day in social relations and in everyday life. These are incontestable and considerable. Simply put, these changes operate *within the system* whose precise function is to control evolution and make sure that the changes never initiate open contradictions.

4. Speaking rigorously, this principle has nothing to do with science or constituted technics. One must separate "the" technic from its absolute use, so as to reveal its concrete efficacy, wherein it is always the technique for something: training and rational exercise.

8. Requiem for the Media

1. Marshall McLuhan, *War and Peace in the Global Village* (New York: McGraw-Hill, 1968) 5.

2. Hans Magnus Enzensberger, "Constituents of a Theory of the Media" *The Consciousness Industry* (New York: The Seabury Press, 1974) 96–128. Originally published in the *New Left Review* (Autumn 1970).

3. This political economy of the sign is structural linguistics (along with semiology and all its derivatives, of which communication theory will be discussed below). We know that, in the general ideological framework, structural linguistics is today's master discipline, informing anthropology, the human sciences, etc., just as political economy did in its time; it's postulates profoundly informed all of psychology, sociology, and the "moral and political" sciences.

4. In this sense, the expression "consciousness industry" which Enzensberger uses to characterize the present media, is nothing but a dangerous metaphor. It supports his entire analytic hypothesis, which is to extend to the media the Marxist analysis of the capitalist mode of production, to the point of rediscovering a structural analogy in these relations:

dominant class	dominated class
producer-entrepreneur	consumer
transmitter	receiver

5. In fact, Marxist analysis can be questioned on two very different levels of radicality: insofar it is a system of interpretation for the separated order of material production and insofar as it is a system of interpretation for the separated order of production (in general).

In the first case, the hypothesis of the non-pertinence of the dialectic outside the field of its "origin" should logically be extended: if the "dialectical" contradictions between productive forces and relations of production largely efface themselves in the field of language, signs and ideology—*maybe they have never truly been at work in the field of material production either*, since a certain capitalist development of productive forces was able to absorb them, not every conflict of course, but the revolutionary antagonisms at the level of social relations. What is therefore the validity of these concepts, if not a purely conceptual coherence?

In the second case, it is at the root itself (and not in its diverse contents) that the concept of production should be questioned, with the separated form that it institutes, with the schema of representation and of rationalization that it imposes. It is undoubtedly there, at the extreme, that one must go.

6. One finds this type of reductive determinism in Bourdieu and in the phraseology of the Communist Party. It is without theoretical value. It makes of the *mechanism* of democratization a revolutionary *value* in itself. That the intellectuals repudiate mass culture does not suffice to make a revolutionary alternative. The aristocrats frown on bourgeois culture in the same way: this never sufficed to make the latter anything but a class culture.

7. [ORTF. French radio and television headquarters. *Trans.*]

8. Thus the institutions of power and of the state according to whether they are in the grip of capital or if the people have taken them over, empty themselves or are filled with revolutionary content, without their form ever being interrogated.

9. Enzensberger, *op. cit.*, 105, 108.

10. *Ibid.*, 97.

11. *Ibid.*, 107.

12. [See Bertolt Brecht, "The Radio as an Apparatus of Communication" (1932) in John Willett, ed. *Brecht on Theatre* (New York: Hill and Wang, 1964) 51–53. *Trans.*]

13. Enzensberger, *op. cit.*, 97–98.

14. This is not a question of "dialogue," which is never anything but the functional adjustment of two abstract speeches without response, wherein the two "interlocutors" are never present one to the other, but only their stylized speech.

15. We can see that taking the ORTF in May '68 would have changed nothing in itself, other than to scuttle the ORTF as such: the entire technical and functional structure of it reflects the monopolistic use of speech.

16. [Roland Barthes, *S/Z* trans. Richard Miller (New York: Farrar, Straus and Giroux, 1974) 4. *Trans.*]

17. Multifunctionality evidently changes nothing here. Multifunctionality, pluridisciplinarity, polyvalence in all its forms are the responses of the system to its

own obsession with centrality and uni-equivalence. They are reactions of the system to its own pathology, but they leave its logic untouched.

18. Enzensberger interprets it in this way: "'Medium is the message' is a *bourgeois* proposition. It signifies that the bourgeoisie has nothing left to say. Having no further message to transmit, it plays the card of medium for medium's sake. If the bourgeoisie has nothing left to say, 'socialism' would do better to keep quiet."

19. This distinction has no meaning in relation to the media. We can give them credit for having largely contributed to its effacement. The distinction is linked with an order characterized by the *transcendence* of politics, and it has nothing to do with what is announced in many forms as the *transversality* of politics. But we should not be fooled: the media only contribute to the liquidation of the transcendence of politics so as to substitute their own transcendence, that abstraction of the form of the mass media that is definitively integrated and offers nothing more than the structure of conflict (Left/Right). Transcendence in the mass media is therefore a reduction of the traditional transcendence of politics, but it is still much more than the new transversality of politics.

20. This form of "exposure" or "propagation" is also to be found in the fields of science and art. Generalized reproducibility obliterates the process of work and of meaning so as to deliver contents as a model of itself (cf. *Diogène* nº 68 (1969); Raoul Ergmann, *Le miroir en miettes*; Baudouin Jurdant, *La vulgarisation scientifique*).

21. We should note that this labor always doubles a work of selection and of reinterpretation at the level of group adherence (Lazarfeld's *two-step flow of communication*). Hence the highly relative pregnancy of the contents of the media and the multiple resistances that it provokes. (We should ask ourselves, however, if these resistances intend, even more than the contents, toward the abstraction of the media itself: in this sense, Lazarfeld's double articulation would, since the second articulation is a network of *personal* relations, opposed to the generality of the media's messages.) Significantly, this "second" reading, wherein group membership opposes its own code to that of the transmitters (cf. Umberto Eco's thesis, discussed below), not to neutralize it, to "reduce" its dominant ideological contents in the same way as critical or subversive *contents*. To the extent that the first (cultural models, systems of imposed values without alternative or response, bureaucratic contents) are homogeneous with the general mass mediated form (non-reciprocal, irresponsibility) and integrate themselves therein through redoubling, there is as an effect of over-determination and therefore a pregnancy greater than the dominant ideological contents. This "passes" better than the subversive contents. But it is not essential. It must be recognized that the *form* of transgression does not pass "more or less;" it is radically denied by the form of the mass media.

22. For Walter Benjamin, in "The Work of Art in the Age of Mechanical Reproduction," the reproduced work becomes increasingly "designed for reproduction." For Benjamin, therefore, the work passes from ritual to "politics." The "exhibition value" revolutionizes the work of art and its functions.

23. [An agreement reached by representatives of the CGT and Georges Pompidou in May 1968. *Trans.*]

24. Jerry Rubin, *Do It* (New York: Simon and Schuster, 1970) 234.

25. The two terms are so minimally present, one to the other, that it is necessary to create the category of "contact" to theoretically reconstitute the group!

26. The developed form of this opens logically onto analysis in terms of classical political economy. In *La communciation de masse* (S.G.P.P, 1971), Burgelin discusses mass communication as a "*market* of messages," repeating all the schemas of liberal economy: competition, offer and demand, equilibrium, needs and consumer "choice," etc. This is the *unchanged* extension of bourgeois political economy, just as Enzensberger extends *unchanged* the critique of that political economy.

27. Enzensberger, *op. cit.*, 119, 127.

28. *Ibid.*, 97.

29. Here again, Enzensberger, who analyzes and denounces this integration of control circuits, meanwhile connects with this incorrigible idealism: "Naturally [!] such tendencies go against the grain of the structure, and the new productive forces not only permit, but indeed demand [!] their reversal"(108). Feed-back and interaction are the *logic* of cybernetics, and there is the same illusion in underestimating the possibilities of the system for integrating these "revolutionary" innovations as in underestimating the capacity of capitalism to develop the forces of production.

30. Enzensberger draws his argument from the fact that Xerox retains its monopoly on photo-copying (the possibility of general "free press") and only rents at exorbitant rates. But having our own Xerox or short wave-length is inessential. The true monopoly is never that of technical means but that of speech.

31. Enzensberger, *op. cit.*, 110.

32. This is why the *individual* amateur cameraman remains in the separated abstraction of *mass* communication. Through this internal dissociation between the two authorities, the entire code and all of the dominant models engulf and seize his practice.

9. DNA or the Metaphysics of the Code

1. [Jacques Monod (1910–1976) shared the Nobel Prize in Medicine with François Jacob and André Lwoff in 1965 for his work in genetics. See Jacques Monod, *Le hasard et la nécessité: essai sur la philosophie naturelle de la biologie moderne* (Paris: Seuil, 1970). *Trans.*]

2. *Planning Programming Budgeting System*: an apparatus processing information for all projected and operational ends.

3. [François Jacob, *La Logique du Vivant: une histoire de l'hérédité.* (Paris: Gallimard, Tel, 1970). *Trans.*]

4. In "archaic" exchange, nothing is left out of meaning or objectified as non-living. No nature, inert, submitted to an abstract and unitary principle of reality. Ambivalence acts on all things. What is left of exchange, of communication, of meaning in Monod's theory? The "stereospecific complex" revived by Morin in molecular Eros. This mode of nuclear affinity, founded on covalence and reading information, is the reduction of all exchange: coded similitudes or non-similitudes are the image of cyberbetic social exchange.

10. The Mirror of Production

1. Marx evidently played an essential role in rooting this productivist metaphor. Marx radicalized and definitively rationalized the concept of production, he "made it" dialectical, and gave it its title of revolutionary nobility. It is in large part through unconditional reference to Marx that this concept pursues its prodigious career.

2. Karl Marx, *The German Ideology* (New York: International Publishers, 1947) 16.

3. *Ibid.*, 7.

4. See Jean Baudrillard, *For a Critique of the Political Economy of the Sign* [1972] trans. Charles Levin (St. Louis, MO: Telos Press, 1981).

5. "Notes on Wagner" in *Theoretical Practice* 5 (Spring 1972) 51–52.

6. Pierre Naville, *Le nouveau léviathan* (Paris: Riviàre, 1954) 371.

7. Karl Marx, *Contribution to a Critique of Political Economy* (New York: International Publishers, 1904) 33.

8. Another great disjunction on which the critique of political economy articulates itself: the technical and social divisions of labor—subjected to the same analysis. Transfiguring the technical division as both sides of the social division, it preserves with the same blow the fiction of an ideal distribution of labor, of a "non-alienated" concrete productivity, and it universalizes the technical mode and technical rationale. Thus the dialectic of productive forces and relations of productivity: everywhere the "dialectical" contradiction ends in a Mobius strip, though in the meantime it has had the time to circumscribe the field of production and to universalize it.

9. Karl Marx, *Contribution to the Critique of Political Economy*, *op. cit.*, 298–299.

10. Karl Marx, *Grundrisse* (London: Pelican, 1973) 527.

11. We will come back to this reciprocal neutralization of the theory and the object in relation to the rapports between Marxist theory and the workers' movement.

12. This is not to say that they have *never existed*: another paradox to which we will have to return.

13. The same for nature: not only the exploitation of nature as productive force, but the over-determination of nature as referent, as "objective" reality, by the code of political economy.

14. Karl Marx, *Manuscripts of 1844*. [Unlocatable. *Trans*.]

15. Herbert Marcuse, "On the Concept of Labor" *Telos* 16 (Summer 1973) 11–12.

16. Easton and Guddat, eds., *Writings of the Young Marx on Philosophy and Society* (New York: Anchor, 1969) 322, 332.

17. Karl Marx, *Capital* vol. 1 (Moscow: Foreign Languages Publishing House) 42–43.

18. *Ibid.*, 177.

19. Engels, always a naturalist, goes on to praise the role play by labor in the transition from ape to man.

20. Marcuse, *op. cit.*, 22.

21. *Ibid.*, 15.

22. *Ibid.*, 25.

23. Walter Benjamin, "Theses on the Philosophy of History" in *Illuminations* trans. Harry Zohn (New York: Schocken, 1969) 259.

24. Paul Lafargue, *The Right to be Lazy* trans. C. Kerr (Chicago: Kerr, 1917) 9.

25. Insofar as it conceives of man as the union of a soul and a body—which took place, as we know, in an extraordinary "dialectical" flowering during the Christian Middles Ages.

26. This autonomization is the key which turns Marxism toward social-democracy, the key to its present revisionism, and to its total positivist degradation (which also includes bureaucratic Stalinism as well as Social Democractic liberalism).

27. Marx, *Capital, op. cit.*, III, 799–800.

28. Marcuse, *Eros and Civilization* (New York: Vintage, 1962) 178.

29. See Julia Kristeva, *Sèméiotikè: recherches pour une sémanalyse* (Paris, Seuil, 1969).

30. Marx, *Capital, op. cit.*, I, 43–44.

31. *Ibid.*, I, 195.

32. For example, this passage from Marx on the social hieroglyph: "Value, therefore, does not stalk about with a label describing what it is. It is value, rather, that converts every product into a social hieroglyphic. Later on, we try to decipher the hieroglyphic, to get behind the secret of our own social products; for to stamp an object of utility as a value is just as much a social product as language" (*Capital, op. cit.*, I, 74). The entirety of this analysis of the mystery of value remains fundamental. But far from only being valuable for the distributed and exchanged product of labor, it already works for the product of labor (and for labor itself) understood as a "useful object." The utility (that of labor as well) is already this socially produced and socially determined hieroglyphic abstraction. The entire anthropology of "primitive" exchange forces us to shatter the natural evidence of utility and recreate the historical and social genesis of use value as Marx did exchange value. Only then will the hieroglyph be totally deciphered and the spell of value be radically exorcised.

33. Why not?

11. Marxism and the System of Political Economy

1. Louis Althusser, *Reading Capital* trans. Ben Brewster (London: Verso, 1979) 124.

2. *Ibid.*

3. *Ibid.*

4. *Ibid.*, 125.

5. Lukacs' concept of "reification" undoubtedly constitutes the only attempt at critical theoretical development between Marx and the Situationists.

6. Marx, *The Poverty of Philosophy* (New York: International Publishers, 1936) 42.

7. From this comes the artificial oligopoly on which the real monopoly is stabilized. Similarly, bipartisanism is the optimal political form for the functioning of monopoly power by a single class; and the peaceful coexistence of two powers (soon three) is the stabilized form of world imperialism.

8. See "Fetishism and Ideology" in Baudrillard, *For a Critique of the Political Economy of the Sign, op. cit.*, 88–101.

9. Economically, this process culminates in the virtual international autonomy of finance capital, in the uncontrollable play of floating capital. Once currencies are extracted from every productive caution, and even from all reference to the gold standard, general equivalence becomes the strategic place of manipulation: real production is subordinated to it everywhere. This apogee of the system corresponds to the triumph of the code.

10. This division is already in place in the universities and *grandes écoles*.

11. See for example the establishment, in the United States, of an indefinite salary-unemployment that neutralizes entire groups as producers, while maintaining them as consumers. This is no longer a question of the strategy of the "reserve army of capital," but of testing everyone and, as in school (this society sends everyone to school), of social availability and transformation (at a cost of enormous financial "sacrifices," but who would not make sacrifices for the reproduction of the system) of whole categories into idle and parasitic clients of the system. No longer wild exploitation, but tutelage and relegation.

12. But one can always ask if this demobilization, this virtual *lock out* responds to the secret exigencies of the calculus of productivity, therefore of the system itself in its reproduction (since it extends to the point of financing nonproductive marginality), or if it really constitutes, through disinvestment and growing defection, a model of subversion.

13. Through "scientific" analysis, linguistics and semiology direct the social exclusion of speech, which defends the code: the life and death of the system is played out, in a less spectacular though nevertheless political way, in the code.

14. But one can also intend to pass simply to the other side of the line to become the marked term, to change positions without breaking the code: the "white" black, etc.

15. To the point of appearing archaic before technocratic reformism: hours of their choice, job enrichment, non-line assembly. The unions resist innovation. Justly, but on a conservative basis.

16. This would mean that the traditional contradictions have no more than an apparent meaning: but perhaps they never had anything more than that?

17. The planetary extension, of the economic and political kind, of capitalism is only the "extensive" modality of this deepening of capital. Significantly, the analysis of "imperialism" is generally limited to this level.

18. Pierre Bourdieu and Jean-Claude Passeron *Reproduction in Education, Society and Culture* (1970) (London: Sage Publications, 1977).

19. See Jean Baudrillard, *The Consumer Society: Myths and Structures* (1970) (London: Sage Publications, 1998).

20. The autonomy of faculties is, as we know, the best way to align them with capitalist productivity; even the independence of colonized countries was the best way to perpetuate and modernize their exploitation.

21. Thus idealist simulation and materialist simulation meet up: their common schema is the separation of authorities. Under the jurisdiction of one among them (the same schema in the semiological reduction). (cf. *Nouvelle Revue de psychanalyse* n° 2)

22. This confusion institutes itself, here again, by creating it beside totalitarianism, which is to say total control, the total control of the class, under the sign of reason, through an organizational authority. Class consciousness, this idealist vision, has in fact only a single mode of objective existence, the party. It is not the class which, in its own movement, offers the party or the organization as dialectical mediation of its practice, it is the bureaucracy itself which, through the extension of its power, secretes class consciousness as its ideology. Lukacs, when he wrote *History and Class Consciousness*, was not anti-Stalinist. He was in the Stalinist movement. He offered the bureaucracy its philosophy of History, a reflexive philosophy of the class as a Subject, through which the triumphant bureaucracy was able to historically idealize its totalitarian practice.

23. In this regard, Lukacs' beautiful dialectic, of *History and Class Consciousness*, takes on an entirely ambiguous meaning: the rational vocation of class as subject of history, the articulation of this process across the consciousness that the class has of itself: everything is here for hypostasizing the being of the class, for the triumph of a reality principle and of the representability of the class, and therefore fundamentally for the triumph of the party. At a first level, this dialectical and "spontaneous," collective class consciousness seems to contradict the bureaucratic process (which the Stalinists, always superficial, violently attacked). But at a deeper level, there is a collusion between a *rationalist* theory of consciousness and the formal *rationality* of bureaucracy. It is not an accident that Lukacs' dialectical and spontaneous theory appeared in the same moment that the bureaucratic monopoly of the party was reinforced. His theory does not fundamentally object to this process since, sealing a reflected essence, a class rationality, a for-itself of the Subject of History, it necessarily establishes a logic of representation and of identification with an ideal authority (in some way the "ego ideal" of the class). This authority can only be the organization and the party. The paranoiac machine of bureaucracy corresponds profoundly with the imaginary Subject of History. (In the same way that the idealization of the subject of consciousness is contemporary, throughout all of Western history, with the extension of the rational control of the State. The same operation rebounds in Lukacs at the level of the class.) Stalinist again, he wrote *The Destruction of Reason* to denounce the irrationality of fascism. But fascism is irrational only for bourgeois democracy; in fact it incarnates a limit for paranoid rationality, a limit from which nothing can protect "dialectical rationality" when it falls into the imaginary transcendence of a subject, the proletarian class. The *exchange value of labor*—the level of exploitation and dialectical contradiction—cannot be built on such an abstraction (with Stalin, it will build itself logically). Marxist theory preserves the *use value* of labor at one level, a level irreducible to the positive of value, mirror of a human positivity of labor, wherein the proletarian class, slipping from negative to positive, comes to recognize itself. Use value, here again, plays the villain in Marxist theory.

24. Here referencing Kalivoda's *Marx et Freud* (Paris: Editions Anthropos, 1971).

25. Similarly, Christian History, the Christian concept of historicity, is born from the failure of parousia.

26. Socialism in one country would be the realization of this qualification in which the proletariat is located, from this substantialization of negativity, of which history, as the *final* dimension, becomes the objective dimension. Initially, the negative subject of the historical dialectic, then simply the positive subject of the positivist history of the revolution. This enormous side-slipping only becomes possible and is only explained by the passage from utopia to the historical *epoché*.

27. [A Situationist slogan from May 1968. *Trans.*]

28. It is not true that Marx "dialectically surpassed" utopia, conserving its "project" in the "scientific" model of revolution. Marx wrote *Revolution according to the Law*, and did not perform the dialectical synthesis of this necessary term and of the passionate, immediate, utopian demand for the transfusion of social relations, because any dialectic between these two antagonistic terms is empty. What historical materialism surpasses while conserving is quite simply political economy.

29. It took a long time to sketch the outline of a work which, once completed, would return to oblivion and nothingness. We know that it's false: the sketch is already the entire work, there is nothing else.

12. Strike Story

1. [Confédération générale du travail. The major association of French trade unions. *Trans.*]

2. Even blackmail, every element under a sharp eye, between Israel, the Arab states and on the backs of the Palestinians. "Either you liquidate the Palestinian resistance, or we liquidate you." A colonial situation par excellence: the colonists always seeking, and often succeeding, in deploying their police through the colonized.

3. *Le Monde* (15 May 1973).

4. The stage is that of missile programs, of the Concorde, of military programs, of the inflation of the industrial park, of social and individual infrastructural equipment, of programs for development and recycling, etc. One must produce no matter what, at any price, according to constraints of investment and development (and no longer exactly as a function of the rates of surplus value). In this reproductive planning, the masterpiece of the genre promises to be anti-pollution, wherein the entire productive system recycles itself through the elimination of its own wastes—the gigantic equation resulting in nothing—not nothing though, rather the greater glory of reproduction.

5. Thus, through the same effect on the terminological level, the entire world becomes specialized workers (signal men-specialized for the heavens, the CDR no longer want to be the specialized workers of the *Union pour la défense de la République* [a right wing political party]; the auxiliary specialized workers in teaching, etc.) from the moment when the word is stretched from the vocubulary of the factory.

6. The entire problem of birth control, of biological "reproduction," remains to be analyzed in the same sense. It is to the extent that procreation begins to be

perceived as a pure and simple dimension of the reproduction of the system that it becomes insupportable and that it is collectively questioned.

7. This theory wants to save this concept by giving it a definition larger than Marx himself did, by implicating the "middle classes" in it: an illegitimate attempt at integrating "modern sociology" in an unchanging Marxist theory.

8. But does this illusion dissipate in the salary guide, there precisely where the "code" of exchange value becomes evident? Yes and no. If the salary is experienced as equivalent (even insufficient) to the labor, it does not efface the illusion; it remains within the internal logic of production. Also, of course, if the salary appears as what it profoundly is—"the political price paid for participation in the world of work"—not as the equivalent of labor power but as a sign of the division of labor and as a designation of the general code of labor. In this sense, demands for equal pay for everyone (or its variants: the struggle against qualifications, etc.) effectively surpass its economic aspect: it intends, in a misdirected form, the end of the division of labor (which is to say of labor as a social relation) and the end of the law of equal footing, fundamental for the capitalist system, of the equivalence of salary and labor power. It targets, therefore, indirectly, the form of political economy.

But salary is a sign, an element of the code in a still more radical sense. There is a fundamental law which regulates social discrimination in the material of labor: against every lived appearance (the laborer offers his labor to the capitalist), *the capitalist offers labor to the laborer* (the laborer, himself, offers *capital* to the capitalist). *Arbeitgeber* in German. The entrepreneur "offers labor"; the worker, *Arbeitnehmer*, "takes work." In the material of labor it is the capitalist who offers, who has the initiative of the gift, which assures him, just as in the schema of the primitive gift, a complete social preeminence, a superiority which goes well beyond economics. The refusal of labor, in its radical form, is the refusal of this symbolic domination, of this humiliation of the awarded thing. At this level, labor, the gift and the "grip" of labor functions directly as code. And the salary is the mark of this poisoned present, the sign which summarizes the entire code. It sanctions this unilateral gift of labor. It transforms the employee into a "receiver of goods" (a consumer), which is to say once again into an inferior, in the dominant terms of the social relation—or again the salary is that by which capital symbolically "redeems" the domination that it exerts through the gift of labor. To refuse labor, to contest the salary, is therefore to question the process of redemption and compensation, which is to say the entire symbolic functioning of the capitalist system (far more than economic since, at the limit, capital can function economically with less and less labor and the salary system is considerably more flexible).

But one can only say that the system suppresses use value only if one admits that it once existed, that there have been real needs, real use values, from "productive" labor. Use value might therefore not have always been only exchange value's alibi (at base the "Critique of the Political Economy of the Sign"!).

Besides, if it was, why would the system undermine itself by liquidating it? Didn't it only fulfill its own law, the law of value, the perfection of that law (the radicality of exchange value) being at the same time its own death? Another Marxist perspective!

9. Which is not true in the order of discrimination. In the order of the difference through signs, racism, sexism, etc. everything is on one side and nothing on the other. The principle of exclusion (and of oppression) which functions across the code and signs, is much more radical than the principle of exploitation.

13. The Dramatization of Economics

1. The American Senate went so far as to evaluate what it would cost to return water to the degree of purity that it had before the European conquest of America (the "1491 norm," Christopher Colombus having as we know disembarked in 1492): $ 350 billion dollars [1974]. But the billions of dollars hardly matter, because what the Senators, who don't give a damn about water, were really calculating was the price that it would cost to return the system itself to the original purity of primitive accumulation, to the golden age of labor power. The 1890 norm, or 1840?

In the same way, the current monetary system dreams of gold and of the Gold Standard, as a stabilizer or regenerator of fiduciary values. Because free and unlimited speculations on the basis of the loss of referent / gold—present state of things—tempts catastrophe at every moment: arbitrary, inflation so gigantic that the authority itself of money teeters and loses all credibility. Here again, a cyclical regeneration through referentiality, a "critical" regeneration is necessary so that financial exchange won't pass to the end of their irreality, where they would destroy themselves.

2. The homology posed by Saussure between signifier and salary on the one hand, and signified and labor on the other, is verified here at a much more advanced level than that imagined by Saussure. In the sense that today every necessary relation is abolished between salary and labor, as it is between signifier and signified. Production and the sign simultaneously lose their reference. And the escalation begins with this loss of referent.
— Production, which is no longer linked by "needs" or even by profit, enters into unlimited productivity.
— Salary, which is no longer linked (even less in the conscience of the employees) through equivalence and labor—value, enters into the game of unlimited political demands.
— Similarly the game of signifiers enters into an unlimited combination, from the moment they are no longer indexed by a "real" signified.

3. Inflation is to currency what the escalation of salaries is to labor power. In both cases, the same disengagement triggers the same excitement and the same structural crisis. Disengagement of salary with the "just" value of labor power (it's use value for the system) —disengagement of currency speculation with real production and its standardization (gold). Inflation in salaries and monetary inflation both result in the same loss of reference. They are inseparable. And the energy crisis offers both an alibi and a perfect dissuasion at once: henceforth, inflation, a structural crisis within the system, can be blamed on the Arabs (and others) overbidding, on the price of raw materials, "naturalized" in Arab terms—and the disaffection of the productivist system, which expresses among other things the "maximalist salary challenge," will be able to be stopped, frustrated by the blackmail of poverty, which is to say by the *blackmail of use value*, of the economic system itself.

4. The same twist for the threat to withdraw their bank deposits and gold reserves from Western banks.

5. The tacit coalition of the two Greats manipulating the Arabs so as to neutralize Europe and Japan and to thereby secure their world economico-political monopoly (see *Le Monde* January 1st, 1974).

6. But, look: simulation is not dissimulation! It is useless, for example in politics, to imagine that the Right manipulates the Left or inversely: this again raises a nostalgia for politics and for a retrospective truth of Right and Left. No, the impression of the total simulacra of the "political life" comes precisely from the perfect commutability of Right and Left in a regulated opposition emptied of all ideological substance.

7. Communist party members and orthodox Marxists are now the only ones who still cling to a real (petit-)bourgeois ideological discourse. The supporters of Marxism are the only ones with red fears. There is a near total discursive substitution between the Christians and the Marxists (cf. the week of Marxist Thought, the theme "Is there a revolutionary morality?" To the extent that all the others became Marxists, the Marxists become Kantians. The Christians say: "the ethical location is displaced: from individual conscience to the group confronted by historical necessities": class revolutionary morality. At the same time, Lucien Sève, Chairman of the French communist party says: "Every class society always essentially contradicts the Kantian moral imperative; to treat man as an end and not a means." And, to the Marxist who defends "the dignity of labor and personal dignity…polluted by the capitalist system in agony"(!), the Christian reproach of "overvaluing labor, neglecting what remains of will to power in every man even in a socialist society, not denouncing development at all costs strongly enough," and he demands that "we not only treat man as a being with needs, but as a being with desires." Only a Christian can say that today. And before that, the Marxist trembles, and shits in his shorts from ideological concupiscence. He will need another fifty years to get there.

N.B.—Look. If the Marxists are not even Christians, the Christians, and everyone who talks about a "desiring being" and of "revolutionary ethics" are still only Christians.

15. Animals Sick from Surplus Value

1. See *Science et avenir* (Juillet 1973).

16. Death Trick

1. Cryogenic freezing, sealing yourself in a gel so as to be resurrected, is the limit form of this practice.

2. See Michel de Certeau, Dominique Julia, and Jacques Revel, "La Beauté du mort" *Politique Aujourd'hui* (December 1970).

19. Death to Savages

1. Hence also, in "The Mirror of Production": "This is why there is properly speaking neither necessity or rarity in the primitive order, from which all symbolic strategy intends to exorcise the apparition of the law [...] consumption of the surplus and deliberate anti-production when accumulation threatens to shatter reciprocity and to make power surge up."

How do we conceive of this "exorcised risk"? Is it the lot of primitive societies, of a preventative wisdom? Is it still an ethnocentric position to attribute the "intention" to archaic societies (even if this intention is deferred to unconscious activity) to elude the risks of power, since such an intention would suppose knowledge of the risks and the reflective experience of what one can do? To say that symbolic exchange intends to block the emergence of power, is this not to defer to a preparatory experience of non-reciprocity?

Ethnocentrism is also dialectical: doesn't it reintroduce it to say that symbolic exchange is the negation of the power relation (the other present at the heart of the same)?

21. The Spiraling Cadaver

1. [Jean Baudrillard distributed this text in the university during the month of May.]

22. Labor Story

1. "Those who give the best of themselves"; disgusting, it's deservedly the inverse, this work is the worst, everyone agrees;

"... has the right to an equitable share": that's all? What the hell, all or nothing. And certainly not the "right" or "equitable," which is always the part left to the dog;

"... they too": now that beats all. The others have already had their share (equitable), so who hasn't? How is this possible? Absurd. Like he said. All the people are equal but some are more equal than others.

Etc. etc. but that's essentially it.

2. The worker welded to the yap of John Wayne.

23. Value's Last Tango

1. Besides, the present strike naturally takes on the same aspects as labor: the same suspense, the same weight, the same absence of objectives, the allergy to decision, the same turns of power, the same mourning for energy, the same indefinite circularity in the strike today as in the strike of days gone by, the same situation in the counter-institution that is the institution: the contagion grows, the circle is closed—after that it will be necessary to emerge elsewhere. Or rather, no: Take this impasse itself as the basic situation, to return indecision and the absence of objective as an offensive situation, as a strategy. Seeking at all costs to tear themselves from this mortal situation, from the mental anorexia of the university, the students only reinsert themselves in the energy of an institution in an outmoded coma. This is forced survival, it is the medicine of despair, practiced today on institutions as on individuals, and that everywhere is the sign of the same incapacity to confront death. "One must push what is collapsing," said Nietzsche.

24. The Magic Struggle or the Final Flute

1. [Censor [Gianfranco Sanguinetti], *The Real Report on the Last Chance to Save Capitalism in Italy* (1976) trans. Len Bracken (Fort Bragg: Flatland Books, 1997). *Trans.*]

2. [The Italian Communist Party secretary. *Trans.*]

3. Insofar as they are *revolutionaries*, things are of course very different, and there is a lot to say about this. Between the immorality of capital and the vitality of the exercise of power, and the incurable morality that henceforth forbid the exercise of political power to the communists (the two historically growing together), another path had been engendered by the proletariat in the 19th century, in the crushed insurrections, and singularly in the Commune, a direct defiance of power with death. Marx has been reproached for his lack of interest in the worker's struggles except after they have been crushed (*The Class Struggles in France, 18th Brumaire, The Commune*). No fool, Marx. Because in the end, that's when they become interesting: when the subject of history is crushed. For once Marx is *immoral* and pushes something in the destruction of what it holds most dear: this linear finality or

dialectic of Reason, this victorious proletarian reason—perhaps it profoundly understands the absurdity of all this and of taking power? Perhaps he understood power, as Lenin and Stalin eventually did, and, behind the ascendant calculation of history, estimated that the elimination of the "class" (the senseless, immediate elimination of the class-subject, without waiting for the rational elimination of the dominant class) was still the only possible defiance. Fundamentally, it was only the good proletariat, like the good Indian, who died. It's true for the bureaucracy, which founded its cynical strategy on the eternity of the dead proletariat. But it's true in another sense, deadly for all power and all bureaucracy. At certain moments in history, the proletariat acts out its own destruction (against Marx himself, cf. the Commune) and this in exchange for no present or future power, but against all power. This does not enter into any dialectic, is forever unnamable, but somewhere the energy of this death shows through today in the derision of all the institutions, including the revolutionary institutions, that thought they buried it.

A Note on the Texts and Translation

Aside from the interview at the beginning, all of these texts originally appeared in the journal *Utopie*, published between 1967 and 1978. Some were published without the signature of their author. Most were collected by Hubert Tonka in *Le Ludique et le policier et autres textes parus dans Utopie* (1967/78) (Paris: Sens&Tonka, 2001). Many were republished by Baudrillard during the 1970s and 1980s in other books. Several have already appeared in English translation by a number of different translators. Excluding "Our Theater of Cruelty," all of the translations published here are new and my own. I nevertheless benefited from consulting many of the previous versions of these texts. Mark Poster's translations were particularly helpful in tracking down citations. My greatest debt, however, is to Vanessa Corrêa, for all of her gifts.
— Stuart Kendall

"À propos d'*Utopie*," interview with Jean-Louis Violeau, May 1997. Paris: Sens&Tonka, 2005.

"Utopie dialectique" *Utopie* 1 (May 1967) 54–5; trans. by Gary Genosko as "Dialectical Utopia" in *Uncollected Baudrillard* (London: Sage Publications, 2001) 58.

"L'Éphémère…" *Utopie* 1 (May 1967) 95–97; translated by Timothy Dylan Wood as "Ephemeral and Durable" in *Uncollected Baudrillard op. cit.*, 56–7.

"Le ludique et le policier" *Utopie* 2–3 (May 1969) 3–15; translated by Paul Patton as "Police and Play" in *Uncollected Baudrillard op. cit.*, 61–69.

"La Pratique sociale de la Technique" *Utopie* 2–3 (May 1969) 147–55; translated by Paul Hegarty as "Technique as Social Practice" in *Uncollected Baudrillard op. cit.*, 45–51.

"L'utopie a été renvoyée…" *Utopie* 4 (October 1971) 3–4; translated by Gary Genosko as "Utopia: The Smile of the Cheshire Cat" in *Uncollected Baudrillard op. cit.*, 59–60.

"Conte de grève 2" *Utopie* 4 (October 1971) 24–27.

"Requiem pour les media" *Utopie* 4 (October 1971) 35–51; reprinted in *Pour une Critique de l'économie politique du signe* (Paris: Gallimard, 1972); translated by Charles Levin as "Requiem for the Media" in *For a Critique of the Political Economy of the Sign* (St. Louis: Telos, 1981) 164–84.

"L'ADN ou la métaphysique du code" *Utopie* 4 (October 1971) 57–61.

"Le miroir de la production" *Utopie* 5 (May 1972) 43–57; reprinted in *Le Miroir de la production ou l'illusion critique du matérialisme historique* (Paris: Casterman, 1973); translated by Mark Poster as "The Mirror of Production" in *The Mirror of Production* (St. Louis: Telos, 1975)17–51.

"Le marxisme et le système de l'économie politique" *Utopie* 6 (February 1973) 5–44; reprinted in *Le Miroir de la production ou l'illusion critique du matérialisme historique op. cit.*; translated by Mark Poster as *The Mirror of Production, op. cit.*, 111–167.

"Conte de grève 3" *Utopie* 7 (August 1973) 26–43.

"La dramatisation de l'économique" *Utopie* 8 (February 1974) 6–17.

"La campagne BNP" *Utopie* 8 (February 1974) 45–48.

"Les animaux malades de la plus-value" *Utopie* 8 (February 1974) 14–17; "Les animaux malades de la plus-value 2" *Utopie* 9 (April-May 1974) 14–17; substantially rewritten as "The Animals: Territory and Metamorphosis" translated by Sheila Faria Glaser in *Simulacra and Simulation* (Ann Arbor: University of Michigan Press, 1994) 129–41.

"Trompe-la-mort" *Utopie* 9 (April-May 1974) 18–23.

"Sur l'échec de la prophétie… ("Les élections '74") *Utopie* 10 (June-July 1974) 7–17.

"La prise d'otage" *Utopie* 13 (March-April 1976) 5–9.

"À mort les sauvages" ("Dies irae") *Utopie* 13 (March-April 1976) 34–37.

"Porno-stéréo" *Utopie* 13 (March-April 1976) 87–95; reprinted in *De la Séduction* (Paris: Galilée, 1979); translated by Brian Singer as "Porno Stereo" in *Seduction* (New York: St. Martin's Press; London: Macmillan; Montreal: New World Perspectives, 1990) 28–36.

"Le cadavre en spirale" *Utopie* 14 (May-June 1976) 10–15; reprinted in *Simulacres et Simulation* (Paris: Galilée, 1981); translated by Sheila Faria Glaser as "The Spiraling Cadaver" in *Simulacra and Simulation op. cit.*, 149–154.

"Conte de travail 3" *Utopie* 14 (May-June 1976) 19–24.

"Le dernier tango de la valeur" *Utopie* 14 (May-June 1976); reprinted in *Simulacres et Simulation, op. cit.*; translated by Sheila Faria Glaser as "Value's Last Tango" in *Simulacra and Simulation, op. cit.*, 155–157.

"La lutte enchantée ou le flute finale" *Utopie* 16 (April 1977) 6–9; reprinted in *Le PC ou les paradis artificiels du politique* (Cahiers d'Utopie, 5. Fontenay-sous-Bois: Cahiers d'Utopie/Quotidienne, 1978) 9–27; reprinted in *La Gauche Divine* (Paris: Bernard Grasset, 1985); translated as "The Enchanted Battle or the Final Flute" by Mark Lajoie in *Uncollected Baudrillard op. cit.*, 91–96.

"Castrée le veille de son mariage" *Utopie* 17 (December-January 1977–78) 2–10; reprinted in *Le PC ou les paradis artificiels du politique* (Cahiers d'Utopie, 5. Fontenay-sous-Bois: Cahiers d'Utopie/Quotidienne, 1978) 29–55; reprinted in *La Gauche Divine* (Paris: Bernard Grasset, 1985); translated as "Castrated on his Wedding Night" by Mark Lajoie in *Uncollected Baudrillard op. cit.*, 96–103.

"Notre théâtre de la cruauté (sur le terrorisme Mogadiscio)" *Utopie* 17 (December-January 1977–78) 17–24; reprinted in *À l'Ombre des majorités silencieuses ou la fin du social* (Fontenay-sous-Bois: Cahiers d'Utopie, 1978); translated by John Johnston as "Our Theater of Cruelty" Semiotext(e) (1982), 4(2): 108–115; reprinted in *In the Shadow of the Silent Majorities, or The End of the Social and Other Essays* Foreign Agents Series. (New York: Semiotext(e), 1983).

Other Semiotext(e) Titles by Jean Baudrillard

Simulations

In the Shadow of the Silent Majorities

Forget Foucault

Looking Back on the End of the World

Ecstasy of Communication

Fatal Strategies

The Conspiracy of Art